30-DAY CONSEC
THE BLESSED VI]

THE MOST POWERFU   ...SSION

ROSARY, OUR MOST POWERFUL
WEAPON AGAINST SATAN

by Peter D. Lee

Copyright © 2021 Peter D. Lee

CONTENTS

FOREWORD

5 Reasons to do Marian Consecration

1. It pleases Jesus to entrust yourself to her.
"Never be afraid of loving the Blessed Virgin too much. You can never love her more than Jesus did." – *St. Maximilian Kolbe*
"Jesus honored her before all ages, and will honor her for all ages. No one comes to Him, nor even near Him, no one is saved or sanctified, if he too will not honor her. This is the lot of Angels and of men." – *St. Maximilian Mary Kolbe, Martyr*
2. On the Cross, Jesus commanded us to take Mary into our homes (our hearts).
"If anyone does not wish to have Mary Immaculate for his Mother, he will not have Christ for his Brother." – *St. Maximilian Kolbe, Martyr*
"Mary seeks for those who approach her devoutly and with reverence, for such she loves, nourishes, and adopts as her children." – *St. Bonaventure, Doctor of the Church*
3. Mary's greatest desire is for our greater unity with her Son, Jesus.
"We never give more honor to Jesus than when we honor his Mother, and we honor her simply and solely to honor him all the more perfectly. We go to her only as a way leading to the goal we seek – Jesus, her Son." – *St. Louis Marie de Montfort*
"The reason why Christ is unknown today is because His Mother is unknown." – *Blessed Cardinal John Henry Newman*
4. Mary cares for her Children and entrustment to her Immaculate Heart is the easiest way to heaven.
"If you invoke the Blessed Virgin when you are tempted, she will come at once to your help, and Satan will leave you." – *St. John Vianney*
"If you ever feel distressed during your day — call upon our Lady — just say this simple prayer: 'Mary, Mother of Jesus, please be a mother to me now.' I must admit — this prayer has never failed me." – *Blessed Mother Teresa*

"Love our Lady. And she will obtain abundant grace to help you conquer in your daily struggle." – *St. Josemaria Escriva*

5. There is no more perfect way to holiness and to Jesus than through our Mother Mary.

"The greatest saints, those richest in grace and virtue will be the most assiduous in praying to the most Blessed Virgin, looking up to her as the perfect model to imitate and as a powerful helper to assist them." – *St. Louis Marie de Montfort*

"Have you strayed from the path leading to heaven? Then call on Mary, for her name means "Star of the Sea, the North Star which guides the ships of our souls during the voyage of this life," and she will guide you to the harbor of eternal salvation." – *St. Louis-Marie Grignion de Montfort, The Secret of the Rosary*

Ad Jesum Per Mariam!
To Jesus Through Mary!

DAY 1

MARY, OUR MEDIATRIX AND AUXILIATRIX

"Will put enmities between thee and the woman, and thy seed and her seed: she shall crush thy head, and thou shalt lie in wait for her heel" (Genesis 3:15).

Pope Pius IX proclaimed in the Dogma *"Ineffabilis Deus"* (1854) that in God's work of redemption, Jesus is inseparable with Mary. The Second Vatican Documents "Lumen Gentium", #62 also says that because Mary shared all the sufferings of Jesus, the one Redeemer, she, therefore, earned the title "Co-Redemptrix". At the foot of the Cross, Jesus gifted Mary the title "Mediatrix" for the people of God (1Timothy 2: 5). In John 19: 25-27 says: *"He saith to his mother: Woman, behold thy son. After that, he saith to the disciple: Behold thy mother. And from that hour, the disciple took her to his own."* Again, the Document "Lumen Gentium" explained that Jesus gave us Mary before dying on the Cross because the people of God, who are the "brethren of Her Son," needs a Mother, as they continued the journey on earth where they are surrounded by dangers and difficulties until they are led into their blessed home in Heaven. 1 Timothy explains: *"For there is one God, and one mediator of God and men, the man Christ Jesus: Who gave himself a redemption for all, a testimony in due times"* (1 Timothy 2: 5-6). The Greek word: "One" in 1 Timothy 2: 5 has two meanings:

1) *"Heis"* which is One and Inclusive.
2) *"Monos"* which is One but Exclusive.

In what way is Mary, the one mediator between God and man, being interpreted?

Is it inclusive or exclusive?

If it were exclusive, no one else can share the work of redemption with Jesus Christ. If it is inclusive, it means that God allows others to share in the one mediatorship of Jesus Christ. Since St. Paul himself coined the title "One Mediator" in 1 Timothy 2: 5, and he also wrote: *"I consider it a privilege to share what is it still wanting in the sufferings of Christ for the sake of His mystical body of Christ, the Church"* (Colossians 1: 24). Therefore, it is clear that the "One Mediatorship" of Christ is not exclusive but inclusive. And since Mother Mary shared all the sufferings of Jesus Christ, She, therefore, could share the "One Mediatorship" of Christ as Mediatrix of Graces in the redemption of mankind.

Being a Mother, the Virgin Mary will do everything to protect Her children from danger, especially from the attacks of Satan.

St. Bridget wrote in her biography, Jesus promised that everything she would request from Him through the intercession of His Mother, Mary, will be granted because of Her obedience to Him. Jesus told St. Bridget: "Whatever petitions you present to Me through my Mother shall not be refused. And I promise graciously to hear all those who ask any favor of Me in My Mother's name, though they may be sinners, if only they have the will to amend their lives."

Saint Alphonsus Liguori said: "It was befitting that Eternal Father should preserve Mary from the stain of original sin, for He destined her to crush the head of that infernal serpent, which, by seducing our first parents, entailed death upon all men; and this is Our Lord foretold: *'Will put enmities between thee and the woman, and thy seed and her seed: she shall crush thy head, and thou shalt lie in wait for her heel'* (Genesis 3: 15). But if Mary was to be that valiant Woman brought into the world to conquer Lucifer, certainly it was not becoming that he should first conquer Her, and make Her his slave; but it was reasonable that She should be preserved from all stains, and even momentary subjection to Her opponent."

St. Augustine, in his commentary on Genesis 3: 15, said: "Since the devil is the head of original sin, this head it was that Mary crushed; for sin never had any entry into the soul of this

Blessed Virgin, which was consequently free from all stains." St. Bonaventure, likewise, added that "It was becoming that the Blessed Virgin Mary, by whom our shame was to be blotted out, and by whom the devil was to be conquered, should never, ever for a moment, have been under his dominion."

Pope Leo XIII, in his Encyclical "Adiutricem Populi" (1895), indicated: "For thereafter, by the divine plan, she so began to watch over the Church, so to be present to us and to favor us as Mother, that she who had been the minister of accomplishing the mystery of human redemption, would be likewise the minister of the dispensation of that grace, practically limitless power being given to her."

Belluacensis and Cesarius, ancient Church historians, tell us of a story of a young man who lost all out of his great neglect and regained everything back through the help of the Blessed Virgin Mary. The story was that a noble youth having lost by his vices the wealth left him by his father, became so poor that he was obliged to beg. He quitted his native land, that he might live with less shame in a distant country where he was unknown. On this journey, he met one day an old servant of his father, who, seeing him so cast down by the poverty he was suffering, told him to cheer up, for he would take him to a prince who was so liberal that he would provide him with everything he needed. Now, this wretch was an impious sorcerer. One day, he took the youth with him to a wood on the borders of a moor, where he began to address some invisible person. The youth asked to whom he was speaking. "To the devil," he answered; and seeing the youth terrified, bade him not to fear. Continuing to speak with the devil, he said: "This youth, oh my master, is reduced to extreme necessity, and wishes to be restored to his former condition." "If he will obey me," said the enemy, "I will make him richer than before; but in the first place, he must renounce God." At this, the youth shuddered, but urged on by that cursed magician, he yielded, and renounced God. "But this is not sufficient," said the demon; "he must also renounce Mary; for it is to her that we attribute our greatest losses. Oh, how many souls she has snatched from us, and led back to God and saved!" "Oh, this I will not do," exclaimed the youth; "deny Mary! why she is my only hope. I would rather be a beggar all my life." With these words, he left the place. On his way, he happened to pass a church dedicated to Mary. The unhappy youth entered it, and kneeling before her altar, began to weep and implore the Most Holy Virgin that she would obtain the pardon of his sins. Mary immediately began to intercede with the Son for that miserable being. Jesus at first said: "But that ungrateful youth, my mother, has denied me." But seeing that his mother still continued to entreat him, he at last said: "Oh, my mother, I have never refused thee anything; he shall be pardoned, since thou dost ask it." The citizen who had purchased the inheritance of that prodigal was secretly present at this scene, and beholding the mercy of Mary towards that sinner, he gave him his only daughter in marriage, and made him heir of all his possessions. Thus that youth recovered, through the intercession of Mary, the favor of God, and even his temporal possessions.

Some people in the desire for material gain, even for a good cause of having to support their family, would sell their souls to the devil. We have heard of stories of actors and actresses, singers, famous sports personalities, politicians, and businessmen, making a pact with the devil in exchange for wealth and fame. Later on, they only lose more than what they have bargained for. Remember, no one can ever give you what you want in life, except God. The devil cannot do anything without God's permission, so even if the devil promises you anything, but if God says no, he cannot do anything.

When in dire needs, let us return to Jesus and Mother Mary, repent and entrust to Her care, both spiritual and material.

MEDITATION

"Mary is called the Co-Operatrix with Her Son in our justification because God has committed to Her keeping all the graces that He has destined for us. All men, present, past, and to come, should regard Her as the negotiator of the salvation of all graces" (St. Bernard).

PRAYER

Oh loving Mother, behold me, your child. The Lord has given you in His infinite mercy and confidence, help me to give thanks to Him for gifted me with your motherly love and protection. Oh loving Mother, I thank you for the good You have done for me, a miserable sinner. From many dangers you have delivered me from, oh my Queen! How much light and how many mercies you have obtained for me from God, through your most powerful intercession. I cannot give you anything in return, but only to praise and love you and Jesus Christ, our Lord. Amen.

DAY 2

THE ROSARY IS A MINI-BIBLE

"And in the sixth month, the angel Gabriel was sent from God into a city of Galilee, called Nazareth, To a virgin espoused to a man whose name was Joseph, of the house of David; and the virgin's name was Mary. And the angel being come in, said unto her: Hail, full of grace, the Lord is with thee: blessed art thou among women. And she cried out with a loud voice, and said: Blessed art thou among women, and blessed is the fruit of thy womb" (Luke 1: 26-29, 42).

In the Encyclical "Marialis Cultus", Pope Paul VI called the "Rosary is a mini-Bible prayer," because it summarizes the center of the Bible: Jesus Christ's Life, Death, and Resurrection. The Life of Jesus corresponds to the Joyful and Luminous Mysteries of the Rosary, the Death is the Sorrowful Mysteries, and the Resurrection is the Glorious Mysteries. The Catechism of the Catholic Church, #2559, defines prayer as the raising of one's mind and heart to God or the requesting of good things from God. When we pray the Rosary, we lift our mind and heart by reflecting on the three Biblical Mysteries of the Rosary: the Life, the Death, and the Resurrection of Jesus Christ.

The Rosary is both Vocal and Contemplative prayer:

The Rosary is Vocal prayer: St. Mathew defines it is a "book of prayer", he says: *"Watch ye, and pray that ye enter not into temptation. The spirit indeed is willing, but the flesh weak"* (Mathew 26: 41). Since Satan tempts us persistently every moment, the Rosary becomes a very powerful prayer that can drive away the devil to help maintain our peace in serving God.

The Rosary is Contemplative prayer: Because as the Catechism of the Catholic Church says: *"Contemplation is a gaze of faith, fixed on Jesus"* (CCC #2715). Contemplation is the prayer of the heart. A person who is in contemplative prayer focuses on the scriptural passages then soaks and basks himself in it in the present of God. The person prays to God with a listening heart; it is when we reflect and pray in a contemplative manner that we come to know, love, and serve God better.

The "Hail Mary" is a biblical prayer. It is the angelic salutation of the angel Gabriel to Mary, this is said in Luke: "Hail, full of grace, the Lord is with thee: blessed art thou among women" (Luke 1: 28). This is also the joyful greeting of Elizabeth to Mary: "Blessed art thou among women, and blessed is the fruit of thy womb" (Luke 1: 42). In invoking the prayer "Hail Mary", we ask Mother Mary to intercede for us before God, and to pray for us sinners now and at the hour of our death. Therefore, the Rosary is basically an Intercessory Prayer coursed through Mary to obtain graces from God, similar to what we do when we ask our friends, parents, families, priests, and religious to pray for us to God. Only Mary's intercession is more powerful because She is the Mother of our Lord Jesus Christ, who sits at the right hand of the Father Almighty in Heaven.

We pray the Mysteries of each of the five sections or decades of the Rosary according to the day of the week. On Mondays and Saturdays, we pray the Joyful Mysteries which is the meditation of the Life of Christ. These Mysteries direct us to focus on five essential events in the life of our Lord Jesus:

- The First Mystery – the Annunciation (Luke 1: 26 - 28)
- The Second Mystery – the Visitation (Luke 1: 39 - 56)
- The Third Mystery – the Nativity (Luke 2: 1 - 21)
- The Fourth Mystery – the Presentation (Luke 2: 22 - 38)
- The Fifth Mystery – the Finding of the Child Jesus in the Temple (Luke 2: 41 - 52)

On Tuesdays and Fridays, we pray the Sorrowful Mysteries which is the meditation of the Passion and Death of Jesus. There are five key events to meditate upon:

- The First Mystery – the Agony in the Garden (Matthew 26: 36 - 56)
- The Second Mystery – the Scourging at the Pillar (Matthew 27: 26)
- The Third Mystery – the Crowning with Thorns (Matthew 27: 27 - 31)
- The Fourth Mystery – the Carrying of the Cross (Mathew 27: 32)
- The Fifth Mystery – the Crucifixion (Matthew 27: 33 - 56)

On Wednesdays and Sundays, we pray the Glorious Mysteries which is the meditation of the Resurrection of Christ. These Mysteries direct us to contemplate on five important events in both Jesus' and Mary's Life:

- The First Mystery – the Resurrection (John 20: 1 - 29)
- The Second Mystery – the Ascension (Luke 24: 36 - 53)
- The Third Mystery – the Descent of the Holy Spirit (Acts 2: 1 - 41)
- The Fourth Mystery – the Assumption of Mother Mary into Heaven
- The Fifth Mystery – the Coronation of Mother Mary as Queen of Heaven and Earth

On Thursdays, we meditate on the Luminous Mysteries which focus on the Public Ministry of Christ. There are five important events highlighted in these Mysteries:

- The First Mystery – the Baptism (Matthew 3: 13 - 16)
- The Second Mystery – the Wedding at Cana (John 2: 1 - 11)
- The Third Mystery – the Proclamation of the Kingdom (Mark 1: 14 - 15)
- The Fourth Mystery – the Transfiguration (Matthew 17: 1 - 8)
- The Fifth Mystery – the Institution of the Holy Eucharist (Matthew 26)

The exact origin of the Rosary as a prayer is quite unclear.

Although in the third and fourth century, the use of knotted prayer ropes among Christians went back to the time of Desert Fathers, while praying the 150 Psalms. These knotted ropes as accounting devices were used during prayer. It was similar in use to the Jesus Prayer in Eastern Catholic monasteries founded by St. Basil. After the Council of Ephesus in 431 AD, the gradual growth in the use of Marian prayers during the Middle-Ages emerged. Catholic tradition tells us that the Rosary, as we know it now, was given to St. Dominic in a vision by the Blessed Virgin Mary in the 12th century, and was promoted by Blessed Alan de la Roche. St. Dominic received the Rosary from the Virgin Mary, who appeared to him in 1214 in Toulouse, France. While he was at prayer, St. Dominic asked the Blessed Mother for help as the heresy of the flagellants was spreading wide in France and in nearby European areas, all attempts to stop it were unsuccessful. In oppression, the Blessed gave St. Dominic the Rosary with the promise that if the Rosary is prayed while meditating on the Life, the Death, and the Resurrection of Jesus Christ, the heretics will be converted. She told St. Dominic that the Rosary is the mini-Gospel prayer. Then the Blessed Mother appeared to Blessed Alan de la Roche and told: "The Rosary is the greatest weapon for the conversion of sinners." St. Dominic later became the founder of the Dominican Order. The Blessed Virgin Mary was through the Rosary and the Scapular; Jesus was through Mary to save the world.

Many misunderstood our Catholic legacy of praying the scriptural prayer of the Rosary, using the following stereotyped arguments:

First, "Praying the Rosary is not biblical, it is a man-made created tradition of the Catholic Church, which the Bible speaks against in Jeremiah 17: 5, and Mark 7: 13;

Second, in "1 Timothy 2: 5 says, 'There is only one Mediator, Jesus', this verse says nothing about praying to Mary;"

Third, "Matthew 6: 7 says, 'When you pray, do not babble in 'vain repetition' like pagans do, for they think they will be heart because of their many words."

Let us clarify one by one these false allegations:

First, the Rosary is not a prayer to Mary; it is a meditation on the life of Christ. Each Mystery of the Rosary reflects on the biblical events of the Gospels. To say that the Rosary is not biblical, it is not accurate at all. When you look at the components of the Rosary individually, you will see that every part is biblical in nature as a deep meaning contrary to the claim of mindless pagan babbling or vain repetition, that it is often described as. The Rosary is composed of the following prayers: "Hail Mary" or "Ave Maria", the Pater Noster or the Lord's Prayer, which was given to us by Christ Himself. The "Glory Be" or "Gloria Patri", "Credo" or "Creed," which are the various mysteries of faith, and the concluding: "Hail Holy Queen" or "Salve Regina."

Second, when Catholics pray the "Hail Mary" prayer, they are not praying to Mary, but they asking for Her prayers of intercession for us, in the same manner as they may ask friends, families, or the clergy to pray for them. Only Mary's intercessory prayers are more powerful, because She is the Mother of our Lord and sits at the right hand of God the Father in Heaven. The "Hail Mary" prayer is taken straight out of the Bible, off the lips of the Archangel Gabriel, the Messenger of God (Luke 1: 28), and from Elizabeth's word of praise mentioned in (Luke 1: 42) because the child in the womb recognized Jesus as the Messiah: "Hail, full of grace, the Lord is with thee: blessed art thou among women, and blessed is the fruit of thy womb" (Luke 1: 28, 42). The doxology "Gloria Patri" or "Glory Be" is nothing more than the hymn of praise to the Holy Trinity: "Glory be to the Father, and to the Son, and to the Holy Spirit, as it was in the beginning, is now, and ever shall be, world without end. Amen."

Third, the Mysteries of the Rosary are meditated upon while praying each decade. 10 Hail Mary beads with the purpose of drawing the person into a deeper reflection of Christ's joy, sacrifices, sufferings, and the glorious miracles of His life. There is no other prayer in the world richer in biblical and theological meaning, and more profound and spiritually beautiful than the Holy Rosary. It is the chain of prayer that binds us to God. That is why most of the Popes, such as Boniface VIII, Gregory IX, and Innocent IV, from the 13th century down to this day. St. Pius V and John Paul II especially encouraged all Catholics to pray the Rosary daily as a family.

The Rosary is a very powerful intercessory prayer to Jesus through Mary. Among the 15 promises of the Rosary give in 1221 to Blessed Alan de la Roche by the Blessed Virgin Mary, three of them are worth mentioning here because of their great significance. First, praying the Rosary shall be powerful armour against Hell. It will destroy vice, decrease sin, and defeat heresies. Second, praying of the Rosary will cause virtue and good works to flourish. It will obtain for souls the abundant mercy of God. It will withdraw the hearts of people from the love of the world, and will lift them to the desire of eternal things. Souls will sanctify themselves by this means. Third, the soul which recommends himself to Mother Mary by the recitation of the Rosary shall not perish in Hell.

MEDITATION

"A family that prays together, stays together." (Ven. Fr. Patrick Peyton)

"Never will anyone who says his Rosary every day become a formal heretic or be led astray by the devil." (St. Louis Marie de Montfort)

PRAYER

Oh Loving God, You promised to listen to our prayers when we take recourse of the intercession of the Blessed Mother Mary, by using Her scriptural Rosary beads. Among others, You promised the devotees of the Rosary to receive signal graces, special protection from evil, powerful armour against hell, destroy vices, defeat heresies, and cause virtue and good works to flourish. Above all, through the praying of the Holy Rosary, you promised to save us from Hell, and not perish by an unprovided death. As we are in dire need of Your graces every moment of our life, we beg you to listen to our prayers through the most powerful intercession of Our Lady of the Rosary and Christ, our Lord. Amen.

DAY 3

THE EFFECTIVE MANNER OF PRAYING THE ROSARY

"And when you are praying, speak not much, as the heathens. For they think that in their much speaking they may be heard" (Matthew 6: 7).

"And he cometh, and findeth them sleeping. And he saith to Peter: Simon, sleepest thou? couldst thou not watch one hour? Watch ye, and pray that you enter not into temptation. The spirit indeed is willing, but the flesh is weak" (Mark 14: 37-38).

The admonition: "Watch and pray always" is best being applied in praying the Rosary, which is the most popular piety in the 1.3 billion Catholics throughout the world.

What does it mean to "Watch and pray?"

The answer can be found in the Gospel of St. Matthew 26: 39-41, Jesus took Peter, James, and John with Him to the Garden of Gethsemane, where He prayed: "May this cup be taken from Me." After the prayer, He found His disciples sleeping; He was grieved that they could not even pray with Him for one hour and warned them: *"Watch and pray so that you will not fall into temptation. The spirit is willing, but the flesh is weak"* (Matthew 26: 41). In this passage, we hear Jesus lamenting that His disciples could not even "pray and watch" for one hour. We are not better than the disciples; we experience at times our worst temptations than sleepiness when we do our Holy Hours. It is sheer that the meditation of the Sorrowful Mysteries of the Rosary becomes an effective solution. If we pray the Rosary properly, we should spend a good 20 to 30 minutes in silent meditation. It is a good habit to pray the Rosary while waiting for Holy Mass to begin, or when we are at home with some free times, and especially when being caught in traffic on our way to work or home. These are opportune moments for us to spend praying the Rosary rather than falling into idleness, because idleness is the devil's workshop. The vigilant prayer of the Rosary helps us avoid falling into laziness, and to keep our minds and hearts fixed on God. To survive the daily challenges of spiritual warfare, developing a strong devotion to prayer is the only way to remain faithful to God. For in prayer, we continually allow God to cleanse us, teach us, and strengthen us to obey Him. To be able to obey His admonition to "keep watch", we must pray for endurance and freedom from distractions. It is discipline and determination as St. Paul tells us, we must pray without ceasing! Unceasing prayer can be achieved by contemplating the Word of God through the daily prayer of the Rosary. This is the gift and simple solution given to us by the Virgin Mary Herself on how we can fight the incessant temptation of the devil. With the help of the Blessed Mother, the Rosary Prayer can bring us inner peace, strength, greater perfection, and fruitfulness in saving souls.

We are living in a fast-paced world, where the efficiency and worthiness of both man and mother are measured by the speed of response to its gifts and address any requests. Productivity means to speed; multitasking has become the game-changer. Because the speed has become the standard measure for productivity, young people today are turned off with anything that takes too long to do, praying the Rosary or piety that takes too long or requires much focus, turn off many Catholics, especially the young people whom we call in this generation the "Millenials". But not only the "Millenials" exhibit the impatience and distracted of attractions, our generation, too, have somewhat leveled up with the fast-changing world, in church, at Mass, how many get so impatient when the priest gives a long homily or says a long prayer after Mass. How much we want the priest to "KISS", a short word of "Keep it short, stupid." How many sit at the pews in the church to listen to their pastor's homily, but in their mind say: "go ahead, say what you need to say but leave me in peace, I still do I as please". The Blessed Mother comes to us in these times of uncertainty, offering one solution that has proven to solve all kinds of problems from personal to global. It is the Rosary, so simple, so banal that even the devil cannot destroy it. He laughs at the Rosary simplicity but he groans at its effectivity.

In the 10th chapter of the book entitled: "The Secret of the Rosary", St. Louis de Montfort teaches us how to pray the Rosary. It consists of the basic prayers: the Apostles Creed, the Our Father, the Hail Mary, and the Glory Be. Along with these simple prayers is a more important aspect of praying this Marian Psalter, the required interior disposition. How do we do this? St. Louis de Montfort said: first of all, asking the Holy Spirit to help you pray well for yourself for a moment in the presence of God, and open up each decade in this way: pause for a moment or two and contemplate the Mysteries that you are about to honor in the said decade. And then through the intercession of the Virgin Mary, ask God to give you one of the virtues that shines forth most in this Mystery. Try to avoid the following two pitfalls that most people make when praying the Rosary: First, forgetting to ask for the graces we badly need. Whenever we pray the Rosary, be sure to ask for some special graces. Second, having no other intention than to get the prayers over as quickly as possible. It is pathetic to see how most people say the Holy Rosary so fast, mumbling as they do, so that words are not even properly pronounced, yet to expect Jesus and Mary to answer our intentions. It is no wonder the most powerful prayer seems to bear no fruit, and after saying a thousand Rosaries, we are still no better than we were before. When praying the Rosary, we should temper our speed. It may take from 15 to 20 minutes to finish one Rosary, and yet when we open our computer or television or smartphone quite often without any purpose, we can waste so many hours without a second thought. Worse when people fall into the addiction to pornography through the internet, spending hours satisfying their lust. This could lead them to burn and excruciating pain, not only 20 minutes but for all eternity in hell. Wouldn't we rather spend 20 minutes to pray the Rosary which will bring us to eternal happiness in heaven? While praying the

Our Father and Hail Mary, St. Louis de Montfort recommends that we pause or brief intervals throughout its prayer so that we may obtain many graces.

During the Feast of Purification, the Blessed Mother appeared to the three sisters, accompanied by St. Agnes, St. Catherine of Siena, wearing beautiful shining robes and written all over the robes in golden letters with the words "Hail Mary, full of grace." The Blessed Mother came to the eldest sister and said: "I salute you, my daughter, because you have saluted me so often and beautifully. I want to thank you for the beautiful robes that you have made me." The virgin Saints, who were with Our Lady, also thanked the elder sister, and then all the three of the heavenly visions suddenly vanished. An hour later, Our Lady and the same two Saints appeared to them again, but this time Our Lady was wearing green, and Her robe had no lettering and did not gleam. She approached the second sister and thanked her for the robe she had made Her by saying the Rosary. Since the sister had seen Our Lady appeared to the eldest much more magnificently dressed, she asked Her the reason for the change of clothes. The Blessed Mother answered, your sister made Me more beautiful clothes because she had been saying her Rosary better than you. And about an hour later, She appeared to the youngest sister, wearing tattered and dirty rags, and said: My daughter, I want to thank you for these clothes that you have made me. The young sister covered her face with shame, called out: Oh my Queen, how could I dress you so badly, I beg you to forgive me. Please grant me a little more time to make you beautiful robes by saying my Rosary better. The Lady and the two Saints vanished, leaving the girl brokenhearted. She told her confessor everything that had happened, and he urged her to say the Rosary for another year, and say it more devoutly than ever. At the end of the second year, at the same day of Feast of Purification, Our Lady clothed in magnificent robe, and accompanied by the same two Saints who were both wearing crowns, appeared to them again in the evening, She said to them: My daughter, I have come to tell you that you have earned heaven applause, and you will all have the great joy of going there tomorrow. The three sisters cried: our hearts are already, dear Queen, our hearts are already, and then the vision faded. On the same night, they all became ill and being sent to the confessor who brought to them the last sacraments, and then they thanked him for the Holy Practice that he had taught them to pray the Rosary every day.

We learn from this story that it is very important to concentrate on the prayer being prayed and the Mystery being contemplated. St. Louis de Montfort advised: "How can we expect God to listen to us if we ourselves do not pay attention to what we are saying?" It would be almost impossible to pray without distractions, but to pray the Rosary well we must give our best attention to our prayer.

Blessed Hermann would pray the Rosary most attentively and fervently when meditating on the Mysteries. At times he would fall into ecstasy, and the Blessed Mother would appear to him. But as time went on, his fervor went off, and he fell into harrying the Rosary without giving his full attention. This time, when Our Lady appeared to him, Her beautiful face was flawed with sadness. Blessed Hermann was appalled at the change in Her, and Our Lady explained to him, "This is how I looked to you, Hermann. Because in your prayer, this is how you are treating me as the woman to be despised out no importance, why do you no longer greet with your respect and attention, meditating on My Mysteries and praising My privileges?" Blessed Hermann was ashamed; he fell into deep repentance for the poor pebble in his prayer. And with the help of Mother Mary, he regained bigger than he once had. After a moment, he died. Blessed Hermann was privileged to see Mother, and Her appearance was always great beauty and majesty.

Another recommendation from St. Louis de Montfort is "Take the time to read and contemplate on the scriptural mystery of each decade." For example, while praying the first Joyful Mystery of the Annunciation, we could read and contemplate on Luke 1: 26-38. We could do the same at the beginning of each new decade. For the Mystery of the Visitation, we could read Luke 1:

39-56. For the Mystery of Nativity, we could read Luke 2: 1-21, and so on for each decade. For each set of Mysteries, there is a particular day of the week on which to pray them, as I mentioned in the previous rose.

Throughout the course of his writing, St. Louis de Montfort emphasized over and over how those who devoted to the Rosary overcame sins in their lives. He said: "When we pray the Rosary in the state of grace, or at least, with the desire to give up mortal sin, the graces we receive are most effective." It is important to have contrition for our sins, otherwise, our prayers take on the form of false devotion. The unwillingness to amend our lives would be like hiding under the mantle of Mary, while at the same time, crucifying our Lord Jesus Christ. By reflecting on the life of Jesus, especially the Sorrowful Mysteries, we should be moved to repentance for our sins. To pray the Rosary well and receive the graces, we must have the pure intention of abandoning sin and turning to God with a whole heart.

Devotions to the Holy Eucharist and the Holy Rosary are the greatest devotions that cannot be surpassed by any other. These are two pillars of salvation which will anchor the Church to prevent It from sinking into the horrific sea of life on earth. These two pillars are none other than the pillar of the Eucharist, which is Jesus Christ, and the pillar of the Blessed Mother, which is the Virgin Mary, most especially through Her Holy Rosary.

MEDITATION

"There is no surer means of calling down God's blessings upon the family than the daily recitation of the Rosary. For the healing of evils which afflict our times, we do not hesitate to affirm again publicly that we put our great confidence in Mary by praying Her Rosary" (Pope Pius XII).

PRAYER

Oh Blessed Virgin Mary, the final battle between God and Satan will be ended by you. Being the final battle, one will be the loser, and the other will be the winner. The winner goes to Heaven, and the loser goes to hell. Surely we take God's side because not to be with God is to be against God. Oh Blessed Virgin Mary, we entrust ourselves to you as well as our loved ones and those recommended to our prayers. You have given us the Rosary and the Scapular to be the invincible weapons to defeat the inroads of Satan in our lives. Help us, Oh Blessed Mother, to persevere until the end, now and forever. Amen.

DAY 4

ROSARY, THE MOST POWERFUL
WEAPON AGAINST SATAN

"Put you on the armour of God, that you may be able to stand against the deceits of the devil. For our wrestling is not against flesh and blood; but against principalities and power, against the rulers of the world of this darkness, against the spirits of wickedness in the high places. Therefore take unto you the armour of God, that you may be able to resist in the evil day, and to stand in all things perfect. Stand therefore, having your loins girt about with truth, and having on the breastplate of justice, And your feet shod with the preparation of the gospel of peace: In all things taking the shield of faith, wherewith you may be able to extinguish all the fiery darts of the most wicked one" (Ephesians 6: 11-16).

Because we are not fighting flesh-and-blood human beings but principalities of darkness, the fallen angels, we must always arm ourselves with spiritual weapons. The worst thing that can happen to us is to live as though there is no devil relentlessly attacking us, and on the other hand that God does not exist. When we think we are free to do what we like, that there is no God and that Satan does not exist, we become slaves of the devil. Since Satan is a preternatural being and we are human beings. In spiritual warfare, we are the sure losers, but Jesus Christ is available to cast out Satan when it attacks us. Jesus has given us the powerful Ally, His own Mother, to crush the head of the serpent every moment of our life. Mother Mary came to give us two powerful weapons to destroy Satan's kingdom here on earth: the Rosary and the Scapular. Let us take on the armor of God like the young David, who with the sling of the Rosary in his left hand

and the crook of the cross in his right hand, fought against Goliath. This life is nothing but warfare and a series of temptations; we do not have to contend with enemies of flesh and blood, but with the powers of hell. We read in Ephesians that *"For our wrestling is not against flesh and blood; but against principalities and power, against the rulers of the world of this darkness, against the spirits of wickedness in the high places"* (Ephesians 6: 12). Pope Paul VI, in "Deliver us from Evil" (1972), said: *"While man is responsible for all the sins he has committed, yet behind the committal of all sins, is the devil, relentlessly tempting all of us."* The Pope said that one will be surprised to know the number one problem of the Church during his time is not the lack of vocation, or too many heretics in the Church and the life. The number one problem in the Church is "How to stop the devil from destroying the Church." He also said that from the crux of compromise and the Catholic Church, the smoke of Satan comes in. Satan or fallen angels though a preternatural being is only a creature of God, and we, human beings, are simply natural, so in the spiritual warfare, which according to *"Gaudium et Spes"* (1965), #37, started from the moment of creation and will last until the end of times, we have no chance to win this war. No wonder we see today in every sector of our society, Christ is no longer in charge but the devil. Pope John Paul II said: "Many good things are happening in the Church today, we see society built on the structure of sin" (Evangelium Vitae 1995). Therefore, at the micro-level, we see the culture of death so rampant; sex education is mandated from the age of five in all schools, sexual violence everywhere, and corruption as the way of life of the government.

What better weapons could we possibly use to combat them than the Rosary Prayer, which our Queen of Heaven gave us, which has chased away devils, destroyed sins, and renewed the world?

What better weapon could we use than Rosary Meditation on the Life and Passion of Our Lord Jesus Christ?

Abbe Blosius said: "The Rosary, with the meditation on the Life and Passion of Jesus Christ, is certainly most pleasing to Our

Lord and His Blessed Mother, and is a very successful means of obtaining all graces; we can say it for ourselves as well as others, for whom we wish to pray and for the whole Church. Let us turn to the Holy Rosary in all our needs, and we shall infallibly obtain the graces we ask of God to save our souls." In 1481, the Blessed Mother appeared to Venerable Dominic, the Carthusian, who lived at Traves, and said to him: "Whenever one of the faithful who is in a state of grace says the Rosary while meditating on the mysteries of the life and passion of Jesus Christ, he obtains full and entire remission of all his sins."

Our Lady also said to Blessed Alan: "I want you to know that, although there are numerous indulgences already attached to the recitation of my Rosary, I shall add many more to every fifty Hail Marys (each group of five decades) for those who say them devoutly, on their knees—being, of course, free from mortal sin. And whosoever shall persevere in the devotion of the Holy Rosary, saying these prayers and meditations, shall be rewarded for it; I shall obtain for him full remission of the penalty and of the guilt of all his sins at the end of his life. Do not be unbelieving, as though this is impossible. It is easy for me to do because I am the Mother of the King of heaven, and He calls me full of grace. And, being full of grace, I am able to dispense grace freely to my dear children." Saint Peter says: "We must arm ourselves in order to defend against the same enemies which seek to conquer and molest us every day." "Every sin of the devil was crushed by the Humility and Passion of Jesus Christ. He has been nearly unable to attack a soul that is armed with the meditation and mysteries of Our Lord's life. And if he does trouble to such a soul, he is sure to be shamefully defeated" (Cardinal Hughes).

St. Louis de Montfort wrote in *The Secret of the Rosary*: "So arm yourselves with the arms of God – with the Holy Rosary – and you will crush the head of the devil and you will stand firm in the face of all his temptations. This is why even the material Rosary itself is such a terrible thing for the devil, and why the saints have used it to enchain the devils and to chase them out of the bodies of people who were possessed."

Blessed Alan said that, a man he knew, who had desperately tried all kinds of devotions to rid himself of the evil spirit who possessed him but without success. Finally, he thought of wearing the Rosary around his neck, which eased him considerably. He discovered that whenever he took it off, the devil tormented him cruelly, so he wore it day and night. This drove the evil spirit away forever because he could not bear such a terrible change.

Blessed Alan also testified that he had delivered a large number of people who were possessed by putting the Rosary around their necks.

Dominican Father Jean Amat was once giving a series of Lenten sermons in the Kingdom of Aragon when a young girl was brought to him who was possessed by the devil. After he had exorcised her several times without success, he touched his rosary to her, with faith in Our Lady. As soon as he had done this, the girl began to scream and yell in a fearful way, shrieking: "Take them off! Take them off! These beads are torturing me!" The next night, when Father Amat was in bed, the same devils who had possession of the girl came to him foaming with rage and tried to overtake him. However, he was holding his rosary tightly in his hand, and nothing they did could wrench it from him. He managed to beat them with it very well indeed and chased them away, crying out: "Holy Mary, Our Lady of the Holy Rosary, come to my help!" The next day when he went to the Church he met the poor girl — still possessed — and one of the devils within her started to laugh and said in a mocking voice: "Well, Brother, if you had been without your rosary, we should have made short shrift of you!" Then the good Father threw his rosary around the girl's neck without more ado and said: "By the sacred name of Jesus and that of Mary His Holy Mother, and by the power of the Most Holy Rosary I command you, evil spirits, to leave the body of this girl," and they were immediately forced to obey and she was delivered from them.

These stories show the power of the Holy Rosary in overcoming all possible temptations that evil spirit may bring, and all kinds of sins because these Blessed beads crush devils.

The Rosary is the downfall and destruction of Satan's kingdom here on earth. Mary, who reads and penetrates the minds of the princes of the devil, so that a soul who is at the brink of hell, She easily snatches away. The Mother of Jesus Christ is all-powerful, and She can save Her servants from falling into hell. She is the Sun which destroys the darkness of our wild and subtlety. It is She who uncovers our hidden plots, breaks our snares, and makes our temptations useless and ineffectual. A soul who persevered in praying the Rosary will never go to hell. One single sign that She offers to the Blessed Trinity is worth far more than all the prayers, desires, and aspirations of all the Saints. Satan fears most of Mary than all the saints and angels together. He is powerless before Her and before those who pray the Rosary daily. We fear Her more than all the other Saints in heaven together, and we have no success with Her faithful servants. Many Christians who call upon Her when they are at the hour of death, and who ought to be dammed according to our ordinary standards are saved by Her intercession.

Anyone who perseveres in praying the Rosary will obtain the grace to receive the sacraments on fashion communion before death and will go to heaven. Now, we must also tell this: "Nobody who perseveres in saying the Rosary will be dammed, because she obtains for her servants the grace of true contrition for their sins, and by means of this, they obtain God's forgiveness and mercy."

MEDITATION

"The Rosary is the wall to hold back the evils that were going to break upon the Church" (Pope Leo X).

"The Rosary comes from heaven as a means of appeasing God's anger and have imploring Our Lady's intercession" (Pope Gregory XIII).

PRAYER

Oh Blessed Virgin Mary, the Mother of God, it was by the Will of the Father as written in Genesis 3: 15 that you will "Crush the head of the serpent". You have given us the Holy Rosary, our sure automated weapon to destroy the kingdom of Satan here on earth. If every Catholic takes this heavenly weapon every day as a family, Satan should have been bankrupt a long time ago. We beg you, O Blessed Mary, let us promote this beautiful and most powerful weapon, sanctifying our souls and driving out Satan. May you intercede to grant us this desire that through the Rosary, the promise of the conversion of the whole world before Christ's Second Coming will be fulfilled now and shortly through Christ, our Lord. Amen.

DAY 5

TWO POWERFUL ARMOURS FROM MOTHER MARY: THE ROSARY AND THE SCAPULAR

"Always rejoice. Pray without ceasing. In all things give thanks; for this is the will of God in Christ Jesus concerning you all" (1 Thessalonians 5:16-18).

In 1 Thessalonians 5: 16-18, God admonishes us to pray without ceasing, and give thanks in all circumstances. In practice for us, Catholics, this is made possible to the praying of the Rosary. But you might say that other religions also make use of prayer beads like the Rosary when they pray. Yes, some religions use prayer beads when they pray, but these are used merely as a hub to count the prayers or private devotions. For instance, the Hindus, Buddhists, Taoists, and Muslims have beads are strung together, which they hold in their hands, moving their fingers to each bead and counting to prayers as they do. The Hebrew too has the string with 150 nuts to represent the 150 Psalms. However, the Rosary for Catholic is a divine gift given by the Mother of God to humanity to be used by everyone who believes to seek for favor and to know and understand the Life, Death, and Resurrection of Her Son, Jesus Christ.

In 1214, the Blessed Mother appeared to St. Dominic and gave him the Rosary. She asked him that instead of praying the 150 Psalms as the Hebrew does, using beads or nuts and pray the "Hail Mary", "Our Father", and "Glory Be", every decade of the fifteen decades which made up the original Dominican Rosary. A decade refers to ten "Hail Marys", preceded by the "Our Father," and ending with the "Glory Be". Today, we, Catholics, pray the five decades of this prayer with the Rosary.

Our Catholic tradition teaches us that the Rosary is a gift of the Blessed Mother to humanity, given to St. Dominic, a good man, and a Spanish priest, who, during his time, was fighting the spread of the Albigensian heresy. The Albigensian was a dualist religious movement during the Middle-Ages that developed in Southern France. It heretically taught that there were two Gods, the good God of light refers to us Jesus and the New Testament, and the God of darkness and evil refers to Satan or the God of the Old Testament. They taught that anything material was considered evil, including the body which was created by Satan; the soul created by the good God was imprisoned in evil flesh, and salvation was possible only through holy living and doing good works. At death, if the person has been spiritual enough, salvation comes to him. But if the person has not been good enough, he is reincarnated in the animal or another human being. They have denied the resurrection of the body since it was considered evil. They also taught that Jesus was God, but He only appeared as a man here on earth, and frequently suicide was practicing as a way to rid oneself of the evil human body. However, St. Dominic fought against this Albigensian heresy with great difficulty, because the asceticism and humility of its followers compared to the great appliance of the clergy at that time brought many converts to this evangelistic movement.

It was in 1208, while at prayer, the Queen of Heaven appeared to St. Dominic and gave him the Rosary. She told him to pray it and teach all others to pray it to save their souls. It is the one prayer that, the Blessed Mother says, will never fail. She could not stress it enough that it would be through "prayer and penance that souls would be saved!" St. Dominic began to preach and teach the Rosary wherever he went, converting the majority of the heretics in doing so. Later, in the same year, the Queen of Heaven told St. Dominic that "Through the Rosary and Scapular, she will save the world." St. Dominic frequently prayed the Rosary Psalter as he walking along the road and taught everyone he encountered how to pray it. The Rosary became a very popular prayer among ordinary parks because of its ease and simplicity.

As the Blessed Mother promised, that the simple prayer preserved the faith of the people, and have it squashed the Albigensian heresy during the Saint's time.

When it was first introduced in the 12th century, this Marian Psalter consisted of 150 "Hail Mary," which was said only in the first part: "Hail Mary, full of grace, the Lord is with thee, blessed art thou among women, and blessed is the fruit of thy womb." That's it. But in 1475, blessed Alan de la Roche, with his Confraternities of the Rosary added the prayers of the Creed: "Pater", "Ave Maria", and "Glory Be", and the Scriptural Mysteries: Joyful, Sorrowful, and Glorious in every decade of the Rosary as how we pray today. Then the Rosary continued to develop to be aligned with the Church's Magisterium. Its scriptural basis was established citing Genesis 3: 15. The "Proto-Evangelium" clearly explains that the Blessed Virgin Mary as the Woman appointed by God to "crush the head of the serpent." This scriptural passage reads that there shall be perennial the enmity between you; the serpent and the Woman, Mother Mary; its offspring and Her offspring, She shall crush its head, and it waits for Her heels. As such it is Genesis 3: 15, we begin to understand the tradition of the apparition on 1208, when Mother Mary, the Co-redemptrix, holding the Baby Jesus, our "One Redeemer", gave the Rosary to St. Dominic and instructed him to pray it; then with Scapular, She also told him: "One day, through the Rosary and the Scapular, She will save the world."

We, Catholics, believe that there is only One Mediator, Jesus Christ, the God-man, who ransomed us from sins. We also believe that by His Passion and Death on Mount Calvary, Christ already saved collectively humanity. But our Catholic faith also teaches us that our salvation is not automatic, it is freely subjective and personal, and it simply means we can individually accept or reject God's redemptive up on Mount Calvary.

St. Bernard said that man prefigured in the image of Adam, and woman prefigured in the image of Eve; both have collaborated for our damnation, so it would be another man, Jesus, the new Adam; and another woman, Mary, the new Eve. What had been destroyed would be restored to their cooperation. Doubt-less to say, Jesus alone was all-sufficient for our redemption. Yet, its sex should take part in our redemption when both took part in our corruption. St. Anselm explained that God created man without His consent, and when he was lost by sin, He could not redeem it without his cooperation.

Therefore, Mary is called co-operatrix with Her Son in our justification, because God has committed to Her keeping all the graces that He has reserved for us. St. Bernard affirmed that all men, past, present, and future, should regard Her as the means and negotiator of the salvation of all ages.

In 1571, during the famous Battle of Lepanto, the second part of "Hail Mary" was added. In that year, St. Pius V ordered Don John of Austria to rally the people to pray the Rosary while the battleships fought the decisive war in Lepanto against the Muslim aggressors. Lepanto was the last bastion of Christianity during the Muslim conquers of Europe. After the people of Aus-tria obeyed the Pope, they rallied in the main street of Vienna to pray the Rosary, the Blessed Mother together with Her angels routed the Muslim fleet, sinking and destroying most of their battleships, and never again to regroup in retaliation against the Christian fleet. The second half of the prayer of the "Hail Mary" became the battle cry for those who invoked the help of the Mother of God and the Mother of the Church at the hour of great peril, and indeed it does: *"Holy Mary, Mother of God, pray for us, sinners now and at the hour of our death. Amen."*

Two years after the Jubilee year of 2000, Pope John Paul II added the Luminous Mysteries or the Mysteries of Light to the Rosary, which contemplates the public life of Jesus Christ.

Nowhere in the history of humanity have we seen the blatant and opened practice of satanic rituals and their abolished activ-ities perpetrated at times by influential people than now. It is as if they are proclaiming victory in all facets of life, and that evil reign supreme in all parts of the world. Pope Paul VI prophesied that "From the cracks of the Church, the smoke of Satan comes in."

Catholic parents today are panicky for they see their faith disintegrating inside out of the Church. Their children and grandchildren have already lost their faith with sex education imposed in schools as early as in kindergarten. The sexual revolution has spread not only in almost all countries but also in all ages. When one loses purity, one becomes blind in his faith, because Jesus said: *"Blessed are the pure, they shall see God"* (Matthew 5:8). Therefore, if we lose purity, we do not see God. In the Acts of the Apostles, St. Peter warns the Jews during Pentecost: *"Save yourselves from this perverse generation"* (Acts 2: 40). This admonition is true for today. Our Redeemer made it possible that we could truly realize this warning. He sent His Mother, the co-redemptrix, to us, using the Rosary and Scapular to save us. The time of St. Dominic was no different from our time.

In 1917, in Fatima, our Blessed Mother told the three children: "Many souls are going to hell because no one prays and does penance for them." With the consecration to the Hearts of Jesus and Mary and living the communion of reparation lifestyle, the message of prayer and penance to save souls from being damned is fulfilled. Three things were mentioned by the Blessed Mother to the Fatima that needed to be prevented: First, from souls going to hell; Second, from the terrible war that will annihilate many nations, leaving millions of people dying in minutes and envying the dead; Third, for the Church and the Popes to suffer more persecutions.

Virgin Mary appeared to St. Dominic and requested the same prayers and weapons: the Rosary and the Scapular. The Blessed Mother clearly asked to consecrate Russia and the world to Her Immaculate Heart. The sign of consecration is by wearing the brown Scapular and praying St. John II's prayer of total consecration: *"Totus tuus Maria, ego sum, omnia mea, tua sunt"*, which is *"all I am, is yours, all I have, is yours."* The Blessed Mother also said: "Sin no more." This we can do by repenting and making reparation. The sinless grace-filled lifestyle is what we call the communion of reparation lifestyle. Four letters summarize this lifestyle: "CARE", a short word of these words: C is for Confession. We need to confess our sins and go to confession regularly to promise to "sin no more" to God who loves us so much; A is for Adoration. We need to prolong our union with Jesus really, truly, and substantially present in the Eucharist in all the tabernacles throughout the world by visiting and adoring His true presence at least an hour every day. We do this in reparation for our sins to seek healing from both our spiritual and physical infestation and sickness; R is for Rosary. Our Lord said that pray always so as not to fall into sin. He sent us His Blessed Mother with Her Rosary to teach us how we can do this simply as often as we can, so that temptation of Satan will affect us; E is for Eucharist. Each time we receive the Holy Communion, we are empowered by Him to face and do anything for His greater glory to salvation of souls, and the honor of the Blessed Mother. The Blessed Mother promises that through the Rosary and Scapular, She will save the world. In Fatima, the Blessed Mother told the three children: "I want everyone to wear the Scapular as a sign of consecration to My Immaculate Heart." The Scapular is for: First, it is a sign of salvation; Second, it is a protection against danger; Third, it is a pledge of peace; Fourth, whoever dies wearing the Scapular, will not suffer eternal fire; Fifth, on Saturday that follows after the person's death, the Blessed Mother will take the soul to Heaven if that person dies wearing the Scapular and had been faithful to it. In 1942, Pius XII said: "To wear the brown Scapular is a sign of consecration to the Immaculate Heart of Mary." Truly with the Rosary and the Scapular, the Blessed Mother shall save the world.

With the help of Mary and the Rosary, we need not fear. Nobody can take away the Rosary. We will have the Rosary no matter what, because all it takes is the ability to pray until the end of times, this weapon against evil. Padre Pio called the Rosary the weapon, and when Mary gave it to St. Dominic, She referred it as the battering-ram against heresy. One of the Popes in the Middle-Ages called it "The skirts of the devil". Remember this: "The Rosary is the solution to the evils of modern times. No matter what happens, we can trust in Mary's protection through the Rosary. This should be a comforting thought that at the end of the day, keep saying the Rosary, the Blessed Mother will take care of you. What can go wrong if Mary is on our side? Who is better in taking care of us than the Mother of God Herself? Mary is the greatest creature of God, and the bridge between God and creation. In Her, God became man. The Rosary is the solution to the times in our personal life and the life of the Church in the world. We are simply willing to pray and trust in the mercy of God, as Pope Pius IX said: "Give me an army saying the Rosary and I will conquer the world."

MEDITATION

"The Rosary is the greatest weapon against evil. Nobody who perseveres in saying the Rosary will be damned because She obtains for Her servants the grace of true contrition for their sins, and by means of this, they obtain the forgiveness and mercy of God" (St. Dominic).

"The Scapular is made for everyone; it is a pledge of salvation" (Our Lady of Mt. Carmel, 1254).

PRAYER

Oh Loving Mother Mary, You are the Mother of the Church, we are all members of the Church under our Baptism. We are under siege everywhere inside out, the loss of faith and they seem to be so commonplace nowadays. We can all panic and feel desperate, but knowing you never abandon us as confirmed by Isaiah 49, we never are discouraged. You have given us two weapons: the Rosary and the Scapular, by meditating upon the Mysteries of the Life, Death, and Resurrection of your Son Jesus in the Rosary; and by renewing our consecration to you daily while kissing the Scapular. We know that Satan, who masterminds all the caves in the world, will one day be totally defeated. We beg you never to abandon us in the hour of evil. You love us so much, and we love you also. We ask this through the most powerful intercession of Our Lady of the Most Holy Rosary. Amen.

DAY 6

ST. LOUIS DE MONTFORT, THE EXTRAORDINARY PREACHER ON THE ROSARY

"Now this is eternal life: That they may know thee, the only true God, and Jesus Christ, whom thou hast sent" (John 17:3).

When we pray the Rosary with the inspiration of the Blessed Virgin Mary, with deepening our knowledge of Jesus Christ, and the assurance of eternal life, every decade of the Rosary allows us to meditate on the Life, Death, and Resurrection of Jesus, the summary of the whole Bible. The knowledge, understanding, and wisdom of Mary taught us that the power of the Holy Spirit is deeper than all the exegesis given us by biblical scholars.

St. Louis de Montfort wrote in his book "Secrets of the Rosary": "If you pray the Rosary faithfully until death, I do assure you that, despite the gravity of your sins, you shall receive a never-fading crown of glory." Even if you are in the brink of damnation with one foot in hell, or even if you are a heretic as obstinate as the devil, St. Montfort asserted, you will be converted later and will amend your life and save your soul if you mark well what I say: "If you say the Rosary devoutly every day until death with the purpose of knowing the truth and obtaining contrition and pardon for your sins."

With the Rosary, we are like young David who slew Goliath with a sling and stone; like young David with a sling of the Rosary in our left hand and the crook of the cross in our right hand, we can overcome all the snares and temptations of Satan as well as obtain all the graces we need from God through the Blessed Virgin Mary.

Why is the Rosary so powerful?

It was through the Angelic Salutation – "Hail Mary full of Grace, the Lord is with you" that brought Jesus to the world, destroyed the kingdom of Satan, and save the whole humanity. Every time we pray the Rosary, Jesus enters and destroys the wiles of Satan in our life, our family, and all those we recommend in our prayers.

St. Anselm said: "When we pray to Mary, we receive more than when we pray directly to Jesus." How could this be? When we pray to Jesus, we receive only what we asked for, for He is the God of Justice and Mercy. But when we pray to Mary, She generally asks Jesus for more graces, more than what we ask from Her, and Jesus will never say "No" to her request, because She is the Mother, She knows our weakness and all the graces we desperately need. When we pray the Rosary and accept all the little crosses Jesus sends us every day, we will become like young David so deadly in fighting Satan who is like the Goliath in our life. We will be a simplest dove; we become unassuming when our only weapon is the Rosary. Yet, it is the deadliest weapon ever sent by God through Mary to destroy Satan. We will be as cunning as a snake; snakes are deadly because of their element of surprise, they always lie in hidden so that the enemy does not know where to find them. We will be as fierce as a tiger; tigers do not balk in the face of the aggression to protect their cubs. When souls are at stake, we should be the same. We will be as strong as the bull; the bull remains constantly strong and unstoppable even in difficult moments. The Rosary prayer warrior stands as strong as the bull defending souls from being lost. We will be as swift as an eagle; the strength of the eagle is in its swiftness, it swoops down on its prey and flies up with it before anyone notices anything. The Rosary prayer warrior is swift in asking Mary to intercede as soon as he notices that a soul is in danger of being lost for eternity in hell.

As an extraordinary preacher of the Rosary, St. Louis de Montfort said: *"Let me but place my Rosary around the sinner's neck, and if he prays the Rosary daily, he will not go to hell."*

Although many of us know the power of the Rosary, however,

its slot destroys it, such as monotony, boredom, and falling into the state of doldrums, destroyed the effectivity of the Rosary. How then do we avoid falling into apathy and laziness when it comes to praying the Rosary? St. Montfort gives us the most effective strategy obtained to the Queen of Heaven. The saint advised that when praying the Rosary, there must be silence, both exterior and interior; moving away from all the noises around you, and silence all distractions or worries you may have within you. Focus alone on the Lord Jesus or Mother Mary in your mind and heart until you have a clear vision of their faces, lifting your heart and mind to God to pray the Rosary, beginning with the Sign of the Cross. Before each decade, pause and meditate on the particular biblical mystery. For example, the First Joyful Mystery is the Annunciation, pause and reflect on the following account from the Scriptures: the Angel Gabriel announced to Mary: "Hail Mary full of Grace, the Lord is with thee, you will become the Mother of God, you had born the Son of God and we will call Him Jesus, great will be His name." Mary said, "How can this be since I do not know man." The Angel replied, "It will be by the power of the Holy Spirit that you will conceive, your cousin Elizabeth, who is barren, is now pregnant in her six months. For with God, nothing is impossible. And Mary said, "Let it be done unto me according to your word." Focus on the message from the Scripture which in the Annunciation is "With God, nothing is impossible," and "With Mary, there is nothing that She cannot obtain from God." Throughout the decade while praying the ten "Hail Mary", offer your own intentions and believe that there is nothing impossible with God through Mary's intercession. Then do the same for the Second Mystery, meditating on the biblical mystery of the Visitation, then on the Third - the Nativity, and the Fourth – Presentation until the Fifth – the Finding of Jesus in the Temple.

Why do we repeat the "Hail Mary" over and over? Because it really has the power to transform our being to heal our sickness and cast out Satan, the answer is "Yes", definitely.

Our Lady revealed to Blessed Alan that while the angelic salutation brought Jesus to redeem and transform mankind, so this same angelic salutation continued to redeem and transform ourselves every time we pray the "Hail Mary". "Hail" comes from the Latin: *"Ave"* which means the new *"Eve"* and it also means Grace. It is the opposite of Eve, our first mother, which means Curse. *"Gratia Plena"* which means *"Full of Grace."* From the moment of conception of Mary in the womb of St. Anne, Mary was already endowed with all the graces Jesus allotted for the redemption of mankind. *"Dominus tecum"* means *"The Lord is with You."* Mary is the eternal Tabernacle where Jesus dwells on earth. Her Flesh is the same Flesh that the Second Person of the Trinity incarnated. Although They are unique Persons, yet inseparable. Pope Benedict XVI said: "The Body of Christ has three meanings: First, Jesus Christ, the God-man, the only Savior. Second, Mother Mary, whose flesh Jesus, the God-man, took Himself to form part of His humanity. Third, it is the Mystical Body of Christ will be the bride of Jesus when He, the Bridegroom comes again in glory." *"Benedicta tu in mulieribus"* which means *"Blessed are you among women".* Of all creatures, no one is more blessed than Mary because our Lord Jesus lived in every part of Her Being. *"et benedictus fructus ventris tui, Iesus"* means "Blessed is the fruit of your womb, Jesus". The Trinity dwelling in Mary's womb is the inexhaustible source and fountain of grace. *"nunc et in hora mortis nostrae"* means *"now and at the hour of our death."* God revealed to St. Catherine of Siena in dialogue 'the two most important moments in man's life'. First, it is the present moment, because every moment is an opportune time to gain merits and save souls. Once an opportunity is missed, it misses forever, and it will be accounted for during judgment day. Second, it is at the Hour of Death, because it is the deciding moment of our eternity in heaven or hell. The demons desperately make their best attempt to bring the soul to hell at the moment of death, but Mother Mary is also present at the same time to save the soul and bring it back to Jesus in heaven. All we need to do is to pray even one "Hail Mary", and heaven opens up to pour out an abundance of graces upon us. It takes only one "Hail Mary", and all of the hell trembles will fear because their days on earth are determined by Her, as it is written in Genesis 3:15, *"She shall crush the head of the serpent."*

When we pray the Rosary and really meditate, it gradually gives us a perfect knowledge of Jesus Christ. Praying the Rosary purifies our souls; it gives us victory over all our enemies; makes it easy for us to practice virtue; it sets us on fire with love for Our Blessed Lord; it enriches us with graces and merits; it supplies us with what is needed to pay all our debts to God and our fellow men; and finally, it obtains all kinds of graces for us from Almighty God.

The Rosary is the Science of Salvation. By meditating of twenty biblical mysteries on the Life, Death, and Resurrection of our Lord Jesus Christ through the intercession of Mary, we come to know more of Jesus Christ than everywhere to study Theology.

The knowledge of Jesus Christ is the science of Christians and the science of salvation; Saint Paul says that it surpasses all human sciences in value and perfection (cf. Philipp 3:8). This is true: because of the dignity of its object, which is a God-man compared to whom the whole universe is but a drop of dew or a grain of sand; because of its helpfulness to us; human sciences, on the other hand, but fill us with the smoke and emptiness of pride; and finally, because of its utter necessity: for no one can be saved without the knowledge of Jesus Christ – and yet a man who knows absolutely nothing of any of the other sciences will be saved as long as he is illumined by the science of Jesus Christ. Blessed is the Rosary which gives us this science and knowledge of Our Blessed Lord through our meditations on His Life, Death, Passion, and Resurrection, which is the content and summary of the Bible.

When we go to confession, our mortal sins are forgiven and the eternal punishment of hell is remitted, but God does not want us to abuse His graces by getting everything free of charge, courtesy of Jesus' Passion and Death on Mount Calvary. He retains some of the temporal punishments due to our sins to purify us. In the Catechism of the Catholic Church says: *"The forgiveness of sin and restoration of communion with God entails the remission of the eternal punishment of sin, but temporal punishment of sin remains. While patiently bearing sufferings and trials of all kinds and, when the day comes, serenely facing death, the Christian must strive to accept this temporal punishment of sin as a grace"* (CCC #1473).

By praying the Rosary, we gain a plenary indulgence that can remit all the temporal punishment due to our sins while here on earth. And if it is applied to souls in Purgatory, it serves as a suffragist for their temporal punishment of their souls after death. One plenary indulgence can be gained each day, by performing the works to which the indulgence is attached; by going to Confession; by receiving Holy Communion; by praying for the intentions of the Pope. The gaining of the plenary indulgence is regulated by the following norms: First, the recitation of a third party only of the Rosary suffices, but the five decades must be recited continuously; Second, the vocal recitation must be accompanied by pious meditation on the mysteries; Third, in public recitation, the mysteries must be announced in the manner customary in the place; for private recitation, however, it suffices if the vocal recitation is accompanied by meditation on the mysteries; Fourth, for those belonging to the Oriental rites, among whom this devotion is not practiced, the Patriarchs can determine some other prayers in honor of the Blessed Virgin Mary.

MEDITATION

Our Lady of Fatima told the three little seers to say the Rosary every day to obtain peace for the world.

Pope Paul VI urged Christians to pray to Our Lady Queen of Peace for world's peace. He wrote in his Encyclical "Mense Maio" that *"This Rosary prayer is so dear to Our Lady and so highly recommended by the Supreme Pontiffs in obtaining world's peace"* (Pope Paul VI).

"There is no surer means of calling down God's blessing upon the family than the recitation of the Rosary" (stated by Pope Pius XII).

"If families give Our Lady fifteen minutes a day by reciting the Rosary, I assure them that their homes will become by God's grace, peaceful places" (Venerable Father Patrick Peyton).

PRAYER

Act of Consecration to the Immaculate Heart of Mary

I, (Name), a faithless sinner - renew and ratify today in thy hands, O Immaculate Mother, the vows of my Baptism; I renounce forever Satan, his pomps and works; and I give myself entirely to Jesus Christ, the Incarnate Wisdom, to carry my cross after Him all the days of my life, and to be more faithful to Him than I have ever been before. In the presence of all the heavenly court I choose thee this day, for my Mother and Mistress. I deliver and consecrate to thee, as thy slave, my body and soul, my goods, both interior and exterior, and even the value of all my good actions, past, present and future; leaving to thee the entire and full right of disposing of me, and all that belongs to me, without exception, according to thy good pleasure, for the greater glory of God, in time and in eternity. Amen. (St. Louis de Montfort).

DAY 7

ANNUNCIATION: GOD OF THE IMPOSSIBLE

"And in the sixth month, the angel Gabriel was sent from God into a city of Galilee, called Nazareth, To a virgin espoused to a man whose name was Joseph, of the house of David; and the virgin's name was Mary. And the angel being come in, said unto her: Hail, full of grace, the Lord is with thee: blessed art thou among women. Who having heard, was troubled at his saying, and thought with herself what manner of salutation this should be. And the angel said to her: Fear not, Mary, for thou hast found grace with God. Behold thou shalt conceive in thy womb, and shalt bring forth a son; and thou shalt call his name Jesus. He shall be great, and shall be called the Son of the most High; and the Lord God shall give unto him the throne of David his father; and he shall reign in the house of Jacob forever. And of his kingdom there shall be no end. And Mary said to the angel: How shall this be done, because I know not man? And the angel answering, said to her: The Holy Ghost shall come upon thee, and the power of the most High shall overshadow thee. And therefore also the Holy which shall be born of thee shall be called the Son of God. And behold thy cousin Elizabeth, she also hath conceived a son in her old age; and this is the sixth month with her that is called barren: Because no word shall be impossible with God. And Mary said: Behold the handmaid of the Lord; be it done to me according to thy word. And the angel departed from her." (Luke 1: 26-38)

St. Bridget once narrated that the Blessed Mother revealed to her in these words: "Even from an infant Mary was filled with the Holy Spirit, and as she increased in age, she increased also in grace. Even from that time she resolved to love God with all her heart, so that he should never be offended by her actions or her words, and for this reason all the goods of earth were despised by her. She gave all she could to the poor. In her food, she was so temperate that she only took what was absolutely necessary to support life. Discovering then from the sacred Scriptures, that this God was to be born from a virgin to redeem the world, her spirit was so kindled with divine love that she desired and thought only of God; and taking pleasure only in God, shunned the conversation even of her parents, that they might not hinder her from thinking on God. And more than all did she desire that the coming of the Messiah might be in her day, that she might be the servant to that happy Virgin who merited being his mother." In Her humility, Mary did not even esteem herself worthy of being the servant of the divine mother. The humility which earned her the favor of God and gifted Her the Divine Motherhood as such.

The Saints are our best sources when speaking about the dignity of Mary, the Mother of God. St. John Chrysostom affirms that God chose Mary for His mother on earth, because He found no one more perfect and holy than the Virgin Mary. There was neither a place more worthy for Him to dwell in than her sacred womb. As St. Bernard also confirms and says that there was no more worthy place on earth than the womb of the Virgin Mary. St. Bernard, in a remark on the great humility of Mary, says: If the angel had said that she was the greatest sinner in the world, Mary would not have been thus surprised; but in hearing those exalted praises of the angel, she was instead greatly disturbed. She was troubled because, being so full of humility, she abhorred every praise, and desired that none but the Creator, the giver of every good, should be praised and blessed. This Mary also said to St. Bridget, speaking of the time when she became mother of God. "I disliked my own praise, and only wished to hear that of my giver and Creator." Seeing the Virgin Mary was so full of fear at the salutation, the Archangel Gabriel encouraged Mary, saying: "Fear not, Mary, for you have found grace with God." Therefore, finally, He now exalts you to be His mother: "Behold, you shall conceive and shall bring forth a son, and you shall call Him

Jesus."

St. Bernard expressed the excitement of the word when he wrote: "Now why this delay? Oh, Lady, the angel awaits your answer! We rather wait for it, who are condemned to death. Behold, Our Mother, to you is now offered the price of our salvation, which will be the Divine Word in you, made man. If you will accept Him for a Son, we shall be immediately delivered from death. Behold, the price of our salvation is offered to you. We are immediately liberated if you will give consent. The Lord Himself – as He is greatly enamored of your beauty – so much more desires your consent, on which He has made the salvation of the world depend" (St. Bernard). St. Augustine beautifully describes the moment of the Incarnation, adds: "Answer quickly, oh Lady, delay no longer, the salvation of the world, which now depends on your consent." Yes, hardly had Mary uttered these words: 'Behold, the handmaid of the Lord, be it done unto me according to your word.' When immediately the Word was made Flesh; the Son of God also became the Son of Mary." St. Thomas of Villanova exclaims as well: "Oh what powerful Fiat! Oh efficacious Fiat! Oh Fiat to be reverenced above every fiat! For by another Fiat, God created the light, the heaven, and the earth; but by this Fiat of Mary, God became man like us."

During the 1976 International Eucharistic Congress in Philadelphia, Cardinal Karol Wojtyla (later Pope John Paul II) explained about the final confrontation of the Church that "We are now standing amidst the greatest confrontation humanity has ever experienced. We are now facing the final confrontation between the Church and the anti-Church, between the Gospel and anti-Gospel, and between Christ and the Antichrist. This confrontation lies within the plans of Divine Providence. It is, therefore, in God's plan, and it must be a trial which the Church must take up and face courageously. We must prepare ourselves to suffer great trials such as will demand a disposition to give up even life with a total dedication to Christ and for Christ. Without prayers, it is impossible to mitigate the coming tribulation, but it is no longer possible to avert it, because only by this, the Church can be effectively renewed. How many time has the renewal of the Church is sprung from the shedding of blood. This time too, it will not be otherwise." So, where are we now?

In 1971, Saul Alinsky, a socialist, published a book entitled: "Rules for Radicals" on how to change society and the world. This book was used by almost all presidents of first world countries as their handbook in changing the world. When being interviewed by Playboy magazine publisher Hugh Hefner about this book, Alinsky gave an over-the-shoulder acknowledgment of Lucifer, the greatest radical because he chose to go to hell and work there for the have-nots. If the majority of the people today will follow these politicians, Jesus is correct to predict: when I come back, will there still faith left on earth. Even if our worst scenario today looks bleak, God cannot be silent forever. Something is about to happen. It is the greatest happening in the whole universe: the Annunciation of the angel to the Maiden Mary.

St. Pope John Paul II wrote: "When Mary said 'Fiat' to the Angelic Salutation, the alliance of the Hearts of Jesus and Mary began." Father Damian Fehlner said: "Outside the order of the Alliance of the Two Hearts, between Jesus and Mary, there is no salvation."

Let us meditate on how the "Hail Mary" of the Rosary, the Angelic Salutation addressed to Mary, changed forever the world. A word that was plunged into despair and hell because of the disobedience of our first parents to God's covenant; it is because of Mary's "Fiat", the Son of God, Jesus Christ – Our Savior, came to save the world. He came to make us, who were lost to sins, once again, adopted sons of the Father of heaven, heirs of heaven, and temples of the Holy Spirit. That is why we are reminded when we read 1 Timothy 2: 5, how with Mary's "Fiat", Jesus became the "One Mediator", and Mary, by Her "Fiat", became in the lower level and always in union with the Passion and Death of Jesus, the Mediatrix of all graces earned by Jesus to save souls. With Mary's "Fiat", heaven was finally opened; with Mary's "Fiat", the great hope was given to man, because finally the Antichrist, who now reigns in the world causing apostasy and great division among the minds and hearts in the world, will be crushed by Mary's feet as prophesied in Genesis 3: 15; and the victory is already assured, it is just a matter of time. With Mary's "Fiat", all in hell trembled with honor, particularly the devils, because from then onwards, Lucifer's days are numbered before his final defeat and captivity; with Mary's "Fiat" and for as long as we remain faithful to pray the Rosary daily, Satan's works, pumps, and temptations will have no power over us.

We read in the Catechism of the Catholic Church, #675, as well as the Gospel of Luke 18: 8, and Matthew 24: 12, that before Christ's Second Coming, the Church must pass through the Final Trial, which will shake the faith of many believers. The persecution that accompanies Her pilgrimage here on earth (see Luke 21: 12 and John 15: 19-20) will unveil the mystery of iniquity in the form of a religious deception offering man an apparent solution to their problems at the price of apostasy from the truth. The supreme religious deception or Antichrist is pseudo-messianism, by which man glorifies himself in place of God. The Catechism of the Catholic Church, #677 continues to say, that the Church, as mentioned in Revelation 19: 1-9, will enter the glory of the Kingdom only through the final pass over. When She will follow our Lord in His Death and the Resurrection, the Kingdom will be fulfilled not by the historic triumph of the Church or through a progressive ascendancy but only by God's victory over the final unleashing the evil which will cause His Bride coming down from heaven. It seldom happens that deputies of the Blessed Virgin Mary, who pray the Rosary daily with fervor fall into apostasy and get involved in diabolical encounters, the Blessed Virgin Mary will keep Her promise: Anyone, who prays the Rosary daily, will not taste the eternal fire of hell, and always die a happy death by receiving the Sacraments before death.

MEDITATION

"Never will anyone who says the Rosary every day be let astray. This is a statement that I would gladly sign with my blood" (St. Louis de Montfort).

"Give me an army saying the Rosary and I will conquer the world" (Pope Bl. Pius IX).

PRAYER

Oh Loving God, You have given us the greatest gift that we have ever received in our lives, Mother Mary. So that while serving Her, She, in turn, will not allow us to fall into temptation. Being free, we can run away from Her protection, but I know that Mother Mary would never forget us until the end of time, even if I try to forget Her.

Oh Blessed Mary, please save my soul and those millions of other souls from the peril of this life, now and forever. Amen.

DAY 8

MARY'S VISITATION GIVES CHARITY

"And Mary rising up in those days, went into the hill country with haste into a city of Juda. And she entered into the house of Zachary, and saluted Elizabeth. And it came to pass, that when Elizabeth heard the salutation of Mary, the infant leaped in her womb. And Elizabeth was filled with the Holy Ghost: And she cried out with a loud voice, and said: Blessed art thou among women, and blessed is the fruit of thy womb. And whence is this to me, that the mother of my Lord should come to me? For behold as soon as the voice of thy salutation sounded in my ears, the infant in my womb leaped for joy. And blessed art thou that hast believed, because those things shall be accomplished that were spoken to thee by the Lord. And Mary said: My soul doth magnify the Lord" (Luke 1: 39-46).

The Virgin Mary's visit to Her cousin Elizabeth was not a worldly show ceremony and a false display. Her visit was nonetheless a show of real concern and love, which brought an abundance of graces. At the Blessed Mary's first salutation, Elizabeth was filled with the Holy Spirit; the baby in her womb, who later would become the Baptist, was delivered from guilt and being sanctified. He gave the sign of joy, exalting in the womb of his mother; he wished to make known the grace received through the Blessed Mother. And his mother Elizabeth declared: "As soon as the sound of your greeting reached my ears, the infant in my womb leapt for joy" (Luke 1: 41). St. Bernard wrote in the meditation of this great moment, that in virtue of the salutation of Mary, St. John the Baptist received the grace of the Divine Spirit who sanctified him. Now, if these first fruits of redemption all passed through Mary, and She was the channel, by which grace was communicated to the Baptist, the Holy Spirit to Mary, and the gift of prophecy to Zachariah, then we have reason to believe, according to St. Bernard, God has ordained, even from that time on, the Virgin Mary to be a universal channel, through which all graces intended for us by God be dispensed.

Let us talk about the charity which is a big correlation on how the Virgin Mary acts:

There are times when offering charity to others we forget that we are doing it for God. There are three ways we can sin against this virtual charity:

First, charity in words;

Second, charity in thoughts;

Third, charity in works or actions.

Charity in words, how do we sin against others in our words?

The Catechism of the Catholic Church, #2476 cites four ways:

First: by false witness and perjury;

Second: by rash judgment;

Third: by detraction;

Fourth: by calumny.

How false witness and perjury works? It is when we make a public statement contrary to the truth which takes on a particular gravity. In court, such a statement becomes a false witness. And when under oath, it is perjury.

Rash judgment is when the moral fault of a neighbor assumed to be true, even tacitly, but without sufficient foundation.

Detraction happens when one, who without an objectively valid reason, discloses a person's faults and failings to others who do not know him.

Calumny is when by remarks contrary to the truth, a person who harms the reputation of another and gives occasion for false judgments to be hurled on the person in question, (according to CCC #2477).

How can we practice fraternal charity in words?

The best disposition and attitude is to abstain from every species of detraction. Detraction is nothing else but the malicious belittling or disparaging of a person's character or work. The person who commits the sin is called "Tale-Bearer", and these sorts of people defile their own souls and end up being hated by all. That is why if you are prone to make negative remarks against people, St. Mary Magdalene de Pazzi says: *"Never utter anything negative in people's absence, what you would not say in their presence."* And if we ever someone speak ill of others, do not encourage this person's lack of charity or even appear please with such language, otherwise, you fall guilty into the same sin. When you hear any kind of ill talk, either approved the person who instigates this conversation or else changes the subject of the conversation, or withdraw from the person who initiates the stop, or at least pay no attention to this person. Thus, whenever we hear a person speaking ill of others, it is necessary to show at least by silence, by a gloomy countenance, and by downcast eyes that we are not pleased with the conversation. Let us conduct ourselves always in such a way that no in the future would dare to attack the character of another in our presence. Let us be careful never to mention to any person that another has spoken ill of him. This kind of tale-bearing sometimes causes disputes and abrasions, which last for a long time. Proverbs warns us: *"Six things there are, which the Lord hateth, and the seventh his soul detesteth: A deceitful witness that uttereth lies, and him that soweth discord among brethren"* (Proverbs 6: 16, 19). Moreover, in our conversation, we must be careful not to wound the feelings of our neighbor, not even in jest. Jests, that offend a neighbor, are opposed to charity. The Lord told us in Matthew that *"All things therefore whatsoever you would that men should do to you, do you also to them. For this is the law and the prophets."* (Matthew 7: 12). Let our words at being affable and meek to all, even to our enemies. Let us never show any emotion of anger when people are rude to us. And when being exalted by others, let us always answer with sweetness, because *"A mild answer breaks anger"* (Proverbs 15: 1).

Charity in thoughts; How do we sin against others in our thoughts?

First: Exert all efforts to banish rash judgments, suspicions, and doubts; to entertain a rash doubt regarding another is a defect; to indulge a position suspicion is a greater fault; and to judge with certainty but without certain grounds that the other has sinned is far more criminal than referring to. The Lord clearly told us: *"Judge not, that you may not be judged, For with what judgment you judge, you shall be judged: and with what measure you mete, it shall be measured to you again"* (Matthew 7: 1-2).

Second: When our neighbor is visited with any infirmity, loss, or calamity, charity obliges us to regret his misfortune, using the superior will. It is the superior will that we particularly need to overcome the feeling of life, and the urge to rejoice at the misfortune, especially of our enemy, because our concupiscence will always get us to take pleasure in hearing that calamity has to befallen those who appall us. But this delight would not be sinful as long as it is resisted by the superior will. Charity obliges us to rejoice at a neighbor's good and to banish envy, which could take the form of a feeling of regret at the good of others in as much as it is an obstacle to our own.

<u>Charity in works or actions; How do we sin against others in our works and actions?</u>

In his book, "Spouse of Christ", St. Alphonsus Liguori explained: "We sin against charity through our works and actions when we refuse to give or provide:

1) Alms to others within our power;
2) Relief to those who stand in need of assistance;
3) Spiritual Alms to those in dire need of losing their souls."

The rule of thumb is to give alms as often as it is within your power. Tobias 12: 9 said: *"For alms delivereth from death, and the same is that which purgeth away sins, and maketh to find mercy and life everlasting."* Be always ready to assess your neighbors in all their necessities, because Our Lord reminds us: *"My little children, let us not love in word, nor in the tongue, but in the deed, and in truth"* (1 John 3: 18). So, how do we do this? St. Mary Magdalene de Pazzi teaches us: As a superior and novice mistress in the monastery, she not only assisted her sisters in their most laborious duties but also offered to perform by herself every work that required extraordinary labor. It became a common saying then in the community that "St. Mary Magdalene de Pazzi labored more than four lay sisters combined." It is worth imitating this woman's charity because whenever she was overcome by fatigue, she would look at Jesus carrying His Cross, and she would be revived to embrace with joy any new labor which her duties required.

The aid that we received from God will be proportioned to the assistance that we gave to our companions. The Scripture affirms this: "And with what measure you mete, it shall be measured to you again" (Matthew 7: 2). Let us have zeal in attaining our neighbor's spiritual good; strive to relieve the spiritual needs of your neighbor, or to contribute to its spiritual welfare. This particular exercise of charity far excels the exercise of charity towards the body, because the dignity of the soul far surpasses the lowly condition of the flesh. Be radical in assisting all according to the best of your ability, by words, by works, and especially by prayers. Because in our common prayer, in our thanksgiving up the communion, and in doing our visit to the Blessed Sacrament, we should never fail to recommend to God all poor sinners, infidels, heretics, and all who live without God. Do not forget to pray for the souls in the Purgatory also, because according to St. Thomas Aquinas, their sufferings surpass all the pains in this life. They stand in the need of our assistance because they no longer help themselves. A certain Cistercian monk appeared after death to another Cistercian of his Monastery and said to him: "Assist me in your prayers, for I can obtain nothing for myself." Let us be particularly careful to practice charity towards the sick, because the merit of serving the sick is far greater than the merit of serving those who are in good health, they stand in greater need of assistance. Sometimes, they feel themselves abandoned by all, by pains, melancholy, and fears. How pleasing it is to God to labor to console them in that state of affliction. Let us learn from the example of St. Ambrose on how we can practice charity towards neighbors who are opposed to us. St.

Ambrose was assigned to an assassin who attempted to take the Saint's life for some of the money that was sufficient to enable the assassin to live comfortably.

Let us turn to the Blessed Virgin Mary, who is the model of both love of God and love of neighbor. Her visit to her cousin Elizabeth, who was happy with the child, was proof of Her love of neighbor and love of God.

St. Thomas Aquinas taught that the love of God and the love of neighbor, both proceed from charity, because charity makes us love God and our neighbor; it is the will of God. 1 John 4: 20 reminds us of this truth that *"If any man says, I love God, and hateth his brother; he is a liar."* Hatred towards our brethren is incompatible with the love of God. That is why an act of charity performed to others is acceptable to Jesus as if the act itself is done to Him as such. In Matthew, Jesus said: *"as long as you did it to one of these my least brethren, you did it to me"* (Matthew 25: 40).

Let us learn from this story of a simple woman named Halen, who had gone to church accidentally and heard the sermon on the Rosary. As she exited the church, Helen bought a Rosary but hid it so that it should not be seen. Afterward, Helen began to pray it, and although she merely recited the prayers without devotion, the Most Holy Virgin infused into her heart such consolation and sweetness that she could not see her beading the prayers of the Rosary. By this devotion, she was inspired by such a horror of her evil life that she can find no peace and was forced to go to confession. She confessed with much contrition that the confessor was amazed. After finishing confession, she went immediately to the altar of the Blessed Virgin to thank for Her advocate. Helen recited her Rosary, and the Blessed Virgin Mary spoke to her from Her image and said: Helen, you have offended God and Me too long with your uncharitable words and actions, promiscuous life, infidelity, and other sins against the love of neighbors. From now, change your life! And I will bestow upon you many of my favors. Helen, in confusion, answered, Oh Most Holy Virgin, it is true that I have been very sinful, but you who are all-powerful, assisted me. I give myself to you and will spend the remainder of my life doing penance for my sins. Assisted by the Blessed Mother, Helen engaged herself in almsgiving by bestowing all her goods upon the poor, helping those who needed assistance, asking forgiveness from all those who she offended against charity, and living a rigorous life of prayer, fasting, and severe penance. She was tormented by dreadful temptation, but she continued to recommend herself to the Mother of God through the Rosary, and always with her aid, came off victorious. She was favored with so many supernatural graces like visions, revelations, and prophecies. At last, before her death, of which she had been warned of a few days previously by Our Lady. The Blessed Herself came with Her Son Jesus to visit Helen. And in death, the soul of the simple woman was seen in the form of a beautiful dove ascending into heaven.

MEDITATION

"When the Holy Rosary is said well, it gives Jesus and Mary more glory, for it is more meritorious than any other prayer;"

"If you say the Rosary faithfully until death, I do assure that in spite of the gravity of your sins, you will receive a never-fading crown of glory" (St. Louis de Montfort).

PRAYER

Behold, Oh Mother of my God, my only hope; behold at your feet a miserable sinner who implores your mercy. You are proclaimed and called by the whole Church and all the faithful the advocate of sinners. You are my refuge; it is you to save me. You know how much your Son desires our salvation; you do know what Jesus Christ suffered to save me. I offer you, oh my Mother, the sufferings of Jesus, His long journey into Egypt, His toils, sweat, the blood that He shed, the torments which caused His death before your eyes upon the Cross. Show your love for this son, while I, for the love of Him, beg you to aid me. Extend your hand to the fallen creature, who asks spirit from you. If I were a saint, I would not ask for mercy, but because I am a sinner, I have recourse to you to bring me back to Jesus, and to live a good life in serving God and neighbor through the end of my life. Amen.

DAY 9

NATIVITY: JEALOUSY, MURDER, ABORTION

"When Jesus therefore was born in Bethlehem of Juda, in the days of king Herod, behold, there came wise men from the east to Jerusalem. Saying, Where is he that is born king of the Jews? For we have seen his star in the east, and are come to adore him. And king Herod hearing this, was troubled, and all Jerusalem with him. And assembling together all the chief priests and the scribes of the people, he inquired of them where Christ should be born. But they said to him: In Bethlehem of Juda. For so it is written by the prophet: And thou Bethlehem the land of Juda art not the least among the princes of Juda: for out of thee shall come forth the captain that shall rule my people Israel. Then Herod, privately calling the wise men, learned diligently of them the time of the star which appeared to them; And sending them into Bethlehem, said: Go and diligently inquire after the child, and when you have found him, bring me word again, that I also may come to adore him. Who having heard the king, went their way; and behold the star which they had seen in the east, went before them, until it came and stood over where the child was. And seeing the star they rejoiced with exceeding great joy. And entering into the house, they found the child with Mary his mother, and falling down they adored him; and opening their treasures, they offered him gifts; gold, frankincense, and myrrh." (Matthew 2: 1-11)

In the years from 37 to 180, Titus Flavius Josephus, the first-century Roman-Jewish scholar, historian, and hagiographer, gave us two whole Scrolls about the Herod the Great. This great historian described the infamous King in the following words:

King Herod was a paranoid tyrant, who ended up killing three of his sons on suspicion of treason; putting to death his favorite wife (of his ten wives); killing one of his mothers-in-law; drowning a high priest; and killing several uncles and a couple of cousins. Further, he revealed in his writings that Herod plotted to kill a stadium of Jewish leaders, and even slaughtered all the innocent male babies and toddlers in a certain village, that is Bethlehem. Here, we can easily see how Herod, being a jealous man, could not accept a competitor. He annihilated those who threat to his throne. That is why when he had been tricked by the wise men was in a furious rage, and he killed all the innocent male babies in Bethlehem and in all the surrounding regions, who were two years and under. St. Augustine spoke of these infants killed by Herod: *"These then, whom Herod's cruelty tore as sucklings from their mothers' bosom, are justly hailed as "infant martyr flowers"; they were the Church's first blossoms, matured by the frost of persecution during the cold winter of unbelief"* (St. Augustine). When someone suffers from jealousy, the community ends up divided, one against the other because jealousy is a strong poison; it is the same poison that we find in the first pages of the Bible in the person of Cain; and out of jealousy for David's victory over Goliath, Saul expressed the desire to kill David. Pope Francis expressed how after hearing the women praise David, Saul's joy turned into sadness and jealousy, and "that great victory begins to undergo defeat in the heart of the king." This is the same worm of jealousy and envy that seeped into the heart of Cain when he killed his brother Abel, the pontiff emphasized that "this is what jealousy does in our hearts." "It is destructive anxiety which cannot tolerate that a brother or sister has something that I have not." And "instead of praising God for this victory as did the women of Israel," observed the Pope, Saul "prefers to withdraw into himself, feeling sorry for himself" and to "stew his feelings in the broth of bitterness." "Jealousy leads to murder. Envy leads to murder," the pontiff continued, adding that "it was this door, the door of envy, through which the devil entered the world."

Highlighting how "jealousy and envy open the doors" to "all evil things," Pope Francis noted that "they also divide the community." The Pope went on to describe that there are two "very clear" things present in the heart of someone who is affected by jealousy, the first of which is that "the envious person, the jealous person, is a bitter person who doesn't know how to sing, how to praise, (or) know what joy is." Looking at someone in this way, considering only what they have and what we don't have, "leads to bitterness, a bitterness that spreads throughout the whole community," the pontiff stated, referring to people with this mentality as "sowers of bitterness." A second approach which "brings jealousy and envy, are rumors," revealed the Pope, emphasizing that when a person sees someone else who has something that they want, the solution is often to put the other person down" so that "I am a bit higher up." "Gossip" is a tool that is frequently used in this situation, observed the Pope, noting that behind every rumor, "there is jealousy and envy." "Gossip divides the community, destroys the community. Rumors are the weapons of the devil." "How many beautiful Christian communities were getting along well" but were divided because one member allowed the "worm of jealousy and envy" to enter their heart, the pontiff lamented. With this jealousy comes "sadness, resentment, and gossip," he explained, highlighting that a person under the influence of envy "kills."

Bringing his reflections to a close, Pope Francis asked for prayer for "our Christian communities so that this seed of jealousy will not be sown between us, so that envy will not take root in our heart" or "in the heart of our communities, so we can move forward with praise to the Lord, praising the Lord with joy."

"It is a great grace, the grace of not falling into sadness, being resentful, jealous, and envious."

What is jealousy?

Jealousy is here taken to be synonymous with envy. It is defined to be a sorrow in which one entertains at another's well-being because of the view that one's own excellence is in consequence lessened. Its distinctive malice comes from the opposition it implies to the supreme virtue of charity. The law of love constrains us to rejoice rather than to be distressed at the good fortune of our neighbor. Besides, such an attitude is a direct contradiction of the spirit of solidarity which ought to characterize the human race and, in an especial degree, the members of the Christian community. The envious man tortures himself without cause, morbidly holding, as he does, the success of another to constitute an evil for himself. The sin, in so far as it bids defiance to the great precept of charity, is in general grievous, although on account of the trifling matter involved, as well as because of the want of sufficient deliberation, it is often reputed to be venial. Jealousy is most evil when one repines at another's spiritual good. It is then said to be a sin against the Holy Ghost. It is likewise called a capital sin because of the other vices it begets. Among its progeny St. Thomas (II-II, Q. xxxvi) enumerates hatred, detraction, rejoicing over the misfortunes of one's fellow, and whispering. Regret at another's success is not always jealousy. The motive has to be scrutinized. If, for instance, I feel sorrow at the news of another's promotion or rise to wealth, either because I know that he does not deserve his accession of good fortune, or because I have founded reason to fear he will use it to injure me or others, my attitude, provided that there is no excess in my sentiment, is entirely rational. Then, too, it may happen that I do not, properly speaking, begrudge my neighbor his happier condition, but simply am grieved that I have not imitated him. Thus if the subject-matter be praiseworthy, I shall be not jealous but rather laudably emulous.

Let us remember what St. Thomas Aquinas said: "All good things belong to God." Therefore, any good thing presents in us or others should not be a source of jealousy nor envy, instead, it should be the reason for us to praise God because we come from nothing, and it is He who lends us these talents. Since jealousy is specie of pride, St. Thomas Aquinas gives us this advice: "Humility is truth and justice."

What is truth?

Truth is knowing that being a creature, I come from nothing, I am good for nothing, and I am worth nothing. But there are good things in me as well and all good things belong to God. To claim these good things as my own, without praising God is theft. Since all good things belong to God, the only thing we can claim our own is our sin.

We also remember that humility is not just the truth, it is also justice.

Justice is to give someone his due. Since all the good things in me belong to God, then all praises are due to God alone. If my neighbor has good things, I should not be jealous because those good things belong to God. Therefore, when we accomplish something good from the talents God has given us, we should rather say "Praise the Lord". Since the only thing we can claim as our own is sin by virtue of justice, because of our mortal sins, we deserve hell. Therefore, what we deserve on earth are all humiliations, punishments, persecutions, and life. And since the greatest punishments and persecutions on earth are not equal to what we really deserve in hell, we should not really feel bad when humiliated or punished. "Put together with all the worst punishments and sufferings on earth, they are not even an iota of the sufferings we deserve in hell" (St. Thomas Aquinas).

Let us recall miracle 85 that is recounted on the fourth part of the Treasure of the Rosary:

There was a rich gentleman, who deeply devoted to the Divine Mother of God, has set apart of his palace an oratory where before a beautiful statue of Mary, he would often remain pray, not only during the day but also during the night. He would interrupt his rest just to go and honor his Beloved Lady. Although his wife was a very devout person, she observed that her husband would leave his bed during the most silent hours of the night and return after a very long time. She started to become jealous and even suspected evil of her husband. One day, she asked her husband if he ever loved any other woman but herself. Smiling and thinking of the Most Holy Virgin Mary whom he loves so tenderly, the husband told his wife that, indeed to us in love with the most amiable Lady in the world, and to this Lady, he would give his whole heart and would rather die than to cease loving Her. Further, he said that if she had known this Lady, she would rather that he loved her more than her (his wife). The man's answer devastated the wife. In sitting anger and jealousy, she took her life one night and left the knife she used lying beside her bed. When the husband came back after his nocturnal visit to the Mother of God, he found his wife in a pool of blood in bed. In horror, the man realized that his wife had destroyed herself out of useless jealousy. In desperation, the man ran to the image of the Virgin Mary and frustrated himself before Her, pouring out his sorrow on Her, begging for help. No sooner than the man said his prayer, he heard a servant-maid calling him frantically to his wife's room. There, in the middle of the bed, still in a pool of her own blood, sat his wife alive. She told him in holding tears that she had died and was before judgment-seat. When the Blessed Virgin Mary intervened before Her Son Jesus gave His verdict, she was given another chance to live and to spend it to make reparation for her sins. The Blessed Mother was her advocate; She gave her a new lease of life. A banquet was celebrated the next day, and from then on, both husband and wife would spend nocturnal vigils before the image of the Blessed Mother praying the Rosary and spending the whole night lifting up songs of praise to the Mother of God, whom they both became very devoted to.

We can see how Mother Mary's intervention is beyond our natural understanding. And as She revealed to St. Dominic and Blessed Alan de la Roche, anyone devoted to Her will not go to hell. Remember that Mary will never be the cause of the downfall of the soul.

St. Bridget revealed to us that when Jesus was still on earth, Mother Mary never refused Jesus anything He asked from Her. Now, She is in heaven, and He will never refuse Her requests for us sinners.

MEDITATION

"The greatest method of praying is to pray the Rosary" (St. Francis de Sales).

"Give me an army saying the Rosary, and I will conquer the

worl" (Blessed Pius IX).

PRAYER

Oh Mother of Holy Love, our life, our refuge, and our hope, you know that your Son Jesus Christ not content with making Himself our perpetual intercessor with the Eternal Father. You also engaged in obtaining for us by your prayers, the Divine Mercy. He ascertained that your prayer should aid in our salvation. He has given such power to your prayers that they obtain whatever you ask. I am a miserable sinner turning to you, oh hope of the wretched. Oh Lady, I hope to the merits of Jesus Christ and through your intercession to secure my salvation. I entirely trust in you that if my eternal were in my own hands, I would like to place it in yours. For in your mercy and protection, I would trust far more than in my own words.

My Mother and my hope, do not abandon as I deserve. Behold, my misery, pitting me, help me, and save me. I confess that I have often, by my sins, shut-out the light and aid that you have obtained for me from the Lord. But your compassion for the wretched and your power with God are far greater than the number and malignity of my sins. It is known in heaven on earth that He who protected by your will, certainly will not perish.

Let all forget me, but may I not be forgotten by you, oh Mother of the Omnipotent God. Say unto God that I am your servant, tell Him that I am defended by you, and I shall be saved. Amen.

DAY 10

INTERCESSORY POWER OF MARY: DO WHATEVER HE TELLS YOU

"And the third day, there was a marriage in Cana of Galilee: and the mother of Jesus was there. And Jesus also was invited, and his disciples, to the marriage. And the wine failing, the mother of Jesus saith to him: They have no wine. And Jesus saith to her: Woman, what is that to me and to thee? my hour is not yet come. His mother saith to the waiters: Whatsoever he shall say to you, do ye. Now there were set there six waterpots of stone, according to the manner of the purifying of the Jews, containing two or three measures apiece. Jesus saith to them: Fill the waterpots with water. And they filled them up to the brim. And Jesus saith to them: Draw out now, and carry to the chief steward of the feast. And they carried it. And when the chief steward had tasted the water made wine, and knew not whence it was, but the waiters knew who had drawn the water; the chief steward calleth the bridegroom, And saith to him: Every man at first setteth forth good wine, and when men have well drunk, then that which is worse. But thou hast kept the good wine until now. This beginning of miracles did Jesus in Cana of Galilee; and manifested his glory, and his disciples believed in him." (John 2: 1-12)

The scenery of Mary and Jesus at the wedding in Cana describes Mary as a true mother. Being a true mother, Mary had the uncanny gift of being sensitive to the needs of people, especially towards Her loved ones, even when not being told. She must have observed that the wine ran out, and Mary was concerned, to whom She turned to: Jesus, Her Son whom she knew could understand, whom She believed in, whom She knew would listen to Her request. Mary must have whispered to Him: "They have no more wine, Son" (John 2: 3). In those days, to run out of wine at the Jewish wedding feast would represent a social catastrophe that would severely damage the family's reputation for years. How well the feast went communicated to guests the family social status and honor. To run out of wine at a wedding feast, therefore, would inflict grave humiliation on the groom's family. It would appear that they were unable to fulfill their role adequately and that they lacked the social connections to preserve their honor. The crisis facing the bride and groom at the wedding feast in Cana gives us insight into how Mary quickly responded to save the couple from gross humiliation. Mary brought this crisis to Jesus, who alone She believed, can solve the problem to prevent a family disaster.

Our Catholic tradition uses Mary's feast of Cana to clearly illustrate Mary's compassion and attentiveness to someone in dire need.

Lumen Gentium describes Mary at Cana being "moved with pity." Pope John Paul II said Mary was "prompted by her merciful heart" to help this family by bringing her concern for them to Jesus: "Having sensed the eventual disappointment of the newly married couple and guests because of the lack of wine, the Blessed Virgin compassionately suggested to Jesus that he intervene with his messianic power."

In these recent times, we have experienced many natural catastrophes such as tsunamis, earthquakes, volcanic eruptions, floods, epidemics, famines, and war. While our immediate reaction would be to call 911, especially in the United States, triple Zero (000) in Australia or 112 in Europe. In fact, we have a host of emergency numbers to call anyone in the world if we get into danger or stuck in life-threatening situations. But we forget to call on that one person that someone who more powerful than any of these man-made created helps, who can prevent and liberate us from any catastrophes: Jesus.

The wedding feast at Cana served as a spring-board for the pattern of Mary's powerful intercession.

Just as Mary at Cana noticed the family's needs before anyone else did, so Mary in heaven continues to notice our needs before we do. And just as Mary at Cana brought those needs to Christ, so does She continues to bring our needs to Her Son through Her intercession.

In his Encyclical *"Redemptoris Mater"* (1987), Pope John Paul II wrote that this scene at Cana clearly shows "Mary's solicitude for human beings, her coming to them in the wide variety of their wants and needs." He continues: At Cana in Galilee, there is shown only one concrete aspect of human need, apparently a small one of little importance ("They have no wine"). But it has a symbolic value: this coming to the aid of human needs means, at the same time, bringing those needs within the radius of Christ's messianic mission and salvific power... Mary places herself between her Son and mankind in the reality of their wants, needs and sufferings.

Why is Mary called *"woman"* by Jesus at the wedding in Cana? Was it the disrespect of Jesus? Let us take a look at the profound meaning of why Jesus called His mother *"woman"* at the wedding feast in Cana.

In John's Gospel, this scene takes place on the seventh day of the new creation week. This leads us to see Jesus and Mary in the light of the creation story. And in this context, Jesus calls Mary *"woman."* With the Genesis stream in the background, this tittle would bring to mind the *"woman"* of Genesis, who is Eve. We read in Genesis 3: 15 that how this *"woman"* played an important part in the first prophecy given to humanity. After the Fall, God confronted the serpent and announced His eventual defeat, saying: *"I will put enmities between thee and the woman, and thy seed and her seed: she shall crush thy head, and thou shalt lie in wait for her heel"* (Genesis 3: 15). These words are known as *"Proto-Evangelium"* or *"First Gospel,"* foretell how one day the woman would have a seed, a son who will crush the head of the serpent. Centuries later, at the wedding feast in Cana, this prophecy begins to be fulfilled. By calling Mary *"woman,"* with a creation story in the background, in the narrative of Saint John's Gospel, Jesus is not merely addressing her politely as He does to Mary Magdalene and the Samaritan woman; rather, He is identifying Mary as the *"woman of Genesis"*. And so, in calling Mary *"woman,"* Jesus is not rebuking or disrespecting His mother, but rather He honors her in a way no woman had ever been honored before. She is the New Eve. The *"woman"* whose long-waited Son will defeat the devil and fulfill the prophecy of Genesis.

Let us consider a particular account which took place in the city of Manaoag in the province of Pangasinan in the Philippines. According to the documented dating back to 1610, one day, a native man, who was walking home, heard Our Lady's mysterious voice; he looked around with great awe and saw the radiant Lady with a Rosary in her right hand and the Baby Jesus in her left arm standing on the treetop. The man fell to his knees, the Blessed Virgin Mary told him to tell everyone in town to pray the Rosary, to place the complete trust in her in all their needs, especially in moments of crisis or catastrophe, and they should not despair because she will protect them from all their miseries. This man was obedient to the Virgin Mary and told the people of the apparition. And soon, right on the spot where Our Lady appeared, a church was built, and a town quickly flourished around it and was called Manaoag. Tradition has it that the town itself was born from the Virgin's call, thus the term *"taoag"* means *"to call"*. This is where the name Manaoag was derived from, which means *"She calls."* The Holy Augustinian Fathers were in charge of this spiritual administration of Managua town from the year 1590 to 1613 according to the Sanctified Decree of Spain. In 1614, the spiritual leadership was transferred to the Dominicans under the patronage of Santa Monica. Our Lady of Manaoag was formally named *"Nuestra Señora del Santísimo Rosario de Manaoag,"* the literal translation is *"Our Lady of the Most Holy Rosary of Manaoag."* This the title given to the Blessed Mother is associated with the Statue of Manaoag of Pangasinan. Dating back to the 16th century, She is the patroness of the sick, the helpless, and the needy in times of miseries. Now, the Statue of Our Lady of Manaoag has a long history of renowned miraculous and pious events that were depicted in the murals all over the church. This is done so that the events will never be forgotten. Deputies come from all over the world with their intentions and petitions, seeking the powerful intercession of the Blessed Virgin Mary. In 1945, during World War II, when it was announced that the Allied forces, led by General Douglas MacArthur, were coming, the Japanese army began to panic for fear of their impending defeat. Apart from the fact that the Japanese Imperial Army was losing many battles everywhere, mainland Japan was short of supply for manpower, armaments, and war materials to replace the weary and exhausted Japanese soldiers who were stationed in the Philippines. In the desperate situation and before dying honorably in the hand of their own Samurai's sword, they wanted to kill every Filipino at hand.

Having been under the oppression of the Spaniards for 400 years, the Filipinos were taught to have deep faith in the Blessed Mother, especially in times of great crisis such as war. During the massive bombing of homes and buildings in Pangasinan, the natives took shelter for months in the Church of Our Lady of Manaoag. The Japanese Imperial Army, who knew there were thousands of Filipinos in the church, sent a squadron of Zero fighter bombers and dropped several bombs in Manaoag Shrine. Inside the church, the natives continually prayed the Rosary and interspersed with the Holy Sacrifice of the Mass. What could have been a great massacre became a great miracle. Through Our Lady of Manaoag's intercession before our Lord Jesus Christ, the bombs, which landed at the roof to the Shrine one after the other, failed to explode. There was no damage of the roof of the Shrine, and not a single one was hurt or killed.

Some of the miraculous accounts regarding Our Lady of Manaoag date back to the early 17th century, the indigenous mountain tribe peoples from Igorot used to burn down newly converted Christian villages, by which the town of Manaoag was not spared. The city was set on fire, and the church with its thatched roof was the last refuge of the people. The leader of the pillagers climbed over the fence and shut flaming arrows to all parts of the church with intention of burning it. However, not a single flame set the church on fire. This miraculous event was famously repeated and nationally reported.

The church of Manaoag is one of the Philippines' most widely revered Roman Catholic refuges. The hilltop location of Our Lady Manaoag Shrine stands up to this day, where tens of thousands continue to flock every year. Not a single after this time that this Shrine is not packed with pilgrims from across the Philippines alone, who come and visit the place where the Blessed Mother's image and where Our Lady calls all Her children for refuge is enshrined.

What is the first word a child usually learns or says? Isn't it "*mama*"? Rarely is the word "*papa*" or any other word for that matter. Why? It is because of that biological bond shared between mother and child spent in those nine months of being physical, emotional, and spiritually together. Then in the early stage of growth, when the child is sick in pain, in need, or hungry, what is its first instinct? It is to cry out for mama! Therefore, it is not or should it not be a natural tendency for us, especially when experiencing grave challenges in life, in danger by the human and natural crisis, should we not have that innate recourse to turn to our Heavenly Mother for help. Yes, we may have all the present concerns or arguments about women having the same rights as men; problems in marriages that bring about the reality of single mothers having to fend for the family alone; problems of poverty that necessitates the practice of responsible parenthood, equal rights, gender equality... each one of us learns to call on someone for help, for most of us that called, went to Mother, Mother Mary. Whether we were heard or helped or understood during a lifetime still, that call we made, went to a mother. Now, Holy Mother, the Church calls on all Her children whether broken or suffering or not in need, capable sick or healthy to turn and call on Her, to anchor themselves to Her pillar of strength as She is now honored, declared, celebrated as an obligatory memorial as Mary, the Mother of the Church. What does this signify? Symbolically, Pope Francis has anchored the Church to Mary, the Mother of God and the Mother of the Church in these perilous times of our human history. Mary as the refuge of the sinners is more than ever the refuge of families. With the Rosary and the Scapular, She ties and binds Her children to Her side as She navigates the turbulent seas before us. At the institution of this great honor of Mary, Mother of the Church on May 21, 2018, the whole Roman Catholic Church will celebrate this title of our Blessed Mother as an obligatory memorial in the Roman calendar and Liturgy, no longer optional as before, but now permanently and yearly, as if, to clearly declare in the midst of war that "the Queen of Heaven has come in full battle gear" to take control of the crisis of the Church as She is Mary, Mother of the Church.

In this millennium, the first of the two pillars in Don Bosco's vision has now clearly appeared inside, the pillar of the Blessed Mother, and the chains by which we, the small ships in the vision, can anchor ourselves to this pillar: the Rosary and the Scapular. Worldwide, we have seen and continue to see the unified efforts of Mary's children to anchor themselves to Mary, the Mother of the Church. Human Rosary chains praying miles and miles around the coast of their countries the Rosary, securing their faith, their family, and their land from every evil attack and possession that is waiting in their midst. Poland led the way, Ireland followed soon, and many other countries will hold this Rosary on the border or the coast soon all over the world.

Beginning of 2017, on the occasion of the centennial anniversary of Our Lady of Fatima, six images blessed by Pope Francis began their missionary journey to the six continents, re-echoing the Virgin Mary's message at Fatima: *"Sin no more."* John Paul II's legacy of consecrating the whole world to the Immaculate Heart of Mary is repeated in each visit of these six International Centennial Pilgrim Statues as every parish, every diocese, and every country is consecrated to the Sacred Heart of Jesus and the Immaculate Heart of Mary by bishops and parish priests. All who participate in the visitation are enrolled and imposed with a brown Scapular as a sign of consecration. Millions have been consecrated and millions more to be done. Reparation vigils will

continue praying of the Holy Rosary are held in all the visit of
Her Centennial Statues in reparation for the sins of abortion,
contraception, desecration of the sacrament of matrimony the
Holy Eucharist, and human life in general. The mission has just
begun for these children of Mary around the world. For two
more years, these six centennial images of Our Lady of Fatima
will travel around the world, bringing the Blessed Mother's call:
"*Sin no more*" in every continent, country, diocese, and parish.
Millions more people will be enrolled, and imposed with the
brown Scapular. Many more Rosary rallies will be organized to
secure every single country along its border and coastlines with
Mary, the Mother of the Church as its help. The clock is ticking,
and the children of Mary, the small ships in Don Bosco's vision,
have a lot more to do to keep the Bark of Peter from sinking.

Our Mother Mary is very much concerned about the volatile
situation of the world today. One false miscalculation from any
of the leaders of the first world countries, the world will go up in
smoke in minutes. The smoke of Satan is whirling around us, it
has entered the crux of the Church, and it is beginning to suffo-
cate many of us.

MADITATION

"*If you wish peace to reign in your homes, recite the family Rosary.*" (Pope Pius X)

"*Even if you are in the brink of damnation, even if you have one
foot in hell, even you have sold your soul to the devil or sorcerers who
practice black magic, and even if you are heretic as obstinate as a
devil, sooner or later you will be converted and will amend your life
and will save your soul if you say the Holy Rosary devoutly every day
until death for the purpose of knowing the truth and obtaining contrition and pardon for your sins.*" (St. Louis de Montfort)

PRAYER

Oh Blessed Mother, you are my refuge. I am your sinful child,
I run to you now for your help and your clemency to ask from
God the Father to pardon for all my sins. I beg for your help that
I may have the strength and humility to all that you asked of me
to amend my life and make reparation to the hour of my death,

for all these offences I have committed against God. I will do that you say, for I know, in the end, it is my soul who will suffer eternal punishment in hell. I no longer fear anything because I have chosen you as my advocate, my refuge, my Mother. Keep me, oh Loving Mother, not only under your mantle but tie securely at your side with the chains of the Rosary and the Scapular, which I promise to pray and wear every single day from now on. I ask this in the Name of Jesus Christ, our Lord. Amen.

DAY 11

VIRGIN MOST FAITHFUL, LOOKS FOR
LOST JESUS AT THE TEMPLE

"And not finding him, they returned into Jerusalem, seeking him. And it came to pass, that, after three days, they found him in the temple, sitting in the midst of the doctors, hearing them, and asking them questions. And all that heard him were astonished at his wisdom and his answers. And seeing him, they wondered. And his mother said to him: Son, why hast thou done so to us? Behold thy father and I have sought thee sorrowing. And he said to them: How is it that you sought me? Did you not know that I must be about my father's business? And they understood not the word that he spoke unto them." (Luke 2: 45-50)

In the account of the loss of Jesus in the temple, we find two questions: *"why hast thou done so to us?"* and *"Did you not know, that I must be about my father's business?"*

After three days Mary and Joseph found Jesus in the temple sitting in the midst of the teachers, listening to them and asking them questions; all who listening to Him were amazed at His understanding and answers. And Mary said to Jesus: *"Son, why did you do this to us? Behold, in sorrow, your father and I had been seeking you. And Jesus said to them: How is it that you sought me? Did you not know that I must be about my father's business? And they understood not the word that he spoke unto them.* There were two events in the Gospel of St. Luke when Mary did not understand but pondered in her heart the mysterious designs of God. The first occasion was when the shepherds visited the Christ child in Bethlehem and told Mary and Joseph all they had seen and heard. Mary is then said to have "kept in mind all these things, pondering them in her heart." The second occasion was when Jesus was found by His parents in the temple after being lost for three days. These two events give us an insight into how God's providence deals with persons that He loves. And God teaches us how we should dispose ourselves to respond to His mysterious ways in our lives just as Mary did. People today want to know everything about their friends, and even the manner on how to deal with them. The problem is many of us want also to treat God in the same way, as if God's supernatural nature could be grasped by our natural mind. This problem is aggravated when God tests our love for Him without revealing His reason for doing so. Remember what Isaiah said: *"For my thoughts are not your thoughts: nor your ways my ways, saith the Lord"* (Isaiah 55: 8). It only means that God tries those whom He loves, and since He loves us all, He tries us all. The God's degree of testing depends on two things:

First, it depends on the level of sanctity to which God wants to raise a soul and on the kind of work He wants that soul to do in the extension of His Kingdom. The higher our call to holiness and the greater the work in the apostolate to which God calls us, the greater will be His testing us, humanly speaking, the more unsolicited will be the trials and difficulties and obstacles God is sure to us, the more is the reward that awaits us.

Second, God has a purpose in everything He does. We might ask that, "why did God allow it?" or "why did Jesus stay back in the temple and let His parents anxiously searched for Him for three days? Let us return to the event of Jesus who after three days was found in the temple by his parents Joseph and Mary. Jesus could have stayed on in Jerusalem by simply telling His parents: *"I am staying in the temple for three days,"* but this is not the case with God. Most of the time, He did not tell us what intends to do; He just does it, then He allows us to figure it out for ourselves. Let us look at an example of St. Paul: He should have asked God so many questions such as "why he had to suffer more than other apostles?" He could not comprehend his sufferings in preaching Jesus Christ to the Gentiles, but because he loved God, he obeyed His will. He could have been fallen into bitterness like many of us so often do, but instead, he became better, he even said in his Letter to Colossians: *"Who now rejoice in my sufferings for you, and fill up those things that are wanting of the sufferings of Christ, in my flesh, for his body, which is the Church"* (Colossians 1: 24). Fortunately, St. Paul has left us something of a record of why he went through during his brief apostolic enterprise. Many of his letters were written in prison, and at least on one dramatic occasion, they were written while he was in chains. Scourged, stoned, left for dead, betrayed, abandoned by friends, hated; and added to all of this, he experienced deep interior sufferings, St. Paul all had to undergo because God had His plans on him.

What are the lessons we can learn in the Finding of Jesus in the Temple?

First lesson: God is Lord. His ways are not our ways! He may send us an illness or take one of our loved ones from us, all in sudden, but He also sends us wonderful people in our lives, our loving spouse, beautiful children, and good neighbors. But just as God gives us wonderful things, people, or situations, He also takes them away from us. Job was the model of righteous man, but he suffered more than the worst criminals during his time. He was gifted and blessed with bounty but in just a blink of an eye, everything vanished, and he was left with nothing but misery. His famous life has been immortalized, *"God has given; God has taken away. Blessed be God!"* (Job 1: 21). God moves in mysterious ways, we learn very well that God's ways are not our ways. This was clearly evident in the experience of Finding of Jesus in the Temple;

Second lesson: God has a purpose for everything He does. We may ask, "Why God act in this way? No one except God knows the full answer. But one thing is sure that God tests His loved ones, not to see them suffer. It may be hard to understand at the present His purpose, but in the end, it is always good and His designs are always just; even more, they are supremely loving and kind.

Venerable Father John Hardon once said that there are only

two mysteries in the universe that cannot be sufficiently explained. One is in Heaven, the Holy Trinity; one is on earth, and that is human suffering. Since the Fall of Adam and Eve, so many explanations had been given about God and human suffering. While we may have sufficient ideas, no one has really succeeded in explaining these two mysteries.

What may be the reason God allows us to suffer? One thing is evident, suffering and trial, especially interior trial call upon our faith in God's goodness as nothing else in life. It is so easy to recite the Apostolic Creed, or thrill to sing our *"Credo in unum Deum!"* when all is well, but there is no melody and no great pleasure in saying *"I believe"* when God is bidding us to accept what we do not understand. The emphasis should be placed on us: "I" do not understand. But what is the essence of faith? It is trusting in God who allows us to suffer to invoke in us the summit of our love. St. John of the Cross explained to us that the suffering of Jesus was more than all the sufferings of the world combined. His immense love for us is shown in how much He suffered to make reparation for our sins and to make us sons and daughters of God, the Father; to give one's life for a friend, and even to give his life for an enemy is what Jesus did, as Jesus is Love. So when do we show that we love God the most? When we love Him for His own sake and not for ours? But these are cheap words. It is bringing these words into action, it is when we make them live that matters. A humble soul fixed only in doing God's Will is able to accept with joy every trial and difficulty. The only satisfaction he receives, the only joy in his heart, is the realization that he is doing as God wants. This is the definition of the perfect love of God. As we read in John 14:16, this is the way that God teaches us in love, that He is the Master, and to love Him, we must obey Him. Those of us who are proud and want God to conform to our own ways, we need this reminder;

Third lesson: The deepest understanding of our faith comes from the experience of suffering and prayer. The Kingdom of Christ is most effectively promoted, and the grace of God is most abundantly poured out on the souls of men by those who have learned the meaning of the apostolate of suffering. From the first to the third century, the Roman Empire, of which Judea is a province, decreed *"Christianis non sunt"*, meaning *"Christianity is not allowed to exist."* Therefore, the killing of Christians was easier than killing flies. When persecutions besieged the Church of God, the Church coined the expression that we should memorize. Let us cherish it: "The blood of martyrs is the seed of Christians". This means that the Church most thrives on the blood of her martyrs. It is not easy to accept this principle of propagation, which the Church prospers on the sufferings of her faithful. Too many people are writhing, struggling with this mystery of God. But there is only one answer, only one-complete and total abandonment to God's Divine Providence.

Let us take the example of this story, in 1962 and 1964, the president of Brazil, Joao Goulart, began to embrace communism and began to install communist into high positions in the government. He thought this was the answer to the widespread poverty and corruption in the largest Catholic country in the whole world. He did not consider a success the millions of babies baptized, over 75% of Catholics going to church amidst the difficulties the people experiencing every day. There are many vocations at the time, many young people, many young men, and women were entering religious congregations. Unfortunately, there was not much comfort and leisure in Brazil because of the strong Catholic identity, and money was not enough to make the life of people more comfortable than what they could afford. The president of Brazil thought that communism would attract more investments and make Brazil very rich. All democracies then were cut tail, a stronger police force was introduced, people were arrested, kidnapped, and unwarranted killings were widespread. In response, Cardinal de Barros Camara encouraged the people to listen to the message of Our Lady of Fatima to pray the Rosary to keep the country free from the danger of communism. President Goulart reacted by mocking the Rosary, saying that "Governmental control, not reciting the prayers of the Rosary, would save Brazil."

A Brazilian woman named Dona Amelia Bastos began gathering many people to pray the Rosary, forming a group called Campaign of Women for Democracy (CAMDE). In a town called Belo Horizonte a group of 20,000 women reciting the rosary aloud broke up a pro-Communist rally. The success of this peaceful protest fed the impetus for the Catholic women to do more. With the help of heaven and the strong influence of Archbishop Cardinal de Barros Camara, Dona Amelia recruited an amazing 600,000 women who marched in Sao Paulo to pray the rosary for peace. They called their protest, "March of the Family with God toward Freedom." under the declaration, "Mother of God, preserve us from the fate and suffering of the martyred women of Cuba, Poland, Hungary, and other enslaved nations." Leone Brizola, a Communist high government official, left in a rage when his planned speech was thwarted by the rattling of 3000 rosaries and the murmuring of the prayers in the assembly hall. Not one life was lost in this most amazing peaceful anti-Communist protest, which is described by many witnesses as, "One of the most moving demonstrations in Brazilian History." Many more rosary rallies were held in major cities despite threats of military action against the crusading women. Under this mounting pressure, on April 1, 1964, President Goulart fled the country along with many members of the government.

We will never fully understand why God allows these things that it does. The Blessed Mother Herself did not understand, but did not mean that She adjusted Her actions to Her lack of comprehension. One lesson that Mother Mary teaches us from Her life as told by the Gospel of St. Luke is the frequent entrance of God into Her life to make demands of Her, and on Her for which She was humanly speaking unprepared.

This was true at the Annunciation. To say the least, she was surprised. And, being told about Elizabeth, her response was the Visitation. But the last thing she had expected was to trek across the hill country of Judea to visit her aged kinswoman who was with child. During Joseph's no doubt long quandary, she was never told to tell him, so she didn't. And did she ever suffer! One of the most painful experiences in life is to think that someone we love thinks ill about us.

At the Nativity of Jesus, The sudden move from Nazareth to Bethlehem was unexpected as well as the reception, or lack of it, in Bethlehem, and the necessary birth of Christ in a stable. The last thing a mother wants when she brings a child into the world is to have that child born, as Christ was, in a barn. The prophecy of Simeon and the flight into Egypt were unexpected, and now the loss in the Temple; but most of all, Christ's strange words to her when He was found, "Did you not know that I must be about my Father's business?"

Therefore, we also should be willing to accept God's plan every day, and for some of us, a large part of the day. We should accept God's visitation, to do what He evidently wants of us. Mother Mary did not know about His Father's business, in the sense of fully understanding why. And this is where Mary, the Virgin Most Faithful, is such a pattern for all of us to follow. She was "most faithful" twice over: most faithful because, unlike Her Son who had the constant vision of God, she had to live by faith; she did not see, and her faith was deep, it was strong; then she is called Virgin Most Faithful because her faith was tried! Believing, she did not comprehend. None of us comprehends the designs of God in our lives, except Mary. What do all these teach us, especially those who are persevering in living the communion of reparation lifestyle? If you are doing, or are attending the monthly reparation vigils, practice some form of asceticism and mortification. "Well, that is very interesting. Keep doing that. But in God's name, be interiorly resigned to God's visitations in your life! Then no matter what you think of yourself, you are close to God."

Surrender what He evidently wants us to give up-and not for a moment or to the least degree hesitate or hold back because we don't comprehend at the moment, in time, He will reveal to you His purpose.

MEDITATION

"When you despise that what is considered to be death here

on earth, then you shall fear what is truly death in the next life, which is reserved for those who shall be condemned to the eternal fire, which shall afflict to the end of those who are committed to it. Then shall you admire those who for righteousness' sake endured the fire that is but for a moment, and you shall count them happy when you understand that fire." (Letter to Diognetus, AD 80 – 200, chapter 10)

PRAYER

Oh Loving God, from the beginning till the end of time, when you created me from nothing to something. You had one great plan to make me a saint to love and serve you for eternity in heaven. Only by following your will like the Blessed Mary, will I be able to realize your divine plan. Oh loving Tender, Divine Providence, and my God, into your hands, I commend my spirit. To you, I commit the most precious interests of my mortal soul and have nothing to fear as long as I do not leave your care. My faults are many, but my hope in you surpasses everything. It has appeared though my weakness greater than my difficulties and stronger than death. Though temptations should have sailed me, I will hope in you. Though I break my resolutions, I will look to you confidently for grace to keep them at last. Though you should take my life like the martyrs, even then I will trust in you, for you are my Father, my God, the support of my salvation. I beg for your blessings that when I lose Jesus your Son through my own fault, but with Saint Joseph and Mother Mary, I may find Him again in the temple, for you live forever and ever. Amen.

DAY 12

BAPTISM OF JESUS, IDENTIFIES HIMSELF TO SINNERS

"Then cometh Jesus from Galilee to the Jordan, unto John, to be baptized by him. But John stayed him, saying: I ought to be baptized by thee, and comest thou to me? And Jesus answering, said to him: Suffer it to be so now. For so it becometh us to fulfill all justice. Then he suffered him. And Jesus being baptized, forthwith came out of the water: and lo, the heavens were opened to him: and he saw the Spirit of God descending as a dove, and coming upon him. And behold a voice from heaven, saying: This is my beloved Son, in whom I am well pleased" (Matthew 3: 16-17).

From the Evangelist, we read that one day as John stood preaching and baptizing on the Jordan, Jesus suddenly appeared and demanded baptism. It was startled, John replied: *"It is I who ought to be baptized by you, but you come to me. But Jesus only answers: Let it be so now; for so it becomes us to fulfill all justice."* And these words John consent to Him to the request of Jesus. *"The heavens opened, the dove descends, and the voice is heard: 'This is my beloved Son, in whom I am well pleased."* When Jesus came to the Jordan, He was fully aware of the extraordinary task that was laid before Him, and of the powers that rose to meet it by the depth of His being. Yet, His first gesture and word were an expression of deep humility. He approached John and asked him to be baptized. The demand for baptism implies that you are ready to accept the word of the baptizer, to do penance, and to willingly accept the word of God, no matter how difficult it might be. So it was no wonder that John was startled at the request of Jesus, and even tried to dissuade the Lord. But Jesus quietly took his place in line, He refused to be an exception, He voluntarily placed Himself within the law that was valid for all.

Since the Fall of man, a barrier had separated us from the beatific vision of God in heaven, but when Jesus came to the Jordan, when He humble lowered Himself to the level of man, for a moment, this barrier was removed. While Jesus stood there and praying, an infinite encounter took place, the heavens opened, and there was an abundant outpouring from God above, which streamed into the Son's human heart.

St. Thomas Aquinas taught that *"Sin is greatest and only evil."* Pope Paul VI clearly wrote: *"Sin is the entry of influence of Satan in us."* When we sin, we become slaves of the devil. Sin is evil because it killed Jesus Christ, our Lord, and God. Sin destroyed the original justice and holiness in us. Because of the influence of Satan and the misuse of human freedom, we see God's masterpiece, totally deformed and brought lower than any other creature He has created. Seeing mankind stuck in the mud of his own sinfulness and unable to free himself, God must have been so moved by compassion and love that it impelled Him to send His only begotten Son to save us from sins.

As Christians, we reflect upon and celebrate the baptism of Jesus in three significant ways: First, Liturgically, at the conclusion of the Christmas season; Second, Devotionally, as the First Luminous Mystery of the Rosary; Third, Theologically, as the scriptural prism for the meaning of Christian baptism.

The baptism performed by John the Baptist was meant theologically as a sign of repentance of sin and conversion to a new way of life, it's reasonable to ask: Why did Jesus, as the sinless Son of God, receive baptism? Jesus' baptism had these meanings:

First, the baptism of Jesus marks the inauguration of His public ministry, His coming out from the hidden life into a life of growing popularity on account of His preaching, miracles, healings and proclamation of mercy and forgiveness;

Second, the baptism of Jesus is the beginning of His mission of Redemption through this public religious act;

Third, the baptism of Jesus brought the descent of the Holy Spirit to anoint Jesus as the Messiah or the Christ, which in Greek means "the Anointed One."

In this dramatic scene, we already grasp the identity and function of the Most Blessed Trinity and the plan of salvation. We see the Father as the One who begets and sends the Son to redeem the human race; the Son as the obedient servant who accomplishes the will of the Father to redeem mankind; and the Holy Spirit as the Sanctifier who empowers the mission of redemption.

Let us look at the Liturgical meaning of the Feast of the Baptism of the Lord. First of all, it marks the end of the Christmas season, typically celebrated on a Sunday, it moves to a Monday if Christmas falls on a Sunday. In the Trinitarian relationship, the Baptism of Jesus revealed His fundamental identity as Redeemer. It constituted partly the Epiphany of the Lord to the Gentiles. In the early Church, the visit of the Magi, the Baptism of the Lord and the miracle at Cana together constituted the meaning of Epiphany, for each of these three events revealed, manifested and unveiled who Jesus was. Devotionally, the Baptism of Jesus is presented in the Luminous Mystery, revealed the power of the Rosary, otherwise, known as the mini-Bible. The Holy Rosary is not only a Marian prayer, the contemplation of the mysteries of the Life, Death, and Resurrection of Jesus shows Jesus' salvific power against sin. As Mary is the tabernacle, the salvific power is not in the tabernacle but in the Sacred Host, the Eucharistic Jesus. Jesus' Baptism as part of the Luminous Mystery is above all, presenting the power of Jesus in interceding between God and man and redeeming man from his sin and the consequence of his sins. When Our Lady appeared to St. Dominic in 1214, She revealed to him that even the devil admitted that the Rosary is the weapon which he fears most, because when properly pray, it has the power to destroy his kingdom. After the Holy Sacrifice of the Mass, the Rosary is the most fearful prayer against Satan and his offspring.

There are profound parallels between Jesus' Baptism and our own. As Jesus revealed Himself as the Beloved Son at the Jordan, so, too, we receive a new identity in Baptism as adopted children of the Father. The fruit of Christ's Resurrection is the victory over the power of sin and death, but the victory over the power of Satan is the divine invitation for us to share in the life of the Trinity. We should renew often our Baptism Promise to renounce Satan and to obey the Father, our Creator; Jesus Christ, our Redeemer; and Holy Spirit, our Sanctifier. At the moment of our spiritual rebirth in the font, God, the Father beholds us with delight, exclaiming: *"This is my beloved son; this is my beloved daughter with whom I am well pleased."* Christianity first and foremost is about whom we have become in Christ before it is about what we do or how we act. This saving act of spiritual adoption draws us into the very life of God and His merciful grace.

In the book Jesus of Nazareth, Pope Benedict XVI offers another insight into the significance of the Baptism of the Lord. He tells us that the baptismal action to the repentant sinners by John the Baptist was noticeably different from any other religious rituals that had preceded it. The Baptism he offered the crowds that came from Jerusalem occurred only once; it signified a radical break from a former life of sin and a new way of thinking and acting. The crowds responded to John's Baptism as a reaction to his fiery preaching against sin and the call to conversion.

Pope Benedict sees Jesus' Baptism as an expression of His fundamental submission to the will of the Father and His complete identification with sinners. By submersion in the waters of the Jordan, Jesus is publicly seen as one in need of repentance and forgiveness himself, although He has no need of it in actuality. Jesus is already embracing the enormous weight of humanity's sinfulness, just as He will do again in a definitive and final way on the cross when He took mankind's sinfulness, labeled then as a criminal and blasphemer. Jesus' Baptism is seen also as a prelude of man's forgiveness for all his sins on the Cross when Jesus pleaded as mediator to God, His Father: *"Father, forgive them, for they do not know what they are doing."* The mysterious events at the Jordan River already foreshadow the saving acts of Christ's death and resurrection.

Looking at the icons of Jesus' baptism of the Eastern Church, Pope Benedict notes the connection between the Baptism of the Lord and the Paschal Mystery by depicting the waters of the Jordan "as a liquid tomb having the form of a dark cavern, which is, in turn, the iconographic sign of Hades, the underworld, or hell." Just as the Lord descends into the swirling waters of death at His baptism, He goes down to the netherworld after His crucifixion to rescue the souls of lost humanity. In this descent, this complete identification with sinners, we grasp the radical humility of Jesus. He is the One who empties himself, not clinging to His equality with God but becoming a slave for the sake of our salvation.

Christianity is the only world religion that believes the omnipotent and mysterious God humbled himself to become one of His own creatures, embracing the fullness of our humanity in order to redeem us from inside our own nature and condition. The Church has never gotten over the wonder of this divine condescension. We celebrate the Word made flesh not only in the glory of Christmas but in the fullness of the liturgy, prayer, and moral life of the Christian tradition, (in his book "Jesus of Nazareth").

In his homily on the Feast of the Baptism of Jesus, Pope Benedict XVI related that Jesus shows His solidarity with us in order to tell us that if we accept Him in our life as our Redeemer, He can uplift us and lead us to the height of God the Father. Jesus truly immersed himself in our human condition, lived it to the end, in all things saved sinners, and was able to understand our weakness and frailty. For this reason, he was moved to compassion, he chose to "suffer with" men and women, to become a penitent with us. This is God's work, which Jesus wanted to carry out: the divine mission to heal those who are wounded and give medicine to the sick, to take upon himself the sin of the world.

No matter how terrible a crime we may have done in this life, if we renew our baptismal promise to God, if we repent, ask forgiveness in confession, and do penance for our sins, God in His infinite mercy will extend clemency to our soul; Have a deep and constant devotion to the Blessed Mother for she is truly the refuge of sinners.

MEDITATION

"The Most Holy Virgin in these last times which we live, has given a new efficacy to the recitation of the Rosary to such an extent that there is no problem, no matter how difficult it is, whether temporal or above all spiritual, in the personal life of each one of us, of our families... that cannot be solved by the Rosary. THERE IS NO PROBLEM, I TELL YOU, NO MATTER HOW DIFFICULT IT IS, THAT WE CANNOT RESOLVE BY THE PRAYER OF THE HOLY ROSARY" (Sr. Lucia, seer of Fatima).

PRAYER

Oh Great Mother of God, I now see that in gratitude I have shown in God for many years by committing of my highness crimes. I deserve no less than hell, but with the Passion and Death of Jesus, your Son, a new collaboration in His Passion and Death, you merited my salvation. Through the Baptism of Jesus, He took my sins and washed it away, that I may become again the adopted children of God.

Oh Blessed Mother, remind me always to renew my baptismal promise to renounce Satan and to accept Jesus in my life as my Savior through your powerful intercession. With this promise, I intend to live a graceful lifestyle and a sinless lifestyle. This is only possible with your help, oh Blessed Mother, who is the refuge of sinners. I ask this through Christ, our Lord. Amen.

DAY 13

"I will put enmities between thee and the woman, and thy seed and her seed: she shall crush thy head, and thou shalt lie in wait for her heel" (Genesis 3:15).

Miracles happen every day to the sensitive and prayerful. These occurrences are quite evident that not so sensitive or pragmatist. These events are extraordinary, but are they? For us who believe in the Virgin Mary and the power of the Rosary, nothing is really extraordinary because nothing is impossible with God, especially if we implore the heart of the Mother of God.

In Genesis 3: 15, the perennial enmity in this world is between the woman (Mary) and the serpent (Satan); Mother Mary representing God while Satan representing Lucifer. It has been already announced that the woman will crush the serpent's head as it lies down and waits for her heel to crush it. God desires all to be saved (1 Timothy 2:4). Like every mother, the Blessed Mother will do everything it takes in Her power to save Her children when they become wayward or fall into danger of losing their souls.

Mother Mary's coming at Fatima revealed three challenges and critical problems that must be resolved right away if we want to live peacefully on earth:

First: Eschatology. This deals with death, judgment, heaven, and hell. Our Lady of Fatima said: *"Pray much and make sacrifices for sinners, for many souls go to hell because there is no one to make sacrifices for them."*

Second: Peace or War. To save souls from the eternal punishment of hell and temporal punishment of war, persecutions, and tribulations, the Blessed Mother warned that men must stop sinning. This is contained in the second part of "Lucia's Memoirs" dated August 31ˢᵗ, 1941, the Blessed Mother said: "But if people do not cease offending God or do not stop sinning, a worse war (World War II) will break out during the Pontificate of Pius XI. When you see an ideal human by an unknown light, know that this is a great sign given you by God that He is about to punish the world for its crimes by means of war, famine, and persecution of the Church and of the Holy Father;"

Third: Persecution or Respect of the Church and the Pope. Again, in the book "Lucia's Memoirs" written on January 3ʳᵈ, 1944, sister Lucia wrote: "We saw in an immense light that is God, there the Holy Father passed through a big city half in ruins and half trembling with halting step, afflicted with pain and sorrow, he prayed for the souls of the corpses he met on his way; having reached the top of the mountain, on his knees at the foot of the big Cross, he was killed by a group of soldiers who fired bullets and arrows at him, and in the same way there died one after another the other Bishops, Priests, men and women Religious, and various lay people of different ranks and positions. Beneath the two arms of the Cross, there were two Angels, each with a crystal holy water font in his hand, in which they gathered up the blood of the Martyrs and with it sprinkled the souls that were making their way to God. In 2 Peter 3: 9, we read: *"God is patient not wishing for any to perish."* To prevent and avert this inevitability of going to hell, having bigger wars, more persecutions, and tribulations of having the Pope shot dead leading to greater persecution of the Church, we need to follow the Message of Fatima which can be summarized in three parts: First part, using "COR", the short word of Consecrate Russia and the world to the Heart of Mary and Jesus, using the acronym "C" for Consecration, "O" for Offering a solution, "R" for Reparation; Second part, Pius XII likewise urged us to consecrate ourselves, family, parish, diocese, country, and the whole Church to the

Hearts of Jesus and Mary. He further explained in his 1956 Encyclical *"Haurietis Auas"*; Third part, in the global level, the consecration of Russia particularly and the world to the Immaculate Heart of Mary, side by side with the Sacred Heart of Jesus, be performed by the Pope and the bishops of the world. The Fatima Message of July 13, 1917, the Blessed Mother said: *"In order to save them, God wishes to establish in the world devotion to My Immaculate Heart."* Our Lady decided that the Holy Father makes more explicit during the Holy Year of Redemption, the act of instruction of May 7, 1981, which had been repeated in Fatima on May 13, 1982. On March 25, 1984, at St. Peter Square, while recalling *"Fiat"* uttered by Mary at the Annunciation, Saint John Paul II and spiritual union with the bishops of the world had been convoked beforehand entrusted all men and women and all peoples to the Immaculate Heart of Mary. Significantly, this is the same consecration formula which the bishops and priests prayed when the International Centennial Images of Our Lady Fatima made Her visit during the 100 Jubilee Anniversary to consecrate the dioceses and parishes to the Immaculate Heart.

This is the heartfelt and powerful prayer:

O Mother of all men and women, and of all peoples, you who know all their sufferings and their hopes, you who have a mother's awareness of all the struggles between good and evil, between light and darkness, which afflict the modern world, accept the cry which we, moved by the Holy Spirit, address directly to your Heart. Embrace with the love of the Mother and Handmaid of the Lord, this human world of ours, which we entrust and consecrate to you, for we are full of concern for the earthly and eternal destiny of individuals and peoples. Immaculate Heart! Help us to conquer the menace of evil, which so easily takes root in the hearts of the people of today, and whose immeasurable effects already weigh down upon our modern world and seem to block the paths towards the future!

From famine and war, *deliver us.*

From nuclear war, from incalculable self-destruction, from every kind of war, *deliver us.*

From sins against the life of man from its very beginning, *deliver us.*

From hatred and from the demeaning of the dignity of the children of God, *deliver us.*

From every kind of injustice in the life of society, both national and international, *deliver us.*

From readiness to trample on the commandments of God, *deliver us.*

From attempts to stifle in human hearts the very truth of God, *deliver us.*

From the loss of awareness of good and evil, *deliver us.*

From sins against the Holy Spirit, deliver us, *deliver us.*

Accept, O Mother of Christ, this cry *laden with the sufferings* of all individual human beings*, laden with the sufferings* of whole societies.

Help us with the power of the Holy Spirit to conquer all sin: individual sin and the 'sin of the world', sin in all its manifestations.

After Saint Paul II prayed this Fatima Consecration, immediately its global effects were made evident as seen in the following international events:

On May 13, 1984, one of the largest crowds in Fatima history gathered at the Shrine to pray the Rosary for peace. On the same day, an explosion at the Soviet's Severomorsk Naval Base in Russia, an installation 900 miles from Moscow, destroyed two-third of all the missile stockpiles of the Soviet's Northern Fleet, the blasts also destroyed the workshop that maintained the missiles and killed hundreds of scientists and technicians. Western military experts called it the worst neighbor disaster of the Soviet's Navy suffered since World War II. After this explosion, the Soviet's Generals believed they could not anymore rule the world, and that ended practically the Soviet power. On December 20, 1984, the Minister of Defense of Soviet Union Dmitry Fedorovich Ustino, who masterminded the invasion plans of Western Europe, suddenly and seriously died from heart failure. On March 10, 1985, the Chairman of the Presidium of the Supreme

Soviet, Konstantin Ustinovich Chernenko died from heart failure. On March 11, 1985, Mikhail Gorbachev was selected as the new General Secretary of the Soviet Union. On April 26, 1986, the Chernobyl disaster also known the Chernobyl accident, this was the inadvertent explosion of a nuclear reactors core during an emergency shutdown while undergoing power failure test. The radioactive materials released in the atmosphere, contaminated a large part of Western USSR in Europe, which after these days, the scientists said that still continues to show signs of nuclear contamination. On May 12, 1988, an explosion wrecked the only factory that made the rocket motors of the Soviet's deadly "SS24 Long-Range missiles which carried ten nuclear bombs each. On August 29, 1989, sister Lucia affirms in correspondence that the consecration *"has been accomplished"* and that *"God will keep His word."* On November 9, 1989, the Fall of the Berlin Wall. November – December, 1989, the Peaceful revolutions in Czechoslovakia, Romania, Bulgaria, and Albania. In 1990, the East and West Germany are unified. On December 25, 1991, is the Dissolution of the Union of Soviet Socialist Republics.

In 2015, the US-North Korea standoff escalated with North Korea threatening to nuke the USA, Japan, South Korea, Guam, and other US allies. The US retaliated with equal nuke called threats, urging Japan, South Korea, NATO, India, and the Philippines to join forces with her. On the occasion of the Centenary Anniversary of Our Lady of Fatima, Pope Francis, on January 11, 2017, blessed the six international pilgrim statues which the Alliance of the Holy Family International and Human Life International in Vienna brought to the six continents to re-echo the Blessed Mother's appeal for prayer and penance. The first to receive Her in Asia were Hong Kong, Taiwan, the Philippines, Singapore, Japan, and South Korea. These countries shared implement political status because of threats of nuclear aggression from North Korea. In South Korea, the tension was high when the Image of Our Lady of Fatima arrived as North Korea had just sent failed nuclear missiles to the coast of the United States.

The Korean air was figuratively ringing, heavenly charged with tension and fear; the ordinary people expressed this in the reception of the Blessed Mother's image. The charged atmosphere could be felt wherever the International Centennial Pilgrim Image of Our Lady of Fatima went: weeping, wailing, and people plowed to the streets worship paths, the men and priests who were carrying Her could hardly move for people stood to block Her way, wanting to touch the garment of the Image. Opened door Masses in National Park had to be arranged but thousands came to hear the Masses in Her honor. The churches were not big enough to hold thousands of the faithful who came to welcome and pray to the Blessed Mother.

The time of miracle happened, on April 27, 2018, the world was rocked and shocked by the news that North and South had come to a truce through a denuclearizing the entire Korean Peninsula, and to start working and officially ending the Korean War. Many are overjoyed with this news, others, how, are skeptical, but the fact remains, the Blessed Mother has kicked the door open for North and South Korea to start burying their hatred.

With the visit of Her International Centennial Pilgrim Images, the Blessed Mother managed to rally Her children to pray and make reparation for peace to reign again in the Korean Peninsula.

Mother Mary always keeps Her promise. Peace is possible; it is the one miracle that can happen with the help of the Blessed Mother. This only proves to show that any problem we have individually or collectively, when course to Our Lady of Fatima will be heard by God without fail.

Let us beg the Father for the fullness of grace that we need from the Holy Spirit, begging through the Blessed Mother's help that these virtues and graces make us truly better Christians and Catholics, would you becoming emissaries of peace, love, and unity among people and nations, ending all atrocities against life, and the threat against the sanctity of family life. Some political will be inspired and will be sent by the Holy Spirit to initiate the move for peace to end these abuses and atrocities that obscured the moral fiber of every person and nation on earth. And we are seeing some of them now, these are valiant spirit-filled men and women, but their initiatives will remain moot if we, all of us, will not contribute what we all can do "pray and do reparation" in answer to our Blessed Mother's call for peace. She answers and makes miracles happen.

MEDITATION

"There is nothing that Mother Mary could not obtain from Jesus Christ, if we pray the Rosary" (St. Bernard).

PRAYER

Oh Blessed Mother, Our Lady of Fatima, the whole world is sitting on a ticking bomb that can detonate any time because evil has corrupted the minds of some political leaders, eager to destroy the world with just one nuclear bomb. You promised that with pray and penance, with consecration and reparation to your Immaculate Heart and in union with the Sacred Heart of Jesus, you will grant peace in the world, our nations, our dioceses, our parishes, and our families. You only promised to prevent souls from going to hell and the further persecution of the Church and the Holy Father. We renew a total consecration of ourselves, our family, and our country to you, and through the intercession of the heart of St. Joseph. We ask this in the name of the Sacred Heart of Jesus, Our Lord. Amen.

DAY 14

PROCLAMATION OF THE KINGDOM OF GOD

"And after that John was delivered up, Jesus came into Galilee, preaching the gospel of the kingdom of God, and saying: The time is accomplished, and the kingdom of God is at hand: repent, and believe the gospel" (Mark 1: 14-15).

In his writing, St. Mark highlights the relation between Jesus' miraculous activity and the awaking of faith in the people He encounters. With the sign of healing that He carries out for the sick, Jesus tries to awaken the faith of the people. The scene of the people of the whole town huddled in front of the house where Jesus was, suffering from both physical and spiritual miseries, constituted so to speak the vital environment where Jesus's mission was carried out. When Jesus came to preach and minister to the people, He did so in their means, He was not at all detached from the people by stood right in the midst of the crowd. The greater part of Jesus' public life was spent on the road, amidst the people to preach the Gospel, to heal physical and spiritual wounds, to proclaim the Kingdom of God which belongs to the poor in body and spirit. The captive audience of the kingdom of God is the crowd of people laden with suffering. It is humanity furrowed by toil and trouble, directed to this poor humanity is the powerful liberating and renewing action of Jesus Christ. And so, once the Sabbath had ended in the late evening, what did Jesus do afterward? He went out by the gate of the city and retired to a place to pray. The disciples then went out to find Him and wanted to take Him back to the city for many more miserable and sick people had come. But what did Jesus answer? Let us go on to the next towns that I may preach the kingdom of God there also. This was the way the Son of God preached the kingdom of God, and this will be the way of His disciples to take to the road, the road signifies the Church's mission of going fort. The mission of the Church is one of movement and never in static nature.

In Genesis 3: 15, we read of the perennial enmity between Satan and the woman: *"She shall crush your head as it waits for her heel."* In this world, there are two kingdoms constantly battling with each other to gain souls: The Kingdom of God and the kingdom of Lucifer. Of course, we know that Lucifer is a fallen angel, and God created the angels, but there is one Creator or God. This is the moment of truth; all of us have to make a choice, for God said: *"If you are not with me, you are against me"* (Matthew 12: 30).

Sister Lucia of Fatima wrote to Cardinal Carlo Caffarra in 2004, we are now in the final battle between Satan and Mary: "The final battle between the Lord with Mary and the reign of Satan will be about the Marriage and the Family. Do not be afraid because anyone who works for the sanctity of Marriage and the Family will always be fought against and opposed in every way, because this is the decisive issue." Then she concluded: "Nevertheless, Our Lady has already crushed the head of the serpent."

In his Encyclical *"Familiaris Consortio"*, St. John Paul II pointed out that the Family is the Unit Cell of Society and the Domestic Church. Whoever and whatever prelate says that the family is not the Domestic Church, he should refer to this Pope which now is Saint to check his theology. And if Marriage and the Family are kept holy, we have a holy society, the holy Church, but if Marriage and the Family are broken, it is found then that we have or will have a broken society and a broken Church. Satan could destroy the whole world if he succeeds in breaking Marriage and the Family life.

Sister Lucia told father Augustine Fuentes, her spiritual director, in 1957 that we are in the last battle for three reasons: First, the Devil is already engaging the whole world in a decisive battle against the Virgin. It is a final battle where one is the victor and the other is the loser. We are already being called to take a side, either for God or for the devil; one thing is certain that there is no middle ground, no neutral possibility: *"If you are not for God and you are neutral, you are for the devil!"* Second reason, Mary said that God is giving the world the last two remedies to survive: the Holy Rosary and devotion to the Immaculate Heart of Mary by way of consecration and reparation: *"These are the last two remedies and there will be no other!"* (Sr. Lucia Dos Santos); Third reason, because in the plans of the Divine Providence, God is going to chastise the world, He always exhausts all other remedies first. When He sees that the world pays no attention whatsoever, then as we say in our imperfect way of talking with a certain fear, He presents us the last means of salvation, His Blessed Mother.

In the book "Jesus of Nazareth", Pope Benedict XVI spoke about the Kingdom of God having three dimensions: The first dimension is the Christological Dimension, he wrote: Here we see that "The Kingdom is not a thing, it is not a geographical dominion like worldly kingdoms. It is a person; it is he. On this interpretation, the term 'Kingdom of God' is itself a veiled Christology. By the way in which he speaks of the Kingdom of God, Jesus leads men to realize the overwhelming fact that in him God himself is present among them, that he is God's presence." (Pope Benedict, Jesus of Nazareth, Part 1); The second dimension is the Mystical Dimension, the Pope wrote: "Here we see that The Kingdom of God resides in the heart of man. Church Father, Origen wrote, "those who pray for the coming of the Kingdom of God pray without any doubt for the Kingdom of God that they contain in themselves, and they pray that this kingdom might bear fruit and attain its fullness."; The third dimension is the Ecclesiastical Dimension, he wrote: "Here we see that the kingdom of God is in the here and now, present in and through the Church. Yet it is a mixed reality that will only be perfectly realized at the end of history. This current "mixed" state can be seen as the Church on earth which now grows in the field of the world with both weeds and wheat until the harvest when Christ says he will "tell the reapers, Gather the weeds first and bind them in bundles to be burned. But gather the wheat into my barn" (Matt 13:30).

Let us now reflect on the story of the apparition of Our Lady of Velankanni in Pakistan:

The basilica attracts millions of devotees each year. As in Karachi, these include both Catholic and Hindu residents. Some Catholic devotees from Karachi embark on a spiritual journey to the basilica of Our Lady of Velankanni to ask the Mother for favors and intercessory graces. Three accounts of the apparitions of the Virgin Mary in Velankanni have been documented over the years, and subsequently narrated by her devotees. The first story dates back to the end of the 16th century and is about a Hindu shepherd boy's sighting the Virgin Mary by a pond. She asked the boy for milk for her son, Jesus. The boy readily offered the milk. Locals remain intrigued until the Mother appeared at the site again. Thereafter, the pond was known as "Matha Kulam" or "Our Lady's Pond". The second event is said to have happened a few years later. A crippled boy in Nadu Thittu was apparently cured by the Virgin Mother after he offered her buttermilk. The Catholic residents of a nearby town then built a shrine in recognition of the healing. Today, Our Lady of Velankanni has special meaning for both Hindu and Christian devotees because of the miracles she is associated with, including the 2004 Boxing Day tsunami which caused massive destruction in Tamil Nadu. Basilica officials were quick to report this as a miracle, as 2,000 pilgrims were attending Mass when the town of Velankanni was hit. News sources and official disaster reports showed that the basilica was the only building to escape this large-scale catastrophe.

This report was immediately attributed to the miraculous intervention of Our Lady of Velankanni, because during those times people were praying the Holy Rosary.

Many beautiful stories of devotion coming from the people when prayed for Our Lady's intercession at Velankanni are worth telling. One such story is a Hindu woman who visited Velankanni to pray to Our Lady of Good Health to be blessed with the gift of a child. Nearly a year and a half after her return to Karachi, she gave birth to a boy. A few years later, she and her family completed rituals to fulfill their vow. She cut off four inches of hair while her husband and son shaved their heads. They bathed in the sea as part of the ritual. These practices are taken from the Hindu faith, showing that interfaith exchanges go both ways. Since then, the woman has worn a head-covering during prayer times as a lifelong promise to the mother for the graces received through her son. Another story: There was a lady who would not wear shoes. She would be spotted even at weddings without shoes ... Imagine going everywhere barefoot in Karachi's heat. But that is how she fulfilled her vow and everyone knew about it. Annually, hundreds of devotees come together in the premises of churches across Karachi and in Tamil Nadu to hoist a flag bearing an image of Our Lady of Velankanni and partake in a short prayer followed by other rituals including the distribution of blessed medals by a priest. The ceremony devoted to Our Lady of Velankanni occurs on September 8, which was the birthday of the Virgin Mary. Each year, Our Lady of Velankanni's statue in Karachi is decorated with fresh flowers and streamers. This day sees some members from the Hindu, Zoroastrian, and Muslim communities all venerating the Virgin Mary. As the parish priest told me, "Mary brings everyone together and it makes sense why you would see Muslims here who can tell you a lot about Surah Maryam." Named after Virgin Mary, Surah Maryam appears in the 19th chapter of the Qu'ran. Of course, "Muslims do not partake in novena prayers, but on September 8, they come here to respect Mary as the Mother of Jesus," Rodrigues said.

What do we learn from all these? Whatever it is, that threatens us, our family, our country, our safety, our faith, and our Church. We have the greatest help and weapon that God Himself gave us to survive and win against all these devils: it is the Blessed Virgin Mary. Through Her, the whole world can be converted to the Kingdom of God. Mary is the greatest antidote to the kingdom of Satan.

MEDITATION

"As long as individuals and states refuse to submit to the rule of our Savior, there would be no really hopeful prospect of a lasting peace among nations." (Pope Pius XI wrote in Encyclical "Quas Primus" 1925)

PRAYER

Almighty and Everlasting God, I entrust the cares of countless people who are in need of so much help, I course it to the Immaculate Heart of Your Mother to intercede for these helpless and poor sinners. Please do not allow them to be bitter and hardened in their hearts because of their miserable situation, make them realize how on Calvary your Son Jesus suffered more than all the sick people put together today. Oh Jesus, you silently offered all your pains and tortures as an act of reparation for the salvation of mankind. Help me too, oh Virgin Mary, to unite my suffering as reparation in union with the Passion and Death of Jesus on Mount Calvary for the conversion of hardened sinners, including the members of family. I ask this through the powerful intercession of the Blessed Virgin Mary, in the name of Your Son, Our Lord Jesus Christ, who lives and reigns with you forever. Amen.

DAY 15

THE TRANSFIGURATION OF JESUS

"And it came to pass about eight days after these words, that he took Peter, and James, and John, and went up into a mountain to pray. And whilst he prayed, the shape of his countenance was altered, and his raiment became white and glittering. And behold two men were talking with him. And they were Moses and Elias, Appearing in majesty. And they spoke of his decease that he should accomplish in Jerusalem. But Peter and they that were with him were heavy with sleep. And waking, they saw his glory, and the two men that stood with him. And it came to pass, that as they were departing from him, Peter saith to Jesus: Master, it is good for us to be here; and let us make three tabernacles, one for thee, and one for Moses, and one for Elias; not knowing what he said. And as he spoke these things, there came a cloud, and overshadowed them; and they were afraid, when they entered into the cloud. And a voice came out of the cloud, saying: This is my beloved Son; hear him. And whilst the voice was uttered, Jesus was found alone. And they held their peace, and told no man in those days any of these things which they had seen." (Luke 9:28-36)

Jesus allowed Peter, James, and John to come with Him in Mount Tabor to experience His Transfiguration. He wanted to strengthen their faith for the forthcoming tragedy of His Passion and Death on the Cross. Upon hearing Jesus speaking of His death on the Cross, Peter was horrified and spoke against it. And because of his violent reaction, Peter was rebuked by Jesus with such a stern command: *"Go behind me, Satan!"* (Matthew 16: 21). For seeing the scandal of the Cross, Jesus prepared His Apostles for it during the Transfiguration; He manifested to them His glory that was to come after His tragic Death on the Cross, the glory of His Resurrection. During the Transfiguration, Moses appeared to represent the Law, for it was to Moses, the Law was given; and Elijah to represent the Prophets because he was the greatest prophet who ascended straight into Heaven. Their appearance during the Transfiguration showed how Jesus was to fulfill the Law and the Prophets, which was why Jesus said: *"Do not think that I am come to destroy the law, or the prophets. I am not come to destroy, but to fulfill"* (Matthew 5:17). Then, in order to reassure the Apostles that Jesus is the Messiah, the Son of God, after the appearance of Moses and Elijah, they heard a voice of God the Father saying: *"This is my beloved Son; hear him"* (Luke 9: 35). After this manifestation of His glory, Jesus wanted His Apostles not to tell anyone of this vision until the Son of Man is risen from death, which is until after His Resurrection. The glorified body in which Jesus appeared during the Transfiguration shall be the same glorified body in which we will see Him again in His Resurrection, and finally, on the last day.

During the Angelus Message on August 6, 2006, Pope Benedict XVI explained how the events of Transfiguration display Christ as "the full manifestation of God's light." The Pope continued, this light, which shines forth from Christ both at the transfiguration and after his resurrection, is ultimately triumphant over "the power of the darkness of evil." The Pope stressed that the feast of the Transfiguration is an important opportunity for believers to look to Christ as "the light of the world," and to experience the kind of conversion which the Bible frequently describes as an emergence from darkness to light. "In our time too," Pope Benedict said, "We urgently need to emerge from the darkness of evil, to experience the joy of the children of light!" For Eastern Catholics, the Feast of the Transfiguration is especially significant. It is among the 12 "great feasts" of Eastern Catholicism. Eastern Christianity emphasizes that Christ's transfiguration is the prototype of spiritual illumination, which is possible for the committed disciple of Jesus. This Christian form of "enlightenment" is facilitated by the ascetic disciplines of prayer, fasting, and charitable almsgiving.

A revered hierarch of the Melkite Greek Catholic Church, the late Archbishop Joseph Raya, described this traditional Byzantine view of the transfiguration in his book of meditations on the Biblical event and its liturgical celebration, titled "Transfiguration of Our Lord and Savior Jesus Christ." "Transfiguration," Archbishop Raya wrote, "is not simply an event out of the two-thousand-year-old past or a future yet to come. It is rather a reality of the present, a way of life available to those who seek and accept Christ's nearness."

We can see from the examples of St. Teresa of Avila, St. John of the Cross, St. Mark the Ascetic, and many other Saints, how they would show this nearness to God each time they would fall into ecstasy while at prayer. Why do only the Saints seemingly have this special experience of nearness to God? It is because most of us naturally reject the Cross. No matter how many precautions we can take, there is always one thing that we can never eliminate: human suffering.

Pope Benedict XVI, when he was Cardinal Joseph Ratzinger then Prefect of the Congregation for the Doctrine of Faith, said in "Instruction on Healing" that "We see suffering as the punishment of our sins and that is why we reject it. However, because we are also entitled to joy healing from our suffering is good." He continued, "That is why we have the Sacrament of the Anointing of the sick to heal those who are suffering." But we must remember that suffering acquired a new dimension. After Jesus' Death on the Cross, it became the Divine Gift that must be valued and pressured. Because, for love of us, Jesus had to suffer to redeem us and to make us again the children of the Father in Heaven.

Often, when we experience the Cross and suffering, our first impulse as human being is to groan and complain. Saint John Paul II tells us in his Encyclical "Salvifici Dolores" (1986) that "It is a Divine Gift", because, for God to love us, Jesus had to suffer and to die as an oblation to save us and to make us heirs of Heaven." That why Saint Paul also said in 1 Corinthians that *"For the word of the cross, to them indeed that perish, is foolishness;*

but to them that are saved, that is, to us, it is the power of God" (1 Corinthians 1: 18). The Cross is the power to redeem others, to heal others, and to cast out Satan from others. St. Mark the Ascetic also said that "Suffering purifies us like pure gold purified seven times by fire, it destroys vices that are still hidden in us, it drives out Satan is still lurking in our person, and it heals the brokenness who inherited from our family tree. God, who loves us so much, knows how to test and purify as best as He did with Jesus. So that when tested by fire seven times, we can appear the most beautiful of all beings, it is like the finest flower which must be pounded over and over several times until it becomes the most refined flower, making it the finest bread to become the Body of Christ. However, this understanding of suffering takes time to realize. For example, St. Teresa once complained over suffering sent by the Lord when she said: "If this is the way you treat your friends, sending them inexplicable suffering, now I understand why you have very few friends," she said this before she absorbed the teachings of St. John of the Cross. Later, when she understood that the "Cross is a Divine Gift" that must be treasured and valued, St. Teresa then started asking for suffering daily to save many souls, because of this, she was empowered to do unbelievable feats. The day St. Teresa was denied the Cross by the Lord, she cried out: "Lord, you do not love me anymore!"

On March 12, 2017, Pope Francis reflected on the beautiful faces of Jesus during Transfiguration and the Resurrection, saying that they give us the hope and courage needed to accept the face that comes between the two: the face of the Crucifixion, the Pope said that "Between this two beautiful Transfiguration and Resurrection, there will be another face of Jesus, there will be a face that is not so beautiful. There will be an ugly face, disfigured, tortured, despised, and bloodied. Jesus' entire body is like something to throw away. The Pope explained how there will be two transfigurations, and in the middle is Jesus crucified, the Cross. The Pope encouraged everyone to look at the Cross often, and to remember how Jesus was annihilated to save us, he added that "Jesus was made sin, sin is the worst thing, and sin is an offense against God, a slap in the face of God... And Jesus became sin, he was annihilated." He explained how Jesus to prepare his disciples "not to be scandalized" by seeing him on the Cross, Jesus was transfigured, he said, explaining that it provides the needed assurance "to go forward." The Pope said: "To see this face, so beautiful, so luminous, which is the same that we see in the transfiguration and it's the same one that we'll see in heaven," is needed, he said, but urged them to also think about the face of Jesus on the Cross. That is why we must reflect on St. Paul's words in Romans: *"To share the Cross of Christ, we shall also share in the Resurrection of Christ"* (Romans 6: 5). The Pope then urged faithful to contemplate these two faces of Jesus: "the transfigured one and the one made sin, cursed." The Pope explained how the Transfiguration encourages us to go forward on the path of life, the Christian journey. It also encourages us in the forgiveness of our sins, we've sinned a lot," he said. That is why Jesus was badly tortured because of our sins. But above all it "encourages us in trust," Pope Francis said. "Because if he became sin, he took ours upon Himself, He is always disposed to forgive us. We only have to ask Him."

St. John of the Cross said: "No pain, no gain," "No merit, no soul saved," "No purchasing power, no glory of God, no honor to Mary, and no joy in Heaven."

Let us remember that the 24 karat gold is not pure unless it is tested by fire seven times. In Heaven, we will be happier for eternity if we have achieved a greater perfection here on earth. That is if we have suffered very much on earth for purification. The soul that suffered much on earth is like the 24 karats pure gold, and because of its great purification to suffering, it would experience a greater beatific mission than the soul that has suffered less on earth.

After St. Teresa of Avila died, she appeared to one of her nuns and to tell her that all Saints in Heaven had given another chance would return to earth to suffer more so that they will be closer to Jesus, who is the purest and the most perfect being.

Let take the story of Blessed Bartolo Longo, a Satanist turned

Apostle of the Holy Rosary:

Blessed Bartolo Longo was born in 1841 to a devout Catholic family. When he grew up, he decided to study law. Naples, at that time, was undergoing a tremendous spiritual crisis. Paganism and Satanism of all sorts were abounding. Bartolo was not immune to these influences and became a satanic priest, much to the chagrin of his family who tried their hardest to get him to convert. As Satanism began to torment his mind, his family convinced him to make a good confession. Alberto Radente, a saintly Dominican priest, helped lead him back to the Catholic faith and encouraged his devotion to the Rosary. Bartolo had a miraculous conversion, and in 1870, he became a third order Dominican and chose to live a life in penance for all the terrible sins he had committed against the Church. One day, he nearly succumbed to the sin of despair, feeling that God could never forgive the tremendous sins he had committed against the Church. At that moment, he received divine inspiration and remembered The Blessed Virgin's promise that she would help in all their necessities those who propagate her Rosary. He set out to restore the dilapidated chapel at Pompeii and promote the Rosary to whoever would listen. Pamphlets about the Rosary were distributed to help the people learn to pray this powerful devotion. He tried to find an image of Our Lady of the Rosary worthy of hanging in the chapel, but was only offered a worm-eaten painting with an image that he felt was coarse and not worthy of veneration, however, he accepted it from the convent in which it was stored. As Bartolo continued his work of propagating the Rosary, the chapel's membership grew tremendously and many miracles began to be associated with Our Lady of Pompeii. Cures and spiritual conversions occurred due to the devotions through this new shrine. The people pledged their support to have a large church built that would properly honor Our Lady of the Rosary. In 1894, Bartolo and his wife gave the church over to the care of the Vatican. The original image found in the convent was restored for the last time in 1965 and Pope Paul VI crowned the heads of Jesus and Mary with diadems given by the people of Pompeii. On October 26, 1980, Bartolo Longo was beatified by John Paul II who called him 'the man of the Madonna' and the 'Apostle of the Rosary'.

Let us learn from the life of our Blessed Bartolo Longo to pray the Rosary to receive the heavenly aid of our Holy Mother to save souls. Even a man deep into sin, a Satanist, could still convert and be healed from the curse if he returns to the Blessed Virgin Mary; pray devoutly her Holy Rosary and ask for her powerful intercession.

Let us remember that the Resurrection and Heaven will always be before us, our suffering must never discourage us no matter how prolong they may be. The Transfiguration and Resurrection will also be our reward if we remain faithful to the Lord even amidst the daily Crosses He gives us to carry. Let us never forget that man's life on earth is short: only 70 years for the weak and 80 years for the strong as Psalm 94 tells us. And after that the eternity awaits us.

Let us bear our suffering, always considering it as redemptive, offering it as reparation, and renew with the Passion and Death of Jesus Christ.

Suffering becomes a privilege if we convert it into reparation. Even the great suffering, the pangs of the Cross will disappear after it is converted and offered for reparation for the sins of others.

MEDITATION

Saint Paul teaches us how to view suffering: *"For the Spirit himself giveth testimony to our spirit, that we are the sons of God. And if sons, heirs also; heirs indeed of God, and joint heirs with Christ: yet so, if we suffer with him, that we may be also glorified with him"* (Romans 8: 16-17).

PRAYER

Oh Loving God, you allowed Peter, James, and John to experience your Transfiguration on Mount Tabor, to prepare them to the scandal of the Cross, the most ignominy death ever conceived by man, which you willingly accepted because of your great love for us. You wanted the Transfiguration to serve as a reminder for them so that when the time comes for their own suffering, they would not fall into despair. Instead, they would look forward to the eternal joy in heaven, transfigured, and res-urrected in accordance with the Image of Jesus, the resurrected and transfigured Body. Help us to remember our sufferings that all our pains are redemptive and can be offered for the conversion of sinners, the healing of the sick, and the casting out of demons. As St. Paul encouraged and embraced that our present sufferings are incomparable to the glory that will later be revealed to us. We ask this through the most powerful intercession of the Blessed Virgin Mary, in the name of Jesus Christ, our Lord. Amen.

DAY 16

THE INSTITUTION OF THE EUCHARIST

"For I have received of the Lord that which also I delivered unto you, that the Lord Jesus, the same night in which he was betrayed, took bread. And giving thanks, broke, and said: Take ye, and eat: this is my body, which shall be delivered for you: this do for the commemoration of me. In like manner also the chalice, after he had supped, saying: This chalice is the New Testament in my blood: this do ye, as often as you shall drink, for the commemoration of me. For as often as you shall eat this bread, and drink the chalice, you shall shew the death of the Lord, until he comes." (1 Corinthians 11: 23-26)

Jesus' transformation in his last Seder meal (Last Supper) into the first Eucharistic celebration is described in our Gospel readings today. Jesus, the Son of God, began His last Passover celebration by washing the feet of His disciples, a service assigned to household servants, as a lesson of humble service, proving what He said: *"I came to the world not to be served but to serve"* (Mark 10:45). Jesus followed the ritual of the Jewish Passover meal up to the second cup of wine, from the roasted lamb into the Body and Blood of Christ. Because instead of serving the roasted lamb as a third step, Jesus offered His own Body and Blood as food and drink under the appearances of bread and wine. Then He instituted the Holy Eucharist as the sign and reality of God's perpetual presence with His people as their living, Heavenly Food. This was followed by the institution of the priesthood with the command, "Do this in memory of me." Jesus concluded the ceremony with a long speech incorporating His command of love: "Love one another as I have loved you" (Jn 13:34). Thus, Jesus instituted the Sacrament of the Holy Eucharist at a private Passover meal with his disciples (Matthew 26:17-30; Luke 21:7-23). He served as both the Priest and the Victim in the sacrifice. He became the Lamb of God, as John the Baptist had previously predicted (John 1:29, 36), who, by His death and Resurrection, would "take away the sins of the world."

The early Jewish Christians converted the Jewish "Sabbath Love Feast" of Fridays and Saturdays (the Sabbath), into the "Memorial Last Supper Meal" of Jesus on Sundays. The celebration began with the participants praising and worshipping God by singing psalms, reading the Old Testament Messianic prophecies and listening to the teachings of Jesus as explained by an Apostle or by an ordained minister. This was followed by an offertory procession, bringing to the altar the bread and wine to be consecrated and the covered dishes (meals) brought by each family for a shared common meal after the Eucharistic celebration. Then the ordained Minister said the "institution narrative" over the bread and wine and all the participants received the consecrated Bread and Wine, as the living Body and Blood of the crucified and risen Jesus. This ritual finally evolved into the present-day Holy Mass in various rites, incorporating various cultural elements of worship and rituals.

What is the life message of the Institution of the Eucharist? Archbishop Fulton Sheen taught that we can draw many line messages from the Institution of the Eucharist:

First: We need to render humble service to others. Our celebration of the Eucharist requires that we wash one another's feet, i.e., serve one another and revere Christ's presence in other persons. To wash the feet of others is to love them, especially when they don't deserve our love, and to do good to them, even when they can't, won't, or don't return the favor. It is to consider others' needs to be as important as our own. It is to forgive others from the heart, even though they don't say, "I'm sorry." It is to serve them, even when the task is unpleasant. It is to let others know we care when they feel downtrodden or burdened. It is to be generous with what we have. It is to turn the other cheek instead of retaliating when we're treated unfairly. It is to make adjustments in our plans in order to serve others' needs without expecting any reward. In doing and suffering all these things in this way, we love and serve Jesus Himself, as He has loved us and has taught us to do (Matthew 25:31-ff);

Second: We need to practice sacrificial sharing and self-giving love. Let us imitate the self-giving model of Jesus who shares with us his own Body and Blood and enriches us with his Real Presence in the Holy Eucharist. It is by sharing our blessings – our talents, time, health, and wealth - with others that we become true disciples of Christ and obey his new commandment: "Love one another as I have loved you" (John 13:34);

Third: We need to show our unity in suffering. The bread we partake of is produced by the pounding of many grains of wheat, and the wine is the result of the crushing of many grapes. Both are thus symbols of unity through suffering. They invite us to help, console, support, and pray for others who suffer physical or mental illnesses;

Fourth: We need to receive Jesus without the stain of sin. We need to make Holy Communion an occasion of Divine grace and blessing by receiving it worthily, rather than making it an occasion of desecration and sacrilege by receiving Jesus while we are in grave sin. That is why we pray three times before we receive Communion, "Lamb of God, You take away the sins of the world, have mercy on us," with the final "have mercy on us" replaced by "grant us peace." That is also the reason we pray the Centurion's prayer, "Lord, I am not worthy that You should enter under my roof, but only say the word and my soul shall be healed" (Matthew 8:8). And that is why the priest, just before he receives the consecrated Host, prays, "May the Body of Christ keep me safe for eternal life," while, just before drinking from the Chalice, he prays, "May the Blood of Christ keep me safe for eternal life.";

Fifth: We need to become Christ-bearers and Christ-conveyers: In the older English version of the Mass, the final message was, "Go in peace to love and serve one another," that is, to carry Jesus to our homes and places of work, conveying to others around us the love, mercy, forgiveness, and spirit of humble service of Christ whom we carry with us. That message has not changed, though the words are different;

Sixth: We need to remember eight things Jesus did for us on Holy Thursday and continues to do for us during every Eucharistic celebration: First, remember and regret what Jesus had to go through because of the way our lives are in sin today and every day; Second, remember and rejoice that Jesus' love for us no limit; Third, remember and believe that Jesus has taken care of everything that stands between us God; Fourth, remember and rely on Jesus, our living Lord, was been through all the troubles and trials that one person can experience. Thus Jesus is able to sympathize and help us in our times of trouble and give the best possible answers to our prayers; Fifth, we remember and know for certain that the one who died on the Cross will never leave us or desert us because even if we may desert him, he will not desert us, he will not leave us; Sixth, remember and celebrate the new hope that we have because Jesus is alive, he is our living Lord and Savior who supports us when we are down, strengthens us when we face difficult challenges, forgives us when we fail, and comforts us when sickness and death terrify us; Seventh, remember and change what Jesus has done in giving us a new life and a new beginning to His Death and Resurrection, changes the way we view other people, our world, and our relationship with God. And with God's help, we fill our lives with kindness, patience, tolerance, and forgiveness; Eighth, remember and anticipate that day when we will gather around the throne of God with all the saints who have gone before us.

Jesus said: "*Behold I send you as sheep in the midst of wolves. Be ye therefore wise as serpents and simple as doves*" (Matthew 10: 16). Lays before the wall, the sheep will be lacerated and killed. St. Paul reminds us in Ephesians 6: 12 that in the same way when we "*make disciples of all nations,*" we know we are not fighting flesh and blood but principalities of darkness. Knowing this, how then can we protect ourselves before the evil one? Jesus gave us the answer when he ascended into Heaven, when he gave the mandate for all of us "*to go and make disciples of all* nations." "*Remember, I will be with you until the end of time*" (Matthew 28:20). How is he with us until the end of time? Canon #1-4, Council of Trent (1562) gave us the answer when it says: "*In the Eucharist, Jesus, is really, truly, substantially present, Body, Blood, Soul, and Divinity.*" St. Peter Julian Eymard said that the same Jesus who sits at the right hand of God the Father is really present in all the tabernacles throughout the world as King of kings and Lord of lords. Paragraph 11 of Lumen Gentium teaches that "*The Eucharist is the source and summit of Christian life.*" Therefore, anything we need whether material, physical, mental, moral, spiritual, and psychological can be obtained in the Eucharist.

Let us look at this example. A young woman from Vienna suffering from breast cancer went to the hospital for treatment. The hospital, unfortunately, gave up on her as her condition was already terminal. In desperation, she prayed before the Lord in the Blessed Sacrament and stayed with Him until she found peace. Then she went back to the hospital after some days for a new test. When the lab result came out, everyone was shocked even the poor woman, not a single trace of cancer cells in her body. She was healed off from her cancer. Since then, this young woman became a perpetual adorer of the Eucharist, adoring the Lord for at least two hours a day. Suddenly, the source and summit of the Christian life is not benefited by all Christians because of prejudice.

In the "Spirit of the Liturgy", Pope Benedict XVI outlined the common errors by the Antichrist against the Eucharist:

First error: The Catholics partake in a cannibalistic meal in their Mass;

Second error: The Eucharist is just a symbolic presence of Jesus, not the real presence of Jesus. Therefore, it cannot save because Jesus is in Heaven;

Third error: The argument that if Jesus is really present in many places in all tabernacles throughout the world, then the Catholics are promoting polytheism: many Gods, not monetarism: one God.

Answering the first error or accusation on Catholics are guilty of cannibalism because they eat the real flesh and drink the real blood of Jesus. Pope Benedict clearly outlined that the Body and Blood of Christ that we consume during the Mass is not the raw human flesh which satanic people eat, rather it is the resurrected Body and Blood, Soul and Divinity of Jesus in the Eucharist. As St. Augustine said that we consume the Eucharist not to assimilate the Body and Blood of Jesus into our human flesh and blood, but rather, Jesus assimilates us into Himself, into a supernatural being so that we undergo two transformations: vertical and horizontal. In our life, we become vertically more like God, which because of sin was badly deformed. We become horizontally transformed enabling us to love our neighbor and remove the division that has broken the Mystical Body of Christ due to the sins of anger, greed, pride, lust, sloth, and gluttony. The virtues of love like patience, humility, and meekness attract our fellow men to conversion in Christ.

Answering the second error or accusation on symbolism, Pope Benedict quoted, *"The Jews, therefore, strove among themselves, saying: How can this man give us his flesh to eat? Then Jesus said to them: Amen, amen I say unto you: Except you eat the flesh of the Son of man, and drink his blood, you shall not have life in you. He that eateth my flesh, and drinketh my blood, hath everlasting life: and I will raise him up on the last day. For my flesh is meat indeed: and my blood is drink indeed. He that eateth my flesh, and drinketh my blood, abideth in me, and I in him"* (John 6: 45-57). In response to this teaching, St. John continues: *"After this many of his disciples went back; and walked no more with him. Then Jesus said to the twelve: Will you also go away? And Simon Peter answered him: Lord, to whom shall we go? Thou hast the words of eternal life"* (John 6: 67-69). Pope Benedict said that if Jesus were referring only to the symbolic presence of His Body and Blood, Jesus should have said, "wait a minute, I am just making an analogical and metaphorical statement." Instead, Pope Benedict insisted that His Body and Blood, Soul and Divinity in the Eucharist are really, truly, and substantially present as he stated in John 6:

30-DAY CONSECRATION TO THE BLESSED VIRGIN MARY: THE MOST POWER...

55-56, *"For my flesh is meat indeed: and my blood is drink indeed. He that eateth my flesh, and drinketh my blood, abideth in me, and I in him."* St. Thomas Aquinas teaches in the Suma Theologiae, 11a, q. 75, art. 1-2, that "The words of consecration, pronounced by the priest, change bread and wine into the true body and blood of Christ. This sacrament is not a symbol or sign of Christ's body and blood; it is, in fact, the body and blood of Christ. By the consecration, the substance of the bread and the substance of the wine cease to exist, and there remains only the substance of the living Christ."

Answering the third error that the Catholics are promoting polytheism: many Gods, not monetarism: one God. The Catechism of the Catholic Church also teaches: *"Transubstantiation means the change of the whole substance of bread into the substance of the Body of Christ and the whole substance of wine into the substance of His Blood. This change is brought about in the Eucharistic Prayer through the efficacy of the Word of Christ and by the action of the Holy Spirit. However, the outward characteristics of bread and wine that is the Eucharistic species remain unaltered"* (CCC#1375 and 1376). The Catechism continues and declares that *"The Eucharistic presence of Christ begins at the moment of the consecration and endures as long as the Eucharistic species subsist. Christ is present whole and entire in each of the species and whole and entire in each of their parts, in such a way that the breaking of the bread does not divide Christ"* (CCC#1377). Therefore, the Eucharist's presence in all tabernacles throughout the world does not multiply Jesus, for He is one God.

Archbishop Fulton Sheen gives the following analogy to explain to a little child how Christ can multiply Himself to so many pieces and remain one, he said to the boy: "take a glass mirror, 'who do you see here?' The boy said: 'myself', then he asked the boy to break the glass mirror, and indeed, the boy through the mirror on the cement floor, it broke into several pieces. Then the Archbishop asked the boy, 'who do you see in all the broken pieces of glass mirror?' The boy replied: 'I see myself in all the mirrors.' The Archbishop said: 'the same is true with the Euchar-

115

ist, this only one Christ symbolized by the big unleavened bread, when broken into pieces, it is the same Christ who is in the big unleavened bread, whole Body, Blood, Soul, and Divinity. When broken into pieces, the whole Jesus is really present there, true Body, Blood, Soul, and Divinity." Jesus is truly, really, and substantially present Body, Blood, Soul, and Divinity in the Eucharist. The same Jesus who sits at the right hand of God the Father in Heaven is right here in the Eucharist in all the tabernacles throughout the world as the God of Mercy and Compassion as well as the Perpetrator to continually intercede for us before the Father in Heaven, to beg for His Mercy on our sins, and to avoid the just punishment we deserve because of our sins. He is waiting for us all the time until the end of time to assist us in all our needs.

While at the Mount of Olives, Jesus said to Peter, John, and James that "Would you not wait for me even an hour?" while He talked to His Father to intercede for us, to forgive our sins, to make us adopted children of God once again after we have fallen into grave sins. Matthew 26: 38-40 recounts the scene well, as he says: *"Then he saith to them: My soul is sorrowful even unto death: stay you here, and watch with me. And going a little further, he fell upon his face, praying, and saying: My Father, if it is possible, let this chalice pass from me. Nevertheless not as I will, but as thou wilt. And he cometh to his disciples, and findeth them asleep, and he saith to Peter: What? Could you not watch one hour with me?"* Why should we keep watch with Jesus? Pope Saint John II said that Jesus as the 'One Mediator' (1 Timothy 2: 5), he is interceding for us before the Father in Heaven in all the Masses and Eucharistic Adoration in all the tabernacles throughout the world because of our sins which are greatly offended him. It is for this reason why we adore Jesus in the Blessed Sacrament, truly, really, and substantially present Body, Blood, Soul, and Divinity in all the tabernacles throughout the world in order to seek grace and mercy, we need for our daily life because as Lumen Gentium, article 11 teaches that *"The Eucharist is the source and the summit of the Christian life."* Let us follow the example given to us by

Archbishop Fulton Sheen so that we may be inspired to adore the Lord in the Eucharist for at least one hour each day.

MEDITATION

"He who has not seen Jesus (in adoration) should not partake in consuming the Eucharistic Sacrifice of Jesus." (St. Augustine)

"I have eagerly desired to eat this Passover with you. Lord, you desire us, you desire me, and you eagerly desire to share yourself with us in the Holy Eucharist to by one with us. Lord, awaken in us the desire for you, strengthen us in unity you and with one another, grant unity to Your Church so that the world may believe." (Pope Benedict XVI)

PRAYER

Oh Loving Jesus Christ, King of kings, Lord of lords, I adore you profoundly in the Eucharist in all the tabernacles throughout the world. You remain here as a prisoner of love to help all of us in our daily trials and challenges in life. The same Jesus, who healed, cast out demons, and touched the hearts of hardening sinners, is right here. The same God who protected the Jews from slaughter by the forces of the Egyptians and who accompanied the chosen race to cross the Red Sea is right here. Oh Jesus, as we adore you profoundly in union with the Father and the Holy Spirit, I beg of you in my wretchedness and hopelessness to grant me all the graces I need to be able to continue serving you with all my heart, now and forever. Amen.

DAY 17

THE BLESSINGS OF SUFFERING

"Then he saith to them: My soul is sorrowful even unto death: stay you here, and watch with me. Watch ye, and pray that ye enter not into temptation. The spirit indeed is willing, but the flesh weak" (Matthew 26: 38, 41).

Jesus leaves the upper room with His disciples, goes to the Garden of Gethsemane, and begins to pray. But as He begins His prayer, a great fear assails Him, an oppressive tediousness, and an overwhelming sadness overcome Him. As the sorrow grows in his heart, He begins to fear. Jesus, our Redeemer, overwhelmed with sadness even saying that "this blessed soul was sorrowful even unto death." After saying this, He saw before Him the melancholy scenes of all the torments and ignominies which were prepared for Him. In His Passion, these torments afflicted Jesus one by one. But in the Garden, the buffets, the spittle, the scourges, the thorns, the nails, and the reproaches, which He was to suffer, came all together to torment Him. Jesus embraced them all, but in embracing them, He trembled, agonized, and prayed. And being in agony, He prayed longer. But we asked Jesus, who compels you to submit to such torments? Jesus answered: "the love which I bear for you compelled me to endure them all." How great must have been the astonishment at the sight of omnipotence become weak? A God afflicted, why? It was to save us men, His own creatures. In the Garden, He opened the first sacrifice, Jesus was the victim, He cried: "My *Father, if it is possible, let this chalice pass from me*" (Matthew 26: 39). This was Jesus' prayer which He prayed so much to be delivered from the torments that He was to endure but to make us understand the pain which He suffered and embraced because He loved us, He wanted to teach us that in tribulations we can ask God to deliver us from them, but at the same time, we should conform entirely to His Divine Will and stay with Him *"Not as I will, but as You will"* (Matthew 26: 29). In His prayer in the Garden, Jesus fell prostrate on the ground, clothed with the contemptible garment of all our sins. He felt ashamed to raise His eyes to Heaven, He contemplated every single sin of men that He bore on Himself, and begged from the Father pardon for each one of us them, bargaining with the Heavenly Father's Mercy for these souls in His silent cry of victimhood.

Many people today become angry with God when they begin to suffer unbearably; too often we hear the complaint: "Does Jesus know how much I suffer?" or "He sits in Heaven looking down on my misery doing nothing." or "Why can't He come down and relieve me of my agony and suffering?" Jesus knows about all our sufferings. He sees every facet of our life, and this is what we must realize and remember. He allows us to share in His sufferings so that we can participate in His greatest act of love, our redemption for our sins so that we may once again inherit Heaven which we have lost because of our sins. Jesus was not sparing in His warnings, He told us clearly: *"But unless you repent, you shall all perish"* (Luke 13: 3). But how we begin repenting? Remember one thing that it is not enough to confess our sins to repent, we must repair for our sins by offering sacrifices in reparation for the sins we did against God and men. If we are hurting now then begin to contemplate on the sorrowful mysteries of the Holy Rosary, you will not only find consolation for yourself but also for Jesus whom we hurt most because of our sins.

St. John Paul II explained in his Theology of Reparation, that we can console Jesus even now, although no longer as head of the Mystical Body of Christ for He has risen from death, but now remember as a member of the Mystical Body.

Jesus says in the Gospel of Luke that *"The Son of man must suffer many things, and be rejected by the ancients and chief priests and scribes, and be killed, and the third day rises again. And he said to all: If any man will come after me, let him deny himself, and take up his cross daily, and follow me."* (Luke 9: 22 - 23). Knowing that the time of His death and departure from this world had come and having loved men even to excess, even to that time, Jesus wished to give them the last and the greatest proof of love as He said: *"Jesus knowing that His hour has come, that he should pass out of this world to the Father: having loved his own who were in the world, he loved them unto the end"* (John 13:1). As we read in Luke 22: 15, Jesus was sitting at the table, all on fire with charity, and turning to His disciples, He said: *"With desire I have desired to eat this Pasch with you before I suffer."* It was like saying: "Brothers, no, I have desired nothing during my whole life but to eat this last supper with you. After this, I shall go to sacrifice my life for your salvation." Knowing that Jesus suffered more than all the pains suffered by the martyrs put together. For what? To atone, to prepare for our sins so that no one of those entrusted to Him by His Father would be lost. He suffered all because He loves us. We read in Isaiah that *"But he was wounded for our iniquities, he was bruised for our sins: the chastisement of our peace was upon him, and by his bruises, we are healed"* (Isaiah 53: 5). Remember that when we suffer, God suffered for us first to make reparation for our sins so that we may become once again the children of God.

Let us learn from the story of Our Lady of Guadalupe: Hernán Cortés had accomplished a great military achievement in subduing millions of Indians with only a few hundred soldiers and in bringing Western Civilization to the American shores, but he alone could not convert the Indians. After this fearless commander had demolished, he led an expedition to Honduras. Upon his return to Mexico City, Cortes found political difficulties that required him to sail back to Spain in 1528 to plead his cause in person with the king. Numerous missionaries arrived in Mexico to open churches, schools, and hospitals, but few Indians converted because paganism had struck deep root in their souls, and the harsh treatment of the natives by the earlier Spanish officials had turned the Indians into hostile and suspicious people against foreigners. In order to heal the wounds of oppression, King Charles recalled the abusive Spanish officials and sent Bishop Juan de Zumárraga, a Franciscan Prior, to protect the Indians from the insensitive officials. Unfortunately, the damage was done and Bishop Zumarraga realized that the general uprising was imminent that would wipe out the Spanish presence in Central America. In isolated cases, the natives even killed some Spaniards; the anger of the natives grew more intense as they began burning some centers of the missionaries and even beating to death some of them. The tension was rising by the moment as the Indian pagans were becoming increasingly violent and aggressive. Their numbers were increasing every day as these tens of thousands of natives armed themselves with whatever was inside so that they can kill and drive out once and for all the foreigners. To prevent more killings and violent uprisings that could wipe out the missionaries, Bishop Zumarraga prayed the Holy Rosary earnestly to Our Lady and asked Her to send some Castilian roses as a sign that his prayers had been heard. In one of the most momentous events in all history, the Mother of God, Our Lady of Guadalupe came down from heaven and appeared to a humble Aztec peasant, Juan Diego, in a barren hill, a few miles outside Mexico City. She identified Herself by the word in Nahuatl language (the Aztec language) as *Mother of the very true deity.* By this, She assured the people that as the Immaculate Conception, she will triumph over both the devil as said in Genesis 3: 15 and over one of the most terrible of all the Indian gods: Moloch. It is no coincidence but surely the work of God that the first apparition of Our Lady occurred on December 8th, which was the Feast of the Immaculate Conception. Our Lady asked Juan Diego to go to the bishop, Bishop Zumarraga to request that the church be built at the location of Her first apparition. The bishop responded courteously but was skeptical. Juan Diego felt dejected, his uncle was dying, and the bishop was uncommitted, he failed the beautiful Lady who sent him to speak to the bishop. However, Our Lady appeared to Juan Diego on December 12th, this time was at the bottom of the hill. There, She gave him the message the same message that She continues to give to Her grieving children even to this day, that is "She is the Mother of mercy, of life, and of hope to all who follow the teachings of Her Son and have confidence in Her powerful intercession. To prove Her loving power, the Blessed Virgin performed one of the most illustrious miracles that have become known all over the world. Following Our Lady's instruction, Juan Diego climbed the hill known as Tepeyac to the place of the original apparitions. To his amazement, there he found a field of brilliant fragrant flowers, including Castilian roses, growing in frozen rocky soil, he carefully gathered a bundle of the flowers in his cloak, and then he went off to the bishop. After he had been brought into the presence of the bishop, Juan Diego showed him the magnificent flowers. The bishop fell on his knees because his prayer was answered and looked upon Juan Diego with astounding amazement because he also saw imprinted on Juan Diego's cloak the Image of Our Lady as She had appeared that day. Bishop Zumarrage built the chapel at the miraculous site to house the Image with an adjoining room for Juan Diego. Unknown to the bishop, the location of the chapel was very significant because it was the site of one of the pagan temples that had been destroyed by Hernan Cortes. The miraculous circumstances and the inexplicable powerful attraction of Our Lady's Image drew thousands of Aztecs to the shrine, having been converted in their hearts. By the time they left the shrine of Our Lady, the pilgrims sought out missionaries for baptism. Soon after the apparition of the Virgin of Guadalupe, "conversions began occurring at an astounding rate." The missionaries were in awe of what was happening: "the Indians were coming from everywhere, from faraway lands asking for the sacraments." It was estimated that 9 million more faithful added to the Catholic Church in just a few years.

Let us remember what Gaudium et Spes Documents said: "Even with the greatest invention of science and technology to make the life of man more comfortable than ever, yet the greatest mystery of all is that amidst these achievements, there is one that defies the progress of science and technology how to eradicate completely human sufferings." In other words, until the end of time, suffering will be our human destiny. But we have seen throughout history that suffering is a blessing in disguise.

In his Apostolic Letter "Salvifici Dolores", Saint John Paul II said: "Human suffering is a divine gift to enable man to participate in the greatest act of love of God, who died on the Cross to pay for man's sins that they may enter the Kingdom of Heaven and become heirs of Heaven."

MEDITATION

"As iron is fashioned by fire and on the anvil, so in the fire of suffering and under the weight of trials, our souls receive that form which our Lord desires them to have." (St. Madeleine Sophie Barat)

"If God gives you an abundant harvest of trials, it is a sign of great holiness which He desires you to attain. Do you want to become a great saint? Ask God to send you many sufferings. The flame of Divine Love never rises higher than when fed with the wood of the Cross, which the infinite charity of the Savior used to finish His sacrifice. All the pleasures of the world are nothing compared with the sweetness found in the gall and vinegar offered to Jesus Christ. That is, hard and painful things endured for Jesus Christ and with Jesus Christ." (St. Ignatius of Loyola)

PRAYER

Oh my Jesus, you desire so ardently to give your life for me, your miserable creature. This desire of yours flames my heart with a desire to suffer and die for love of you since you suffered and died for love of me. Oh beloved Redeemer, make known to me your will as I desire to please you in all things. I desire to give you pleasure to correspond, at least in part, to your great love for me, increase this blessed flame within me always so that it may make me forget the world and myself, that from this day onward I may think only of pleasing Your Loving Heart. May you increase my love for you by loving the Cross you send me to make reparation for my sin and to be reconciled with the Father forever in Heaven. I ask this through the most powerful intercession of Our Lady of Guadalupe, in the name of Jesus Christ, Our Lord. Amen.

DAY 18

THE SIN OF PONTIUS PILATE

"And Pilate, calling together the chief priests, and the magistrates, and the people, said to them: You have presented unto me this man, as one that perverteth the people; and behold I, having examined him before you, find no cause in this man, in those things wherein you accuse him. No, nor Herod neither. For I sent you to him, and behold, nothing worthy of death is done to him. I will chastise him therefore, and release him." (Luke 23: 13-16)

Pilate took Jesus and scourged Him. Seeing the failure of his two attempts to save the innocent Jesus from the Jews: sending Jesus to Herod and suggesting that Jesus be released than Barabbas; Pilate tried another, he ordered Jesus to be scourged, and afterward, to dismiss him. Pilate's words were firmed: *"You have presented to me this man, and behold I, having examined him before you, find no cause in this man. No, nor Herod neither. For I sent you to him, and behold, nothing worthy of death is done to him. I will chastise him therefore, and release him"* (Luke 23: 14-16). Listen closely to what Pilate said, he found Jesus innocent, yet, he chastised our Lord, what utter injustice! What did Jesus do? He humbled Himself to except this painful and ignominious punishment in satisfaction for our sins. The executioner scourged every part of our Lord's Sacred Body. Afterward, they continued, without mercy, to lash at the wounds already inflicted, adding more pain after pain. This was in fulfillment of what was prophesied in Psalm 68: 27 that *"and they have added to the grief of my wounds."* We also read in Isaiah that *"He was wounded for our iniquities. He was bruised for our sins"* (Isaiah 53: 5). Alas and most alas, the most beautiful of all men was mangled and deformed that no one can ever recognize him, a mere leper covered with wounds from head to foot. Why? It is because this loving Redeemer wished to suffer the pains that were due to us, as prophesied in Isaiah: *"Surely he hath borne our infirmities and carried our sorrows"* (Isaiah 53: 4). While the executioner scourged Him cruelly, Jesus neither spoke nor complained nor signed. Rather, He patiently bore and offered all to God to appease His anger against us.

The scourging of Jesus is historically proven with medical records to show that the beatings were real and fatal.

William D. Edwards and Associates wrote in detail about these proofs in their article: "On the Physical Death of Jesus Christ", published on March 21, 1986 in the Journal of the American Medical Association, Vol. 256. Edward described that the Romans did not invent crucifixion (the Persians did), yet they did refine it as a technique for torture that would lead to a slow and extremely painful death. When we say pain is "excruciating" we are actually saying, according to the root meaning of the word, that the pain is "from the cross." So severe and disgraceful was crucifixion that it was usually reserved only for slaves, non-Romans, revolutionaries and the worst criminals.

Flogging was a legal preliminary to every Roman execution, and only woman and Roman senators or soldiers (except in cases of desertion) were exempt. The usual instrument was a short whip (flagrum or flagellum) with several single or braided leather thongs of variable lengths, in which small iron balls or sharp pieces of sheep bones were tied at intervals. Occasionally, staves also were used. For scourging, the man was stripped of his clothing, and his hands were tied to an upright post. The back, buttocks, and legs were flogged either by two soldiers (lictors) or by one who alternated positions. The severity of the scourging depended on the disposition of the lictors and was intended to weaken the victim to a state just short of collapse or death. After the scourging, the soldiers often taunted their victim.

As the Roman soldiers repeatedly struck the victim's back with full force, the iron balls would cause deep contusions, and the leather thongs and sheep bones would cut into the skin and subcutaneous tissues. Then, as the flogging continued, the lacerations would tear into the underlying skeletal muscles and produce quivering ribbons of bleeding flesh. Pain and blood loss generally set the stage for circulatory shock. The extent of blood loss may well have determined how long the victim would survive on the cross.

At the Praetorium, Jesus was severely whipped. (Although the severity of the scourging is not discussed in the four gospel accounts, it is implied in one of the epistles (Peter 2: 24). A detailed word study of the ancient Greek text for this verse indicates that the scourging of Jesus was particularly harsh). It is not known whether the number of lashes was limited to 39, in accordance with Jewish law. The Roman soldiers, amused that this weakened man had claimed to be a king, began to mock him by placing a robe on his shoulders, a crown of thorns on his head, and a wooden staff as a scepter in his right hand. Next, they spat on Jesus and struck him on the head with the wooden staff. Moreover, when the soldiers tore the robe from Jesus' back, they probably reopened the scourging wounds. The severe scourging, with its intense pain and appreciable blood loss, most probably left Jesus in a preshock state. Moreover, hematidrosis had rendered his skin particularly tender. The physical and mental abuse meted out by the Jews and the Romans, as well as the lack of food, water, and sleep, also contributed to his generally weakened state. Therefore, even before the actual crucifixion, Jesus' physical condition was at least serious and possibly critical.

Physical violence, anguish, humiliations, mockery, blood, intense pain, both physical and moral, even before the crucifixion, all rendered Jesus' body and soul to be both terribly battered and bruised. Yet, Jesus suffered all these us silently without any compliant whatsoever.

In the scene of the scourging, Pontius Pilate committed two crimes: First, Self-justification (rationalization); Second, Human Respect.

Self-justification or Rationalization is a common sin that we also commit many times, not only Pontius Pilate. Rationaliza-tion is a human act where one devises superficially rational excuses for acts, beliefs, or desires in order to justify one's im-proper or immoral acts. Modern ethics has also termed this act "Consequentialism", which is also condemned by the Catholic Church. Although Pilate knew that Jesus was innocent, he still abandoned and punished Him in a very cruel torture that left Jesus half-dead.

The second sin of Pontius Pilate was the sin of human respect. Because of human respect for the Jewish people, especially the chief priests, Pontius Pilate chose to displease God's Will. Many of us commit this sin of human respect whenever we fear loss of name or esteem, resorting to human consideration and estima-tion rather than of what is good and upright; rendering to man what is due to God. Although human respect is a good thing, when we respect, honor, and appreciate one another. It becomes sinful when we give more respect to human beings than respect to God. For instance, when we are scared to tell the truth about evil of some actions, for example abortion, we are afraid to cor-rect or tell someone not to do the procedure as it is outright murder.

Let us remember that the good end does not justify the evil means. For example, the good end of appeasing the crowd of rebellious Jews, which led Pontius Pilate to self-justification or consequentialism, does not justify the evil means of torturing Jesus and leaving Him half-dead. Emperor Tiberius of Alexan-dria had already warned Pontius Pilate not to intimidate the Jews. Out of human respect for the Emperor and the Jewish people and aware of the harsh criticisms that await him, Pontius Pilate chose to torture Jesus by scourging Him at the pillar.

Although, some people may quote St. Thomas Aquinas' Suma Theologiae which explains the ethical principle of double effect to excuse the crime of Pontius Pilate, remember that there should be a sufficient proportion of good effect for one to tolerate the evil effects. We must be able to distinguish the condemned moral theories of consequence solution and proportionalism from the Catholic moral principle of double effect.

The Catechism of the Catholic Church says that "*A morally good act requires the goodness of the object, of the end, and of the circumstances together. An evil end corrupts the action, even if the object is good in itself (such as praying and fasting "in order to be seen by men"). The object of the choice can by itself vitiate an act in its entirety. There are some concrete acts - such as fornication - that it is always wrong to choose, because choosing them entails a disorder of the will, that is, a moral evil*" (CCC#1755). The Catechism continues, "*It is therefore an error to judge the morality of human acts by considering only the intention that inspires them or the circumstances (environment, social pressure, duress or emergency, etc.) which supply their context. There are acts which, in and of themselves, independently of circumstances and intentions, are always gravely illicit by reason of their object; such as blasphemy and perjury, murder and adultery. One may not do evil so that good may result from it*" (CCC#1756).

After the Second Vatican, it had become very popular, especially among European and American theologians to believe that in determining moral lawfulness, the end or intention could justify an evil act of proportionalism, or the foreseen good effects could justify an action that previously had been judged to be morally evil. These false theories deny that any act can be intrinsically evil by its object alone, apart from its intention and circumstances, even abortion, contraception, adultery, and other intrinsic evils, which the entire moral tradition has condemned, could, in some cases, be morally good by reason of their intention or consequences.

In Encyclical "Veritatis Splendor" (1994), #76, Pope John Paul II emphasized that specifically condemned these theories of consequentialism and proportionalism, he wrote: "Such theories, however, are not faithful to the Church's teaching. When they believe they can justify as morally good deliberate choices of kinds of behavior contrary to the Ten Commandments of the Divine and natural law. These theories cannot claim to be grounded in the Catholic moral tradition. The faithful are obliged to acknowledge and respect these specific moral presets which declared and taught by the Church in the name of God, the Creator and Lord."

Remember this; rationalization or consequentialism, which is the human act to divine superficially rational excuses for one's acts, beliefs, or desires to justify one's improper and immoral acts, is a sin. In fact, it is a mental disorder caused by pride. This is the trickery of human nature. Adam and Eve started it all, when Eve transgressed God's commandment, instead of saying to God, "it is my entire fault. I am sorry." Eve rationalized their immoral actions of eating the forbidden fruit by blaming the serpent. Adam rationalized his immoral action by blaming his wife. Pontius Pilate justified the sin of the injustice be scourging the innocent Jesus by blaming the Jews for their insistence.

Pilate had a good intention or end but made use of the wrong means. How often do we justify ourselves washing our hands like Pontius Pilate when we employ evil means in order to obtain what we want? Let us engrave in our hearts and minds that the end does not justify the means. Let us remember that our good intentions do not make our actions good if we carry out an evil means to obtain what we want.

Today, people continue to do the same thing; the husband justifies his adultery because of his wife's frigidity; the wife justifies her privileged lifestyle because she is lonely; the child justified his addiction to pornography because his parents gave him a smart phone.

The truth remains regardless of how much we try to rationalize our actions, we cannot make something wrong into something right before the eyes of God. Sadly, with simple human respect, we have the tendency of distorting good things and turning them bad. For example, during the Passion and Death of Jesus, Pilate knew that Jesus was innocent, and that he was delivered by his enemies because of their envy. Pilate wanted to save Jesus, but because of human respect, he did not have the courage to go against the wishes of the crowd. So he made an absurd move, he gave the crowd an option to choose between Barabbas, a murderer, and Jesus, the innocent man.

Human respect is basically cowardice, prevents us from fighting for justice and truth, it makes us afraid of what other people would think or say, and it makes us more concerned with our benefits than with what is actually good. This pursuit for human respect often manifests itself in the form of fear that is the fear of not fitting in or of being criticized for thinking or acting differently from other people, especially when it comes to practice the faith. Human respect makes us fear man more than God. It makes us more concerned with what other people think of us than with what God thinks and expects of us. This unholy fear often causes us to make bad decisions because of our desire to avoid upsetting others or being looked down upon by those in authority. In short, with human respect, we care too much about what others might think of us than with what God thinks of us. Our fear of losing human respect can manifest at times in our tendency to remain silent and indifferent. We see people inappropriately dressed at Sunday Mass, but because we fear rejection or ridicule if we correct these people, we say nothing, we keep to ourselves and not get involved. We hear our Lord's Holy Name blasphemed or slandered, or when we hear others call good evil and evil good, and although we know we should speak up against this monstrosity because it offends our Lord, out of fear, we remain silent and pretend we did not see or hear any of these offensive words or actions. There is more when someone is in our care, whether it be a child or an employee, and we know we should correct them because they are doing something wrong, because of human respect, we say nothing out of fear of losing the respect or good favor. We tend to fall into this sort of fear from time to time. It is only natural that we want other people to like us but at what price. Let us remember that our goal should be to always live in God's presence and according to His Will, not in accordance with what other's will and think of us. Although this is easier said than done, just think that God sees all things and knows all. It takes courage to do what is right and to do it for God. It means being brave enough to stand out from the crowd and to not simply take the safer route, the popular route the easy way out of things.

Many people are afraid of being different, or are worried that they may appear intolerant or backwards in their thinking that they might not fit in, or simply they may be afraid of standing up for what is right alone. But remember that Jesus stood out alone because of what is right, because He defended what is right and true.

This is a story of a wealthy and influential person named Jerry (not his real name) who earned respect from his fellow men through hard work and honesty. One day while eating in a restaurant with friend, he was accosted and accused of drug peddling by the police. He was taken into custody and his story appeared in all mainstream news channels. Rumors circulated that he had accumulated his wealth by selling forbidden drugs that grew in the lives of so many people. He and his family who were highly religious abiding citizens were shocked. His friends and the people of the city were scandalized, in short, his name was destroyed. When he appeared in court, he knew he had no chance because the judges were all prejudiced against him. It was at this moment that he and his family reinforced the most powerful prayer, the family's Rosary. Many people came in support of Jerry at the court hearing, but in spite of their lobby, Jerry lost the case, and was sentenced to at least fifteen years in jail. Jerry did not dishearten, he never stopped praying the Rosary, he believed that the Blessed Virgin Mary would bail him out and disproved their accusation. His family also intensified their praying the Rosary and asked close friends and relatives to do the same. In the prison, Jerry experienced the mockery of other inmates because of all the false news every day on television and in the newspapers. Jerry spent many sleepless nights but he held on to his Rosary and prayed as he suffered. Jerry found solace in visiting the prison chapel where he prayed and invoked the help of the Blessed Virgin Mary. He never stopped praying for his accusers. After a month to solve, for whatever reason, the judge who condemned him without sufficient evidence resigned, and the one replaced him reopened Jerry's case. After days of hearing, his case was dismissed for lack of substantial evidence to everyone's surprise, but Jerry was not surprised because he knew that the Virgin Mary would immediately come to his aid. In Jerry's country, anyone suspected of drug pushing has no hope for appeal. The Mother Mary was more powerful than any person, as She turned out the law enforcer who accused Jerry of drug pushing turned himself and admitted that he and his group had made up the story. Jerry attributed it all to the help of the Blessed Virgin Mary who restored Jerry's reputation. Now, Jerry is happily doing what he used to do, promoting the Two Hearts Devotion and joining the parish Rosary with the Legion of Mary.

Let us learn from the example of Jerry, always ask ourselves that *"Am I following God if I do this? Am I doing what the Holy Scriptures and the Church teaching if I do this?"* If we simply follow popular opinion at best, we will always find ourselves trying to fit in with the crowd, at worst, we will find ourselves thinking, believing, and acting in a way that is gravely offensive to our Lord. People tend to judge others according to their own likes or dislikes, or by their own set of fixed ideas. The judging is almost opinion related. Remember, we cannot make everyone happy. If we try to do so, we will just end up exhausted and probably pleasing no one. Our Lord will only judge our actions on how much we have demonstrated our love for Him by following all that He asked. The thoughts and words of men can neither odd nor subtract from our true word. We do not become more or less of the person because praises or criticism of people. Our goodness and the goodness of everyone around us can only come from God.

Let us give up rationalization or our tendency for nurturing human respect. Never fear of being rejected or hurt by another person because we sided with the truth. Let us stand firm in our faith and in what we know is true, because it is better to walk in the right direction even if it means walking alone than to walk with a whole crowd that is headed towards eternal perdition.

The one who walks with God never walks alone.

MEDITATION

"The Most Holy Virgin in these last times in which we live has given a new efficacy to the recitation of the Rosary to such an extent that there is no problem, no matter how difficult it is, whether temporal or above all spiritual, in the personal life of each one of us, of our families... that cannot be solved by the Rosary. There is no problem, I tell you, no matter how difficult it is, that we cannot resolve by the prayer of the Holy Rosary." (Sister Lucia dos Santos of Fatima)

PRAYER

Oh Loving Jesus, help me to defend the truth without being afraid of the consequences. May I be able to overcome human respect and cover this to do what is morally right than good. Pontius Pilate's plan and good intentions did not pull true, the people chose Barabbas due to the manipulation of the chief priest who inside the crowd to choose the criminal. How terribly envy is to make us do such terrible things. Help me, Lord, to learn how to think on my own and not be influenced by the evil schemes of other people. God gave us freedom and made rational creatures so that we can choose what is good. Oh Jesus, pardon me for many times I have given into the snares of the evil one; help me to make good use of my freedom to not be easily swayed by the deceits of the enemy; teach me to overcome the sin of the scandal that is instigating others to commit sin because of my words, actions, and behaviors. I ask this through the most powerful intercession of the Blessed Virgin Mary, in the name of Jesus Christ, Our Lord. Amen.

DAY 19

CROWNING WITH THORNS

"Then the soldiers of the governor taking Jesus into the hall, gathered together unto him the whole band; And stripping him, they put a scarlet cloak about him. And platting a crown of thorns, they put it upon his head, and a reed in his right hand. And bowing the knee before him, they mocked him, saying: Hail, king of the Jews. And spitting upon him, they took the reed, and struck his head. And after they had mocked him, they took off the cloak from him, and put on him his own garments, and led him away to crucify him." (Matthew 27: 27-31)

As if his brutal scourging on the part of the Roman soldiers were not enough, Jesus was labeled a neurotic fool who claims to be a king. He was mockingly donned with a purple robe and was shamelessly struck on the face as if he had done something to merit every ferocity and cruelty. Worse even and with the idea to ridicule him, Jesus was sadistically crowned with thorns. "Crowning with thorns was not an official part of the punishment; it was an initiative of the soldiers themselves, a product of their cruelty and desire to mock Jesus. On the stone pavement in the Antonia tower some drawings have been found which must have been used in what was called the "king game": dice were thrown to pick out a mock king among those condemned, who was subjected to taunting before being led off for crucifixion" (Navarre Bible Commentary to John 15:1-3).

The soldiers fabricated a crown-helmet perhaps using the flexible stems or a plant called *Sarcopoterium spinosum*, or the tree called *zizyphus spina-christi*, both of which have very long thorns, much longer than those of *Acacias*. Medical record shows that the Shroud of Turin reveals 33 wounds in Our Lord's scalp, which the doctors have proven to have bled profusely around 330 milliliters, (10 to 12 percent of the total human blood volume), apart from the blood that Jesus lost in the hematohidrosis and the scourging. The Gospel also reveals to us that after being crowned, the soldiers hammered the crown-helmet into Jesus' head so that it would fit snugly. Jesus also received continuous blows to His head, actions which would have driven these thorns deeply into the highly vascularized scalp and forehead, thereby, producing excessive bleeding. Each blow would have caused Jesus a painful silent scream and a shudder towards His curved spine. The parody of the adoration has begun: soldiers kneeling before Jesus, more blows and spits on His face, bruises, and insults seemingly never-ending.

It is easy to overlook Jesus' physical sufferings associated with the crown of thorns, especially when compared with the brutality of the scouring and the crucifixion itself. It might be easier to meditate on the mockery and humiliation that Jesus received from the Roman soldiers than to meditate on the physical suffering of His crowning with thorns.

However, Doctor Frederick Zugibe, Former Chief Medical Examiners from New York, analyzed the crowning with thorns extended Jesus' physical suffering. This doctor discusses a neurological condition known as *Trigeminal Neuralgia*, which is caused by stimulation or irritation of the two major nerve branches located on the top and sides of the head. This condition causes paroxysmal bouts of pain to the face, which sufferers describe as "knifelike stabs," "electric shocks," or "jabs with a red-hot poker". Trigeminal neuralgia is among the worst pain a human can experience. Once this irritation has occurred, even light touches, facial movements, chewing, talking, or drafts of air across the face can precipitate an attack. The Doctor explained that the condition "is said to be the worst pain that man is heir to. It is devastating pain that is just unbearable in its several forms."

Turning back to the Gospel account of the crowning, Doctor

Zugibe explains in details that "It is important to note that the crown was made by interweaving (plaiting) the thorn twigs into the shape of a cap. This placed a large number of thorns in contact with the entire top of the head, including the front, back, and sides. The blows from the reed across Jesus' face or against the thorns would directly irritate the nerves or activate trigger zones along the lip, side of the nose, or face, bringing on severe pains resembling a hot poker or electric shock lancinating across the sides of his face or deep to his ears. The pain would stop almost abruptly, only to recur again with the slightest movement of the jaws or even from a wisp of wind, stopping Jesus `dead' in his tracks. The traumatic shock from the brutal scourging would be further enhanced with each paroxysmal pain across the face bringing him to his knees. Exacerbations and remissions of throbbing bolts of pain would occur all the way to Calvary and during crucifixion, being activated by the movements of walking, falling, and twisting, from pressure of the thorns against the cross; and from the many shoves and blows by the soldiers."

Despised and humiliated, Pontius Pilate presented Jesus to the infuriated crowd, shouting: "Behold, the man!" (in Latin, *Ecce homo!*). Pilate was trying to pacify the wrath of the multitude by showing them that Jesus had suffered sufficiently and reiterated that he found no crime in him with the implicit intention to let Jesus go.

Each time we commit sin, most especially the worst sin which is disobedience to God's Will or simply pride, we not only offend Jesus but we also add thorns to His already agonizing suffering head from the crown of thorns, not only this, we also add more swords to the Heart of Mother Mary, who "seven swords spears in Her Heart," according to St. Alphonsus Liguori.

According to St. Thomas Aquinas, pride is "the greatest sin in man," "the beginning of all sin," and "Man's first sin." (Summa Theologiae II-II 161, 6-7; 163, 1) He further tells us that "the root of pride is found to consist in man not being in some way subject to God and His Rule." (II-II, 162, 5) Simplifying St. Thomas's words, Peter Kreeft boils it down to this: "'Thy' will be done is the essential prayer of the saint; 'my will be done' is the essential prayer of the sinner." (Practical Theology)

As he did with the whole of his Passion, Jesus willingly accepted his crown of thorns (and the excruciating pain that came as a result) on our behalf. But why? Venerable Archbishop Fulton Sheen explains that "As the scourging was the reparation for the sins of the flesh, so the crowning with thorns was the atonement for the sins of the mind – for the atheists who wish there were no God, for the doubters whose evil lives becloud their thinking, for the egotists, centered on themselves." (The Fifteen Mysteries) Jesus wore the crown of thorns because of our pride, plain and simple.

If we are honest and let the virtue of humility override our pride, we can pray this way: far too often, Lord, has my pride caused me to put on my own crown and ignore Christ's crown of thorns. This pride has taken many forms over the years, both big and small. So many times when I've been in the valley of darkness, God's will was the farthest thing from my mind. Even when I could muster up the strength to say the Lord's Prayer (the "Our Father"), "thy will be done" was nothing more than words. Deep down, I thought my will was better than God's. Yet, the reality is that the crown of my pride is heavy, weighing me down into an abyss of misery. It prevents me from loving Jesus Christ and doing his will through keeping his commandments. (John 14:21). But thanks to God's grace and mercy, I can remove my crown of selfish pride, put on Christ's crown of glory, and become a royal heir thanks to His precious blood that flowed from the crown of thorns.

Sacred Scripture assures us of this:

- "Blessed is the man who perseveres in temptation, for when he has been proved he will receive the crown of life that he promised to those who love him." (James 1:12)
- "I have competed well; I have finished the race; I have kept the faith. From now on the crown of righteousness awaits me, which the Lord, the just judge, will

award to me on that day, and not only to me, but to all who have longed for his appearance." (2 Timothy 4:7-8)

- "Run so as to win. Every athlete exercises discipline in every way. They do it to win a perishable crown, but we, an imperishable one."
- "The Lord redeems your life from the pit, and crowns you with mercy and compassion." (Psalms 103:4).

We have the ancient story of Saint Pachomius, the founder of Christian Cenobitic Monasticism of the Coptic Church. At age 21, Pachomius was swept up against his will in a Roman army recruitment drive, a common occurrence during this period of turmoil and civil war. With several other youths, he was put onto a ship that floated down the Nile and arrived at Thebes in the evening. Here he first encountered local Christians, who customarily brought food and comfort daily to the conscripted troops. This made a lasting impression, and Pachomius vowed to investigate Christianity further when he got out. He was able to leave the army without ever having to fight, was converted and baptized.

Pachomius then came into contact with several well-known ascetics and decided to pursue that path under the guidance of the hermit named Palaemon. One of his devotions, popular at the time, was praying with his arms stretched out in the form of a cross. After studying seven years with Palaemon, Pachomius set out to lead the life of a hermit near St. Anthony of Egypt. It was then that he heard a voice of Jesus who told him to build a dwelling for the hermits who were unprepared to follow the rigorous penance of St. Anthony of the desert. Towards the enemy's life was suffering intense pain in his head and oppressed with interior anguish of mind, Pachomius had recourse to prayer to obtain relief and consolation from God. On this occasion, Our Lord, Jesus appeared to him wearing a crown of thorns, accompanied by Mother Mary with seven swords pierced in Her Heart together with many holy angels and shining with dazzling glory. Mother Mary was holding another crown of thorns and told

Pachomius not to cry because God allows these sufferings and the good would come out of it. The Blessed Mother continued to explain to Pachomius that when God permits suffering to happen, it is to remove: (1) the vices still present inside him, to make his soul holier, more beautiful, and better than before; (2) to cast out the demon is still hiding in his mind causing mental and emotional disorders; (3) to heal his brokenness from his family through his sufferings. Surprised, at this heavenly vision, the suffering servant of God prostrated himself with his face to the ground, when one of the angels very affectionately raised him up and told him that Jesus Christ and Mother Mary have come to console him in his affliction. Jesus and Mary, on intervals, spoke to Pachomius words of heavenly comfort, encouraging him to bear his trials and sufferings with resignation. They assured him that his trials and sufferings were intended for the purification of his soul and for the great increase of merits which was soon to be crowned with corresponding and bliss for all eternity in heaven. They assured Pachomius that these sufferings were not even a small part in comparison with the sufferings of Jesus who told innocent, but out of love, took the sins and punishment of mankind to make all men again children of God. They encouraged Pachomius to accept the crown of thorns out of love and in reparation for his sins and for those who need a conversion to avoid falling into the fires of hell. This vision converted Pachomius, compelled him to go to confession more often and to fast in order to strengthen his will. Since the vision appeared, he spent each day of his life offering prayers and sufferings in reparation to God through the intervention of the Blessed Virgin Mary. Mother Mary taught Pachomius how to pray the Psalter Prayer or Jesus' Prayer with a knotted cord, later in 1214, Mother Mary told St. Dominic to change the Psalter Prayer with its knotted rope, and what we now call the "Holy Rosary." Pachomius is also credited of being the first Christian use and to recommend the use of the prayer rope. A prayer rope is a loop made up of complex woven knots formed in a cross pattern, usually out of wool or silk. Prayer ropes are part of the practice of Eastern-

Catholic and of Eastern Orthodox monks and nuns, and is used to count the number of times one has prayed the Jesus Prayer: "Jesus, Son of David, have mercy on me, a sinner" or, occasionally, other prayers. The effects of these prayers and penitential lifestyle formed Pachomius to become a Great Saint and the pioneer of the first Eastern Catholic Monasticism.

Whenever we feel our pride creeping in, try to have this mental image of Jesus with the crown of thorns and contemplate on what He endured to pay for our sins of pride to simply become more aware or even just to recognize how much we hurt Jesus when our will goes against His will, we have gained the victory over our pride. It is in fighting these small battles, day by day, that allows us to take baby steps toward holiness. For true "freedom consists not in doing what we like, but in having the right to do what we ought." (St. Pope John Paul II).

MEDITATION

"His ignominy has blotted out ours, his bonds have set us free, his crown of thorns has won for us the crown of the Kingdom, his wounds have cured us" (St. Jerome, Comm. in Marcum, in loc.).

"You and I..., haven't we crowned him anew with thorns and struck him and spat on him?... Never again Jesus...never again." (St. Holy Rosary, third Sorrowful Mystery).

PRAYER

Oh Blessed Virgin Mary, according to St. Catharine; you were granted the privilege to suffer all the afflictions of Jesus, which encompasses all the sins of every generation. When Jesus was crowned with thorns, you experienced it, and as a mother, the pain you experienced was seven more times painful than that of your Son. It is because of my pride and pride of all the people in this world that Jesus suffered so much and crowning with thorns. Every time I have the headache or migraine or some other worries to solve which unsettles me, physically or emotionally, please help and teach me to accept them with joy, knowing that Jesus who wore the crown of thorns to save me from hell. He accepted and endured all for my sake. Help me to be more self-sacrificing and to embrace my pains with resignation and faith that you are with me in bearing them all. I ask this in Christ, Our Lord. Amen.

DAY 20

CARRYING OF THE CROSS

"Then therefore he delivered him to them to be crucified. And they took Jesus, and led him forth. And bearing his own cross, he went forth to that place which is called Calvary, but in Hebrew Golgotha." (John 19: 16-17)

We are walking with Mary, contemplating as She did during the time that She was with Our Lord, Jesus, as He was accused, humiliated, judged, and made to suffer the most unthinkable torture. What does Mary see?

Today, we look at the scenes where Jesus suffered in the hands of Pilate and the scribes through the eyes of the Blessed Mother, who stood among the crowd, at first, and later followed Jesus' painful walk to the Stations of the Cross.

Remember, in all these events, Mary stood by Jesus, She was with Him and in Him. Pontius Pilate turned to the Jews, cried out: "Behold, your king!" But they cried out, "Away with him! Away with him! Crucify him!" Pilate said to them, "Shall I crucify your king?" The chief priests answered, "We have no king but Caesar." Pilate shouted back, "Take him yourself and crucify him! I find no crime in him!" So, in front of all the people, Pilate ordered a bowl of water to be brought and he publicly washed his hands in front of them all, saying 'I am innocent of the blood of this just person; see ye to it', (Matthew 27: 24). Then he handed him over to them to be crucified. And so they took Jesus and let him away.

This is what really happens when an innocent man is condemned; he is given over into the hands of his enemies that they may take away his life by the dead, which is most pleasing to

143

them.

The Jews then said, "His blood be upon us and upon our children!" The unjust sentence of death is read in the presence of our condemned Lord. He listens to it and with entire resignation to the judge decree of His Eternal Father who condemns Him to the Cross. Jesus humbly accepts, not for the crimes falsely imputed to Him by the Jews but in atonement for our real sins, for which He offers to make satisfaction by His death.

And from among the crowd where She stood, Mary also heard and listened to the sentence. It was like as if Pilate said on earth, "Let Jesus die," the Eternal Father from Heaven confirmed the sentence, "Let my Son die." The Son Himself answered, "Here I am! I obey and accept the death and the Cross." Our Beloved Redeemer accepted death because of our sins, and by His Death, He obtained life for us.

Now, then, Mother Mary saw the following scenes right in front of Her eyes:

The Roman soldiers removed the cloak of Our Lord which had already stuck to His deep wounds. Blood starts to ooze once again...more painful but silent shudder. They put His own clothes which immediately are stained with His fresh blood. And they put the patibulum, the horizontal beam of the Cross on His shoulders, weighing 35-50 kg, to which His hands were tied by ropes. The weakened and heavily bruised body of Our Lord tried to balance itself to remain standing under this new burden which He willingly carries for us. The journey to Golgotha, around 650 meters from where He was scourged begins. Mother Mary followed, and Our Lord started the journey with His bare soles along the rough, dry and dusty roads, being pulled by the ropes which the soldiers held and pushed by the soldiers to hurry Him up. The weight of the heavy burden finally causes our Lord to fall onto His face towards the ground. More bruises and contusions to his Most Holy Face...Another fall...and another... And so the soldiers forced Simon of Cyrene to help Jesus carry the Cross. Our Lord shows his sincere gratitude to Simon, looking directly into his eyes, perhaps with a small smile...

Thompson and Harrub provide us a summary of the historical and medical details of the carrying of the Cross:

"Archaeological evidence strongly suggests that criminals during the time of Christ were not forced to carry an entire T-shaped cross ... but rather only the crossbeam (known as a patibulum), which would have weighed between 75 and 125 pounds. It was customary, however, for convicted criminals to carry their own cross from the scourging site to the place of crucifixion. Their hands normally were tied (or even left unbound) during the procession, rather than being nailed to the patibulum. The effects of the scourging on Christ's physical condition can be inferred from His severely weakened condition - as demonstrated by the fact that later, Simon of Cyrene would be compelled to carry the patibulum. As a bloodied Christ struggled with that crossbeam, a centurion led the procession, which usually consisted of a full Roman military guard. Measurements indicate that the distance from the praetorium to the site of Christ's crucifixion was approximately one-third of a mile (600-650 meters). The Bible never actually mentions that Christ collapsed under that heavy load. However, consider the possibility that if His hands were tied to the crosspiece and He had fallen, Jesus would have been unable to break the fall. Researchers have speculated that falling under the weight of a crossbeam very likely would have "resulted in blunt chest trauma and a contused heart" (Ball, 1989, p. 83)."From Bert Thompson, Ph.D. and Brad Harrub, Ph.D., in "An Examination of the Medical Evidence for the Physical Death of Christ"

Every day, in one way or the other, we experience the cross, but out of fear, we try to repel and stop the cross by any means, either by avoiding it or by healing the cause. We do not want to suffer the punishment for our sins in this life. At the back of our mind, we would prefer to pay for our debts after life, and to console ourselves with the idea that life ends here on earth, although faith tells us there is life after death. So day in and day out, we reject our cross and adapt rather a painless comfortable lifestyle to eliminate any presence of suffering in our lives. However, Jesus tells us in Luke that *"If any man will come after me, let him deny himself, and take up his cross daily, and follow me"* (Luke 9: 23).

I, sometimes, wonder that as Christ was carrying the Cross, did it ever cross his mind to merely stop and lie down on the dirt road to die right there and then completely finished. I wonder if Jesus was tempted by the thought "I can't take another step."

What about the Blessed Mother? She felt every pain, every wound, and every agony that Jesus did. No mother would just stand there and let her son be hurt or suffer without coming to her child's defense. For most mothers, it would have been the end of that creature that would dare hurt her child. Mother Mary did not just stand there; She stood by Her Son, allowed the Father's will to prevail and for Her Son Jesus to obey.

The fruit of the mystery is perseverance and patience. Jesus was still standing up the brutal plugging and should have left Him dead, His flesh was already mutilated and was profusely bleeding, His body extremely weakened and shaken from the severe blood loss. Yet, somehow, Jesus withstood the pain and kept on going, His Mother may have remained on the sideline, following Her Son every painful step to see Him dying every inch of the way, this was bitter torture for Her.

Mary stifled every cry and never back down in staying by His side, She gave Him strength as He gave Her His. Their eyes locked and their hearts were one. Whether Jesus could or could no longer make it, the Roman soldiers were determined to reach Golgotha; nothing was going to stop them from their final goal of execution. Jesus persevered, so did Satan. Satan was every bit as determined as Jesus that day, and he was getting plenty of help from the bloodthirsty Roman soldiers. In this battle between love and evil, it was beginning to look like Satan would prevail; he had already succeeded in brutalizing the body of Our Lord. But things were not as they seem, for Satan was about to be eternally defeated. In faithful obedience to the Father's will, Jesus persevered and so did Mary. Though it may seem as though the enemy was winning, the truth, he already had lost. Though we may be drained of strength, suffering, and pain, if we remain faithful to the end, Satan will not prevail. In all these, as if Jesus is telling each one of us keep on walking, though life may seem unbearable, "I am with you. I will never leave you. I have been in hell and back for you. There is nothing to fear, look! My Mother shares with you as well, hold on to Her hands and She will stay with you, She will help you.

Following is a story of St. Bridget of Sweden:

There was a rich man with a special devotion to the Sorrowful Mother. He would frequently meditate on the seven sorrows of Mary and on the Passion and Death of Jesus Christ. He was often seen praying the Rosary and would meditate on how Mother Mary participated in the Passion and Death of Her Son. He knew that the Blessed Mother would help him to enter the Kingdom of Heaven. This rich man loved to contemplate on the Sorrowful Mysteries in front of the image of Our Lady of Sorrow. But as time went by because of worldly temptations and concerns, this noble man began to drift away, neglecting as such the praying of the Rosary, likewise, his practice of stopping at the image of Our Lady of Sorrows to pay her homage. He rapidly began to spiral downwards until he reached the terrible point of selling his soul to the devil. Having given up the hope that he would still be saved, this rich man would contend himself by just stopping for a few minutes before the image of the Blessed Mother of Sorrows to touch his Rosary on Her, as every attempt to pray it would send the devil to torture him. St. Bridget further revealed that this rich man grew from bad to worse in his sinful habits, and for years he never approached the sacraments. When the time came for him to face his final hour, Jesus Christ to show him mercy commanded St. Bridget to tell the confessor to go to visit this man, and to strongly encourage him to confess his sin. The confessor went and the sick man said that he did not need to confess as he had often approached the Sacrament of Penance. The priest went a second time, but this poor slave of hell persevered in his abstinent determination not to confess. Jesus again told St. Bridget to tell the confessor to return, and again the priest did so. On this third occasion, the priest told the sick man that the Lord had ordered him to return so many times because He wanted to show him mercy. On hearing this, the dying man was touched and began to weep; he could not possibly understand how he could be saved after having served the devil for 60 years and having burdened with innumerable sins. The priest encouraged him not to doubt but to repent, and on the part of God, he promised him pardon. The sick man had looked upon himself and was already in despair of salvation. Then he again felt sorrow for his sins, giving him the confidence to make a general confession, because deep in his heart, he knew that God had not abandoned him. He made his confession four times that day with the greatest mark of sorrow, and on the following morning, he received Holy Communion. On the sixth day of contrite and resign, this rich man died. After his death, Jesus Christ again told St. Bridget that the sinner was saved, that he was in purgatory, and that he owned his salvation through the intercession of the Blessed Mother. Although he had lived so wicked life, he had persevered his devotion to Her Sorrows, and whenever he thought of them, this man pitted Mary's Sorrow for the Passion and Death of Jesus Her Son. After his conversion for six days before he died, this rich man began praying the Rosary again before the statue of Our Lady of Sorrows as he used to do when he was younger. For this, the Blessed Mother obtained pardon from Jesus by sending the confessor to him before his death. So what is Our Lady's promise to her clients? Anyone who prays the Rosary daily will not die without the Sacraments and will have a happy death. Mary always keeps Her promise, if we promise to pray the rosary daily, our souls will be saved. Mother Mary promises to help us and She only keeps Her promises.

St. Thomas Aquinas was one day visit to St. Bonaventure and asked him from what book he had drawn all the beautiful lessons he had written? St. Bonaventure showed him the image of the Crucified Lord Jesus, which was completely blackened by all the kisses that he had given it, and said, "this book received everything that I write, and it has taught me whatever little I know." In short, "All the saints have learned the art of loving God from the study of the Crucifix."

Every time St. Francis heard the bleeding of the lamb, he felt himself touched with compassion at the thought of the Death of Jesus, the Immaculate Lamb drained of every drop of blood upon the Cross for the sins of the world. Therefore, this loving saint could find no subject on which he exhorted his brethren with greater eagerness than the constant remembrance of the Passion of Jesus Christ.

If we constantly reflect on Jesus Crucified, it will teach us to have a lively fear of sin, and on the other hand, it will inflame us with love for God, which is full of love for us. It will remind us of the great malice of sin which reduce Our Lord to suffer so bitter at death to satisfy the divine justice and the love which our Savior has shown us in choosing to suffer so much to prove to us how much He loves us.

MEDITATION

"See how lovingly he embraces the Cross. Learn from him. Jesus carries the Cross for you: you . . . carry it for Jesus.   But don't drag the Cross. . . . Carry it squarely on your shoulder, because your Cross, if you carry it like that, will not be just any Cross. . . It will be the Holy Cross. Don't carry your Cross with resignation: resignation is not a generous word. Love the Cross. When you really love it, your Cross will be...a Cross without a Cross." (St. Josemaria, Holy Rosary, fourth sorrowful mystery)

PRAYER

Oh Loving Lord, Jesus! We ask you to forgive us for the many times we have caused you to suffer and added a new burden to Your Cross. May we learn how to struggle against ourselves, our disordered passions, out of love for you and may we be able to live daily your words to deny ourselves, carry our cross daily and follow you. We ask this through the most powerful intercession of Our Blessed Mother, Our Lady of Sorrows. Amen.

DAY 21

MARY, MOTHER OF THE CHURCH

"Now there stood by the cross of Jesus, his mother, and his mother's sister, Mary of Cleophas, and Mary Magdalen. When Jesus therefore had seen his mother and the disciple standing whom he loved, he saith to his mother: Woman, behold thy son. After that, he saith to the disciple: Behold thy mother. And from that hour, the disciple took her to his own." (John 19: 25-27)

In the Scriptures, we read that at the foot of the Cross, Mary became the Mother of the Church. Cardinal Robert Sarah, Prefect of the Congregation for Divine Worship and Discipline of the Sacraments from the Papal Decree of March 3, 2018, wrote in his Decree that "Mary became the Mother of the Church when She accepted Her Son's testament of love and welcomed all people in the person of the beloved disciple as sons and daughters to be reborn unto the life eternal." Cardinal Sarah continues to say, "Joyous veneration given to the Mother of God by the contemporary Church, in light of reflection on the mystery of Christ and on his nature, cannot ignore the figure of a woman, the Virgin Mary, who is both the Mother of Christ and Mother of the Church. This celebration will help us to remember that growth in the Christian life must be anchored to the Mystery of the Cross, to the oblation of Christ in the Eucharistic Banquet and to the Mother of the Redeemer and Mother of the Redeemed." St. Augustine and St. Leo the Great all spoke about the maternity of Mary in the Church. St. Augustine said that she is "acknowledged and honored as being truly the Mother of God and of the redeemer" but she must also be considered "the mother of the Members of Christ ... since she has by her charity joined in bringing about the birth of believers in the Church, who are members of its head." St. Leo said that the birth of Christ the head is also the birth of the Church his Body. Thus indicating that Mary is, at once, Mother of Christ, the Son of God and Mother of the Members of His Mystical Body, which is the Church.

As a caring guide to the emerging Church, Mary had already begun Her mission in the upper room, praying with the Apostles while awaiting the coming of the Holy Spirit, which we read in Acts 1: 14. In this sense, in the course of the centuries, Christian piety has honored Mary with various titles such as "Mother of the Disciples," "Mother of the Faithful," "Mother of Believers," and of all those who are reborn in Christ, and also as "Mother of the Church" as is used in the text of spiritual authors as well as in the Magisterium of Popes Benedict XIV and Leo XIII.

Blessed Paul VI, on November 21st, 1964, during the Second Council of Vatican, declared that "Mary most holy Mother of the Church, that is of the whole Christian people, both faithful and shepherds, that they may call her their most beloved Mother; and we establish that with this title the whole Christian people from this point forward should give her greater honor still and entrust to her their prayers." So what is the significance of this faithful Decree? Pope Francis has decreed that the ancient devotion to Blessed Mary, under the title of the Mother of the Church, be celebrated from now on as an Obligatory Memorial in entire Roman Catholic Church. The liturgical celebration "*Mariae Virginis, Ecclesiae Matris*" will be celebrated annually as a Memorial on the day following immediately Pentecost.

In a decree released by the Congregation for Divine Worship and the Discipline of the Sacraments, Robert Cardinal Sarah said, "The Pope's decision took account of the tradition surrounding the devotion to Mary as Mother of the Church." The Cardinal continued, "The feeling of Christian people through two millennia of history has cultivated the filial bond, which inseparably binds the disciple of Christ to his Blessed Mother in various ways." The hope, Cardinal Sarah concluded, is that the celebration of Mary as Mother of the Church "will remind all Christ's disciples that, if we want to grow and to be filled with the love of God, it is necessary to plant our life firmly on three great realities: the Cross, the Eucharist, and the Mother of God."

In this day and age, the challenge of motherhood is greatly intensified. Why is this so? Because children are losing their faith; they no longer wanted to attend Sunday Mass, and they are facing all kinds of social and ethical problems. While it is true that Catholics children, who are home schooled, are generally well grounded in their faith, and there are still many good Catholic schools, colleges, and universities that produce faithful young Catholics. There seems to have been a drastic loss of faith, however, among the youth worldwide. So what is happening? The National Survey, conducted by the Pew Research Center from February 16 to March 14, 2007, revealed a widespread belief that "Today's parents are not measuring up to the standard that parents said a generation ago. The biggest challenge in raising children today, according to parents and non-parents alike, is dealing with the outside influences of society. Among the top specific concerns mentioned are drugs and alcohol, peer pressure and the impact of television and other forms of media. Beyond social influences, other challenges in raising children include teaching morals and values, maintaining discipline, handling the financial aspects of child bearing, of child reading, and dealing with the educational system because of the problems encountered by many of the children in their faith and moral values, overall 70% of Americans said that mothers today have a more difficult job than mothers did twenty or thirty years ago. Nearly two-thirds of those surveys, 63% of them said that they gave up their Catholic faith between the ages of 10 and 17 years old. The Center for Applied Research in the Apostolate (CARA) recently conducted two national studies that provide some insights into these losses; some young Catholics have told CARA that they are leaving the faith for science, believing that the Catholicism is incompatible with what they are learning in high school or at the university level. This Survey may only consider the pressing situation which is consequence here on earth, but what are the ultimate consequences when children lose their faith? Father Gabriel Amorth, Former Chief Exorcist of the Vatican, said, "When the youth lost their faith, immediately, Satan takes advantage." It is no wonder that there are so many young people experiencing diabolical infestations and many are left untreated, if we lose our young people, we lose the future of the Catholic Church.

When Our Lady of Fatima appeared, She said, "more souls are in hell because of impurity than any other sins." A number of exorcists have revealed that the number one entry point of the devil in the diabolical infestations of young people is impurity. Sexual right gifted to us by God is ordained only for married people for the purpose of procreation to create future saints in the kingdom of heaven. In today's demoralized society, more and more young people are abusing the conjugal right. As a concerned, Our Lady also revealed at Fatima that "many souls are going to hell because no one prays and does penance for them." Many families with such easy access to television and the internet have abandoned the family rosary which is the most powerful prayer to keep the family united in holiness and to protect it from diabolical attacks and even laws of faith. When people lost their faith and end up diabolically infested, they suffer tremendously because sin is like a disease; its effect is deadly and pandemic. The worst thing that could possibly happen to these young people is to lose their souls. In God's plan, they are all with Him forever in heaven, but, instead, for all eternity, they end up in hell where the torment and suffering is endless.

Saint John Paul II, who understood deeply the sadness of the Blessed Mother, offered these words of Prayers to Her:

"*O Mother of all men and women, and of all peoples*, you who know all their sufferings and their hopes, you who have a mother's awareness of all the struggles between good and evil, between light and darkness, which afflict the modern world, accept the cry which we, moved by the Holy Spirit, address directly to your Heart. Embrace with the love of the Mother and Handmaid of the Lord, this human world of ours, which we entrust and consecrate to you, for we are full of concern for the earthly and eternal destiny of individuals and peoples. Immaculate Heart! Help us to conquer the menace of evil, which so easily takes root in the hearts of the people of today, and whose immeasurable effects already weigh down upon our modern world and seem to block the paths towards the future!

From famine and war, *deliver us.*

From nuclear war, from incalculable self-destruction, from every kind of war, *deliver us.*

From sins against the life of man from its very beginning, *deliver us.*

From hatred and from the demeaning of the dignity of the children of God, *deliver us.*

From every kind of injustice in the life of society, both national and international, *deliver us.*

From readiness to trample on the commandments of God, *deliver us.*

From attempts to stifle in human hearts the very truth of God, *deliver us.*

From the loss of awareness of good and evil, *deliver us.*

From sins against the Holy Spirit, deliver us, *deliver us.*

Accept, O Mother of Christ, this cry *laden with the sufferings* of all individual human beings, *laden with the sufferings* of whole societies."

Now more than ever, we need Our Mother Mary who is the Mother of the Church. We have to entrust ourselves to the Mother of the Church, just as Jesus entrusted John, His Disciple, to Marry, His Mother. Saint John Paul II invited the whole world, especially earthly mothers to entrust their motherhood totally to the Blessed Virgin Mary, Mother of God and Mother of the Church. He asked us to consecrate ourselves to Her in this prayer of total surrender to the Queen and Mother of the Church. This holy Pope prayed, accept O Mother of Christ, this Christ has laden with the sufferings of all individual human beings, laden with the sufferings of whole societies, help us with the power of the Holy Spirit to conquer all sins: individual sin and the sin of the world, sin in all its manifestations.

We have seen this in the Nazi regime, and more recently in the communist systems based on the Marxist doctrine of human nature, both the systems failed to understand man in relationship to God, they either claim God did not exist or they put man the race or the state in its place, but you cannot ignore the relationship of the person to God. We build our Christian anthropology on the truth of creation that man is made in the image and likeness of God. Man is God's creature, yet, at the same time, he represents God. Being an image of God is a concrete reality that belongs to the human person, it is a reality which has been received as a gift, a reality which reaches its most noble projection in Jesus Christ, who is the perfect image of the Father. At the same time, being an image of God is a mission, a vocation entrusted to each person, so he can make it grow. This humanization leads to an integral liberation, the freedom of the sons and daughters of God. On this foundation of truth will emerge a very different kind of society than that offered by the totalitarian ideologies such as communism. It will be a civilization of person related to God who is the source of love. It will also be different from the dominant Western secular liberal society around us today, based on individualism which ignores God. That society is producing a permissive and decadent civilization of death. The essence of that system can be condemned into one deadly arrogant expression, pro-choice. And so, as an image of God, each person is called by God to grow in that good have received from God, in a response, which is a grace-filled collaboration with Him. But none of us lives alone, we are not islands, we are social beings made to relate to others in a communion of persons, the first and foremost created communion of person exists between a man and a woman, and so, at the very beginning of his discussion of the civilization of love.

In the Letter to Families, Saint john Paul II underlined the truth of Genesis 1: 27, *"God created man to his own image: to the image of God he created him: male and female he created them."* The pope further said, "Human, fatherhood and motherhood, contained in an essential and unique way the likeness to God, which is the basis of the family as a community of human life, as a community of persons united in love. We are at the heart of the mystery of the Holy Trinity, in some way, image in the family, the first and fundamental expression of the social nature of men."

A real mother wants nothing but the best for her children something that will last forever. If our human mother, because of human frailties, could not give the best for her children something that will last forever, let us call on the Heavenly Mother of Jesus, who is also the Mother of all Christian faithful and the Mother of the Church.

There is a story about A six-year-old Protestant boy had often heard his fellow Catholics pray the Hail Mary. He liked it so much that he memorized it and prayed it every day. "Look, mommy, what a beautiful prayer," he told his mother one day. "Do not say it again," replied the mother. "It is a superstitious prayer of Catholics who worship idols and think that Mary is a goddess. She is a woman like any other. Come on. Take this Bible and read it. It contains everything we have to do." From that day on, the boy stopped praying his Hail Mary every day and spent more time reading the Bible. One day, while reading the Gospel, he saw the passage on the Annunciation of the Angel to the Virgin. Full of joy, the boy ran to his mother and said: "Mommy, I found the Hail Mary in the Bible: 'Hail, full of grace, the Lord is with thee: blessed art thou among women'. Why do you call it a superstitious prayer?" She did not answer. On another occasion, he found the scene of Elizabeth's salutation to the Virgin Mary and the beautiful canticle of the Magnificat, in which Mary announced: 'from now on all generations shall call me blessed'. He did not say anything to his mother and began to pray the Hail Mary every day again, as he used to do. He felt pleasure in telling those beautiful words to the Mother of Jesus, Our Savior. When he turned fourteen, one day he heard his family discussing about Our Lady. They all said that Mary was an ordinary woman. The boy, after hearing their erroneous reasoning, could not take it anymore and, full of indignation, he interrupted them saying: "Mary is not like any other son of Adam, stained with sin. No! The Angel called her FULL OF GRACE AND BLESSED AMONG WOMEN. Mary is the Mother of Jesus and consequently, the Mother of God. There is no greater dignity to which a creature can aspire. The Gospel says that all generations shall call her blessed, while you try to despise her. Your spirit is not the spirit of the Gospel or the Bible you claim is the foundation of the Christian religion." The impression made by the boy's words on his mother was so deep that she often wept inconsolably: "Oh, God, I fear that this son of mine will one day join the Catholic religion, the religion of the Popes!" And indeed, a short time later, the son was convinced that the Catholic religion was the only authentic one, he embraced it and became one of his most ardent apostles.

A few years after his conversion, the protagonist of our story found his sister already married. He wanted to greet her and hug her, but she rejected him and said indignantly: "You have no idea how much I love my children. If one of them wanted to become Catholic, I would first bury a dagger in their heart than allow them to embrace the religion of the Popes." Her anger and temper were as furious as those of St. Paul before his conversion. However, she would soon change her mind, as happened to St. Paul on his way to Damascus. It happened that one of her children fell seriously ill. The doctors gave no hope for his recovery. As soon as her brother found out, he looked for her in the hospital and spoke to her with affection, saying: "Dear sister, you naturally want your child to be cured. Very well, then do what I'm going to ask you. Let us pray together a Hail Mary and promise God, that if your child recovers, you will study the Catholic doctrine. And in case you come to the conclusion that Catholicism is the only true religion, you will embrace it no matter what sacrifices this implies." His sister was initially reluctant, but she wanted her son to recover, so she accepted his brother's proposal and prayed with him a Hail Mary. The next day, her son was completely healed. The mother fulfilled her promise and began studying the Catholic doctrine. After intense preparation, she received Baptism in the Catholic Church along with her entire family. How much she thanked her brother that he had been an apostle to her.

This story was told by Father Francis Tuckwell in one of his homilies. "Brothers," he concluded, "the Protestant boy who became a Catholic and converted his sister to Catholicism, devoted his whole life to the service of God. He is the priest who speaks to you now. How much I owe to the Blessed Virgin, Our Lady! You too, my dear brothers, dedicate yourselves completely to serving Our Lady and do not let a single day pass without saying the beautiful prayer of the Hail Mary as well as your Rosary. Ask her to enlighten the minds of Protestants who are separated from the true Church of Christ founded on the Rock (Peter) and against which 'the gates of hell will never prevail'."

Devotion to Mary under the title Mother of the Church is a powerful means of intercession for someone seriously looking for the path of salvation. When Jesus gave John the Apostle to Mother Mary, it was to protect him from being an orphan.

MEDITATION

"The Blessed Virgin is like a good mother who not content with looking after Her children in general, watches over each one separately." (St. John Marie Vianney)

PRAYRER

O loving Mother Mary, Mother of the Church, I entrust myself and all the members of the Mystical Body of Christ to you. Saint John Paul II said, "The mother is the heart of the family. Without the love of the mother, the whole family falls into crisis. The Catholic Church is suffering from crisis because She has abandoned Her devotion to Marry, Mother of the church." Blessed Paul VI said that "The devil has infested the Church from Her cracks of compromise in Her doctrine." We renew our entrustment to you, O Mary, Mother of the Church. We know that once we abandon ourselves to you, you will take care of us. And when we pray our Rosary daily, we will always enjoy your presence, we may experience every day of our life the peace and love of the Mother, whose only desire is our eternal salvation. This She does by bringing us all to Jesus, our Savior. We ask this through the intercession of Mother Mary, Mother of the Church, in Jesus Christ, our Lord. Amen.

DAY 22

PRECIOUS GIFT OF THE CROSS

"And one of those robbers who were hanged, blasphemed him, saying: If thou be Christ, save thyself and us. But the other answering, rebuked him, saying: Neither dost thou fear God, seeing thou art condemned under the same condemnation? And we indeed justly, for we receive the due reward of our deeds; but this man hath done no evil. And he said to Jesus: Lord, remember me when thou shalt come into thy kingdom. And Jesus said to him: Amen I say to thee, this day thou shalt be with me in paradise." (Luke 23: 39-43)

Pope Francis, in his Angelus Message on September 3rd, 2007, said: "Always, even today, the temptation is to follow a Christ without a cross, rather, to teach God the right path. Like Peter, we may say: 'No, this will never happen.' But Jesus reminds us that his way is the way of love, and there is no true love without Christ's self-sacrifice. We must embrace suffering, because as Christ told his disciples: 'Whoever wishes to come after me must deny himself, take up his cross, and follow me.' We, Christians, are called by God not to be absorbed by the world's vision to live an easy life, but rather to go after the path of the Cross to go 'against the current,' pointing out the challenge of self-centeredness found in Christ's words. 'Whoever wants to save his life will lose it; and whoever loses his life for my sake will find it." Pope Francis said: "The golden rule that God inscribed into the human nature created in Christ is the rule that only love gives meaning and happiness to life." Spending our time, talents and our energy only to save and take care of ourselves actually leads to loss, to a "sad and sterile existence," the Pope explained. Whereas, if we live our lives for the Lord, set on fire with love, then our lives will be fruitful and we will have genuine joy.

The Holy Father called out the shame that comes with running away from our responsibilities, being silent in the face of injustice, perpetuating laziness and greed, and being self-interested and selfish. He said: "Shame for all the times that we bishops, priests, consecrated men and women have scandalized and hurt Your Body, the Church, by your end decisions over moral and doctrinal issues, over compromises in doctrine to please others and not to please God." The Pope continued, "We have forgotten our first love, our first enthusiasm and our total availability to the Will of God, His Teachings and Commandments, leaving our hearts and our consecration to rust." Let us reflect on the words of the Pope, as he prayed: "In this shame, we also have hope by praying that the Lord will "not treat us according to our merits but solely according to the multitude" of his mercy. We hope that "Your Cross turns our hardened hearts into hearts of flesh able to dream, to forgive and to love." The Church hopes that she can be the voice that cries in the "desert of humanity" to prepare the way for Christ's second coming without fear of human criticism and persecution that can kill only the body, instead, only beholden to God who alone can both destroy the body and the soul, knowing that God's truth is not based on our own understanding. The Pope also said that we have hope that those faithful to Christ's Cross will "continue to remain faithful like yeast that gives flavor" and "that good will win in spite of Christ's apparent defeat!"

In the celebration of the Eucharist we relive the mystery of the cross; not only do we remember but we carry out the memorial of the redeeming Sacrifice, in which the Son of God loses Himself completely to receive Himself again from the Father and thus find us again, who were lost, together with all creatures. Every time we take part in Holy Mass, the Love of the crucified and risen Christ is communicated to us as food and drink, so that we can follow Him on the way every day, in the concrete service of brothers.

"O Christ, we ask you to teach us to never be ashamed of your

Cross, not to exploit it, but to honor and worship it, because with it you have shown us the monstrosity of our sins, the greatness of your love, injustice of our judgments and the power of your love," he concluded.

So often, we find ourselves getting angry with God when He brings us suffering; we take it as a punishment for our sins as we do not believe we have to suffer. I have noticed that even those who are advancing their faith also fall easily into crisis or lessen their fair board to prayer, because they think that God is being cruel for sending them sickness. They are only prepared and willing to serve God if there is no pain or suffering, only if there is joy and comfortable lifestyle.

So why did God the Father allow His innocent Son to suffer the most gruesome and cruelest torture ever to be conceived by man on Him?

Saint John Paul II, in his Encyclical "Salvifici Dolores," explained how Jesus willingly took all the afflictions of the sins of mankind and the punishments due to their sins without complain, simply because of love. It was love that compelled Jesus to die on the Cross rather than for man to be punished for eternity in hell. It was love that made Him substitute for the sins and punishments of mankind so that we will become once again adopted children of God, and finally enter everlasting life and share the beatific vision for eternity in heaven. In the book "*The Spirit of the Liturgy*," Pope Benedict XVI said: "I could not figure out what symbolism could fit in the events of the life of Christ to manifest His greatest act of love and surpassed by all mankind and angels put together. It is the Crucifixion on Mount Calvary that proves how much God loves us more than anybody else." Of course, we know that when Jesus died on the Cross, He redeemed us from our sins, and finally reopened heaven which for four thousand years was close because of the sins of Adam and Eve. "*I consider it a privilege to suffer what is still wanting in the sufferings of Christ in His Mystical Body, the Church,*" Saint Paul said in his letter to the Colossians 1: 24. In Saint James 1: 2 – 3, he considered, "*My brethren, count it all joy, when you shall fall into divers temptations; Knowing that the trying of your faith worketh patience. And patience hath a perfect work; that you may be perfect and entire, failing in nothing."* Then, in 1 Peter 1: 6 – 7, we read that *"Wherein you shall greatly rejoice, if now you must be for a little time made sorrowful in divers temptations: That the trial of your faith (much more precious than gold which is tried by the fire) may be found unto praise and glory and honour at the appearing of Jesus Christ."*

In the mid 1800's there lived in Paris a good woman who, after her husband died, was left destitute. The widow had an only son, Hubald, who was her pride and joy. Worn down by poverty, sacrifice, and worry, she became critically ill. Calling her son to her bedside she said, "Hubald, son, I am about to die. I would like to make a last will". "Mother", remonstrated the lad, "We've never had less; what can you possibly leave me?" "I have a treasure to leave you," said his dying mother, "Reach under my pillow". Doing so, Hubald pulled out a Rosary. "This is what I leave you, my son," gasped the mother, "I have nothing else, but this Rosary is enough. In honor of your dying mother, promise me that you will say it every day". "I promise," said Hubald, his eyes awash. "I promise never to let a day pass without praying the Rosary on your beads". And so the lady breathed her last. After the funeral, alone and penniless in the world, the young man joined the army and was sent to the Crimea. Hubald proved a worthy soldier, and quickly attained military rank. At the age of thirty he was promoted to Colonel. Unfortunately, his spiritual life did not keep pace with his military advancement. Gradually, through the years, Colonel Hubald had given up all practice of religion and all religious sentiment. Still, he kept his sacred promise to his dying mother, and no matter how busy or stressed, he found fifteen minutes each day in which to finger her beads, and recite the Rosary. At times, he thought regretfully, "If mother only knew what has become of me! My lips mouth the "Our Father" and the "Hail Mary" but my soul has no religion, and I've become so sinful". On September 7, 1855, when the army camped in the vicinity of Malakoff, during the siege of Sebastopol, Hubald lay in his cot. He was thus reflecting on the faithlessness and sinfulness of his life, when he felt a tap on his shoulder. "Colonel, are you awake?" Turning, Hubald recognized the Army Chaplain. As they shook hands, the priest felt the Rosary beads. "I'm so glad to see you praying the Rosary, Colonel. I did not think you so devout". "I'm not, Father. I say the Rosary in remembrance of my Mother" And he proceeded to relate his story. Taking advantage of the emotion of the moment, the good priest spoke words of encouragement and comfort to Hubald, assuring him that God wanted nothing more than to forgive him all his sins. "Colonel, why don't you open your soul in Confession? I assure you that your heart will know the peace and serenity which you no longer believe possible". Touched by grace, the soldier humbly bowed his head, and making a general confession, unloaded years of sin and remorse. As the priest raised his hand in absolution, an indescribable joy flooded Hubald's soul. While he basked in this new found feeling, there was a trumpet blast and the cry; "To arms!" Assembling his troops, the Colonel rode into the fray. There was a fierce battle, men falling on all sides, but hours later the victory went to the French. Among the dead, struck by a fatal bullet, was found Colonel Hubald. In his pocket he had his mother's beads. The Rosary had opened heaven to him.

Remember the promise of Our Lady to Saint Dominic and then to Blessed Alan de la Roche: "If you pray the Rosary, you will never die without receiving the Sacraments." And this is what happened to Colonel Hubald; when he thought he was desperate, a chaplain came to hear his confession and after that he died.

We are all sinners, let us abandon ourselves the Virgin Mary by praying the Rosary daily for our salvation. The Pharisees, with their holier than our attitude, did not receive salvation from Jesus because they had no need of Him. We read in the Gospel of Luke that *"Jesus answering, said to them: They that are whole, need not the physician: but they that are sick. I came not to call the just, but sinners to penance"* (Luke 5: 32-33).

MEDITATION

"They will have the two-edged sword of the word of God in their mouths and the blood-stained standard of the Cross on their shoulders. They will carry the crucifix in their right hand and the rosary in their left, and the holy names of Jesus and Mary on their heart. The simplicity and self-sacrifice of Jesus will be reflected in their whole behavior." (St. Louis de Montfort's Speaking on the Saints of the End Times)

PRAYER

O Loving Jesus, when the cross is heavy and the going gets tough, I find myself on my knees, not knowing where to turn, but I realize the Blessed Mother that you allow me to suffer because you want me to share the joys of redemption. Now, I realize upon listening to the inspiration of Blessed Virgin Mary that when praying the Rosary, it's better to pray for the needs of those who are suffering more in the world. While having the joys of interceding for the thousands of people who die every day, in union with the most powerful intercession of Saint Joseph, I also experience the greatest consolation and peace in my heart amidst all my sufferings, in addition, all my daily trials find their solution to the daily Rosary which I pray with love for you, Mother, in the name of Jesus Christ, our Lord. Amen.

DAY 23

RESURRECTION OF JESUS

"And behold there was a great earthquake. For an angel of the Lord descended from heaven, and coming, rolled back the stone, and sat upon it. And his countenance was as lightning, and his raiment as snow. And for fear of him, the guards were struck with terror, and became as dead men. And the angel answering, said to the women: Fear not you; for I know that you seek Jesus who was crucified. He is not here, for he is risen, as he said. Come, and see the place where the Lord was laid. And going quickly, tell ye his disciples that he is risen: and behold he will go before you into Galilee; there you shall see him. Lo, I have foretold it to you." (Matthew 28: 2-7)

The Resurrection of Jesus was not witnessed by everyone. Jesus did not vindicate Himself to His critics by showing the glory of His Resurrection with blinding rays of light. Instead, as silent as He was born from a womb in the obscure town of Bethlehem, so was He "born" silently from a tomb as to humbly not make a big fanfare of His return.

Despite no one witnessing the actual Resurrection, we know Jesus came back from the dead because of His appearances to His Disciples as He passed through closed doors; He cooked breakfast with them, ate with them, conversed with them; He even allowed Saint Thomas to put his finger into His wounds and His side to disprove the apostle's disbelief.

A peculiar thing in the Resurrection event is that the Scripture never mentions if Christ appeared to His Mother. Although an old manuscript of Saint Bonaventure, entitled *"Meditationes de Vita Christi,"* and in the book *"Life of Jesus and the Bible"* by Saint Anne Catherine Emmerich, and even in the *"Divine Life of the Blessed Virgin Mary, Mystical City of God"* by Ven. Agnes Agreda mentioned the appearance of the Resurrected Christ to His Mother, but we can find nothing of it in Scripture. Some people have problems with non-scriptural ideas, but theologians point out that just because Scripture is silent about something like what happened in the 30 years of Jesus hidden life doesn't mean it did not happen. Remember, Scripture is not a biographical account of all that Jesus did and said.

The Benedictine Abbot, Dom Prosper Louis Pascal Gueranger, founder of the French Benedictine Congregation, which re-established monastic life in France after he had been wiped out by the French Revolution, wrote in his popular book *"The Liturgical Year"*: "The Gospel does not relate the apparition thus made by Jesus to His Mother, whereas all the others are fully described. It is not difficult to assign the reason. The other apparitions were intended as proofs of the Resurrection; this to Mary was dictated by the tender love borne to Her by Her Son. Both nature and grace required that His first visit should be to such a Mother, and Christian hearts dwell with delight on the meditation of the mystery. There was no need of its being mentioned in the Gospel; the Tradition of the Holy Fathers, beginning with St. Ambrose, bears sufficient testimony to it; and even had they been silent, our hearts would have told it to us."

So how did we get the notion that Christ appeared to His Mother? The scholars like to point out that the Gospels indicate Christ was no longer in the tomb when Mary Magdalene went there during the first hours of Sunday. The nagging question is where did Jesus go so early in the morning? Considering the situation, the scholars' answer, is that Christ appeared to His grieving Mother to console Her as soon as He could: *"And why was it that our Savior rose from the Tomb so early on the Day He had fixed for His Resurrection? It* was, *because His filial love was impatient to satisfy the vehement longings of his dearest and most afflicted Mother. Such is the teaching of many pious and learned Writers; and who that knows aught of Jesus and Mary could refuse to accept it?* "(Dom Gueranger, the Liturgical Year, vol. 7, "Easter Sunday:

Morning").

On May 21, 1997, St. John Paul II said: "*Could not the absence of Mary from the group of women who approached the tomb at dawn constitute an indication that she had already met Jesus.*"

As we can see, Christ appearing to His Mother is a small-T tradition that can be found all the way from the Church Fathers down the centuries to Pope John Paul II. It has also found itself ingrained into the arts (e.g. paintings by Juan de Flandes, 1496) and religious culture of some churches. For instance, in the early dawn of Easter Sunday, a re-enactment of the Risen Jesus meeting His Mother is still performed today in the Philippines. It is called the "*salubong*," which means "*welcome encounter.*" There are at least three figures in this re-enactment: Christ, Mary, and the angel. Other women mentioned in the Gospels are included depending on which province is performed. Except for the angel that must be human, all characters are usually statues carried about by people. Mary is dressed in black with a (black) veil covering her eyes. Two processions start from different places: one with Christ, and the other with Mary (and the other women). The separate parades come closer together until they meet. The angel, usually suspended by a harness, is then lowered and removes the veil of Mary, symbolizing the end of her grief when she finally sees her resurrected son. To further emphasize this joy, the black dress of Mary is usually turned inside-out to reveal a resplendent shimmering gold gown.

Different towns in Spain, Brazil, Mexico, and Peru also have their own unique versions, which they call "*Encuentro*" or "*Encounter.*" But the "plot" is the same: Mary, starts from one end of the procession, while the Risen Christ on the other. They come closer and meet in the middle. One town has a truly unique Encounter: they hold a race! The Risen Christ is on one end, while different groups carry the statue of Mary running up the street to meet Jesus – a way of showing how Mary, in haste, was so happy to see again Her Son.

Although the Church has no absolute dogmatic teaching about Christ's apparition to His Mother after the Resurrection, it is found within her customs and culture. We are not forced to believe it, and neither are we committing any heresy if we do not – after all, it is only just a consensus among some theologians. But I, for one, am inclined to agree with these theologians because I ask myself: how could Christ not appear to the Mother He loves only to leave her grieving?

John Paul II said that Christ's Resurrection has the following meanings:

First, Saint Paul saw the Resurrection as the basis of the Christian faith. He saw it as the key stone of the entire edifice of the doctrine and life built up on revelation. In as much as, it is the definitive confirmation of the whole ensemble of truth taught by Jesus Christ. Hence, all the Church's preaching from the apostolic times down the centuries, spanning generations even to the present day, makes its appeal to the Resurrection.

Second, the Resurrection is also a confirmation of all that Christ had done and taught. It was the divine seal stump on His words and life. He Himself had indicated to His Disciples and adversaries this definitive sign of this truth, all the truths, including those most impenetrable to the human mind, find their justification even from the rational point of view in the fact that the Risen Christ gave the definitive proof promised beforehand of His divine authority.

Third, the truth of Christ's divinity itself is confirmed by the Resurrection. In John 8: 28, Jesus said: *"When you shall have lifted up the Son of man, then shall you know, that I am he."* Those who heard these words wanted to stone Jesus because for the Jews the word *"I am"* were the equivalent of the unspeakable name of God. The second Commandment: "Thou shalt not take the name of the Lord God in vain." In fact, when asking Pontius Pilate to condemn Jesus to death, they presented as the principal charge that "He had made Himself The Son of God" as written in John 19: 7. For this reason, the Sanhedrin had to condemn Jesus as guilty of blasphemy. In reply to the high priest's question, Jesus had declared that He is the Christ, The Son of God (Matthew 26: 63 – 65, Mark 14: 62, and Luke: 22: 17).

Fourth, Jesus' Resurrection foretells our very own Resurrection from the dead. Unfortunately and sadly, the Jews refused to believe that Jesus resurrected from the dead. They concocted a plot to kill anyone who preached the Resurrection of Jesus. We had the stories of Longinus, St. Paul, and St. Peter. There are authentic people who attest that Christ resurrected from the dead. For example, if the apostles witnessed the Resurrection of Jesus by mere words, it could have been bias, but if they were willing to go to prison uneven to die as they did then they were credible. Moreover, if the enemies of Jesus were to attest of Jesus' Resurrection from something that happened to them such as healing, the change of heart, and were gladly imprisoned and put to death, this is a proof be unreasonable doubt that Jesus rose from the dead. Even Saint Paul, the archenemy of Jesus and the persecutor of Christians, testified to the truth of Christ's Resurrection. After he saw with his own eyes the Risen Jesus as a blinding light, he was converted, baptized, and then empowered by the Holy Spirit to become a die-hard believer of the Resurrected Christ. Saul was an enemy of the Gospel and a persecutor of the Church. Based on his background, he had no possible motives to accept the Gospel, and every possible motive to continue to reject it. His testimony had all the evidence of truth and sincerity for he had no reason to be untruthful.

Let's take a look at the summary of St. Paul's testimony from the following accounts taken from the Acts of the Apostles. Paul had been a Jew; he was strictly following the law and persecuting Christians: "*About noon, on the road to Damascus, a light from heaven shown around me brighter than the noon sun, I heard a voice speaking to me in Hebrew: Saul, Saul, why are you persecuting me? Saul spoke: who are you, Lord? And Jesus said: I am Jesus, whom you are persecuting*" (Acts 26: 13-15). Those with Paul saw the light but did not understand the words that were spoken. Jesus stated that he had appeared to Saul to make him both a minister and a witness. He was to preach to people how they could receive forgiveness of sins. Suppose on testimony claims specifically that he both saw and heard Jesus as well as He spoke to him, this qualified Paul as an eyewitness, which was essential requirement in order for one to be an apostle as we read in Acts 1: 21 – 22. This meant that Saul was a witness in the same sense as the other apostles; he was able to tell people that he had personally seen Jesus alive after His Death. His supreme testimony came when he was arrested by the Roman soldiers. When asked by Governor Felix and later by King Agrippa about his crime, he said plainly, it is because of his belief in the Resurrection of Jesus Christ that he was persecuted by the Jews. His fidelity as the stature of Christ's Resurrection finally reached its crowning glory when he willingly accepted the verdict of Emperor Nero in Rome to be beheaded in 67 A.D. for his crime of believing that Jesus had risen from the dead. He said in his Letter to the 1 Corinthians 15:14, *"If Christ be not risen again, then is our preaching vain, and your faith is also vain."* Evidently, St. Paul saw the Resurrection as the basis of the Christian faith.

In the meteorology, it speaks of St. Longinus, a centurion whose life was changed forever as he stood transfixed at the foot of the Cross. Longinus was in command of the Roman soldiers who presided over the Crucifixion of the Lord Jesus Christ on Golgotha. According to some Church traditions, Longinus was also the centurion who pierced Christ's side with a spear, in order to confirm His death, after which the wound discharged a rush of blood and water that healed an eye infection which had been greatly troubling him, almost blinding him.

The divine Matthew the Evangelist describes the moment of his conversion to Christianity with enormous power: When the centurion and those with him, who were guarding Jesus, saw the earthquake and the things that had happened, they feared greatly, saying, *"Truly this was the Son of God!"* (Matthew 27: 54).

Soon after the events at Golgotha, St. Longinus would play a major role in helping to establish the truth of Christ's Resurrection. The Jewish elders who had ordered the death of Jesus bribed several soldiers to spread the false report that the Savior's disciples had stolen His body under cover of darkness and made off with it. St. Longinus, who refused to be bribed, insisted on telling the world the true story of how Christ's body had risen into the glory of the Resurrection. After learning that the Roman soldier wanted no part of their conspiracy or their money, the Jews decided to rely on their usual ploy: They would simply murder this truth-telling centurion in cold blood. But Longinus was a man of courage and integrity – and as soon as he heard about the plot against him, he took off his military garb, underwent baptism with several fellow-soldiers and then went to Cappadocia, where he spent many hours in prayerful devotion and rigorous fasting. Responding to the former centurion's compelling piety, many pagans in the region were also converted to the Gospel and underwent Baptism as a result. St. Longinus lived and moved among them freely for a time, then eventually returned home to live on his father's estate. But the deceitful Jews were not finished with him – and their lies soon provoked Pontius Pilate, the Roman governor of Judea under the emperor Tiberius Caesar, to issue a draconian order to his troops: Find this renegade centurion and behead him immediately! However, St. Longinus anticipated a plan against his life. Hurrying out the roadway, he greeted his adversaries as friends. Without letting them know who he was, he invited them back to his own residence. He fed them lavishly, and when they fell asleep, he prepared himself for his execution by praying throughout the night and then clothing himself in a white burial garb. As dawn approached, he drew his loyal companions to his side and instructed them to bury him at the top of the nearby hill. The stage was now set. Moving swiftly, the martyr approached the awakening soldiers and told them: "I am Longinus, the man you seek!" Amazed and mortified by his honesty, the Romans were knocked completely off balance – how could they behead a man of such noble character? But even as they protested against the execution, this greathearted soldier insisted that they should carry out their orders to end his life. In the end, St. Longinus and the two fellow-soldiers who had stood with him at the foot of the cross were taken to Jerusalem and where beheaded, and the centurion's destiny as a martyr for Jesus Christ was fulfilled.

Sighing mournfully over the tragedy they had been required to act out, the execution squad carried Longinus head to Pilate, who immediately sent it on to the scheming Jews. The Jews threw it on the dung heap outside Jerusalem. St. Longinus was dead – but the legends that would follow this courageous warrior had only just been born.

The power of those legends can be seen in another story that has persisted down through the ages. According to the narrative, a blind woman who was visiting Jerusalem in order to pray at its holy shrines experienced a mysterious dream in which St. Longinus appeared and told her where to find his head, which she should bury. The blind woman obeyed instantly, and found a guide to lead her to the dung heap. There she located the saint's head and reverently transported it back to his native land of Cappadocia for burial.

The story of the Roman soldier who watched Christ die and was then martyred himself lives on as a treasured narrative in the long history of the Holy Land saints. The life of this revered Christian reminds us that God the Father does not hesitate to award His saving grace to anyone who sincerely asked for it, including even those who were engaged directly in ending the life of His beloved Son.

The idea that such healing grace is freely available to all has become a central tenet of the Christian faith, thanks in part to the courageous loyalty of the valiant soldier who died for our Lord Jesus Christ.

There is real evidence of Jesus' Resurrection; the Shroud of Turin has been preserved at the Cathedral of Saint John the Baptist in Turin, Italy. It is a linen burial cloth, measuring 14 feet 3 inches in length by 3 feet 7 inches in width. It apparently covered a man who suffered the wounds of the crucifixion in a way very similar to that recorded for Jesus of Nazareth.

The Shroud has undergone more scientific testing than any other relic in human history. The 1978 Shroud of Turin Research Project (STURP) investigation and subsequent investigations were remarkably thorough, and with the exception of the questionable 1988 carbon dating, all the evidence points to it being the burial cloth of Jesus, including the following:

Four contemporary dating tests carried out by various scientists. The vanillin dating test of Dr. Raymond Rogers, the two spectroscopic analyses (of professor Giulio Fanti, et al.), and the compressibility and breaking strength tests (of Fanti, et al.) date the Shroud to a time commensurate with the life and crucifixion of Jesus.

There were also three kinds of extrinsic dating evidence: (1) Dr. Max Frei, who collected dust samples from the Shroud during the 1978 investigation, concluded that the majority of the pollen samples were from the region of Israel (specifically from sedimentary layers from 2,000 years ago near the area of the Sea of Galilee), with six grains from the eastern Middle East (two grains from Edessa, Turkey, and one growing exclusively in Istanbul/Constantinople). The remaining grains came from France and Italy. Importantly, 13 of the pollen grains are unique to Israel and can be found at the bottom of both the Sea of Galilee and the Dead Sea. (2) Roman coins on the eyes of the image of the Shroud, which give evidence that it's highly probable that the image of the man on the Shroud of Turin has two Jewish lepta, minted in A.D. 29 by Pontius Pilate in Judea in the time of Jesus, on his eyelids. (3) 120 coincidences of blood and fluid stains between the Shroud and Sudarium or face cloth of Oviedo give evidence of a date and location of the Stroud's origin similar to that of Jesus.

The blood stains on the Shroud tell a story very similar to the highly unusual crucifixion of Jesus of Nazareth – they were imprinted on the Shroud before the image was made (the opposite of what would need to be done by a forger). The Shroud has deposits of real human blood, according to the experts who studied the blood flecks gathered on the STURP tapes in 1978. They determined that the blood of the Shroud is real human blood.

The image on the Shroud was not formed by dyes, chemicals, and vapors or scorching. The only known explanation for the formation of the image is an intense burst of vacuum ultraviolet radiation emitted from every three-dimensional point of the body in the Shroud. This is suggestive of a resurrection event similar to that described in the Gospels. The combination of the collective evidence is difficult to explain in any way other than the mysterious Shroud is that of Jesus Christ of Nazareth with evidence suggestive of His resurrection in light.

The Shroud of Turin is a challenge to our intelligence. It requires of every researcher that he humbly grasps the profound message it sends to this reason and to his reason and his life. The mysterious fascination of the Shroud forces questions to be raised about the sacred linen and the historical life of Jesus Christ. Since it is not a matter of faith, the Church has no specific confidence to pronounce on these questions. She entrusts to scientists the task of continuing to investigate so that satisfactory answers may be found to the questions connected with the sheet, which according to tradition, wrapped the body of our Redeemer after He had been taken down from the Cross.

For the believer, what comes above all is that the Shroud is the mirror of the Gospel. Whoever approaches it is aware that this Shroud does not hold people's hearts to itself but turns them to Jesus, and so it is right to foster an awareness of the precious value of this image which everyone sees, and no one at present can explain. As explained above, it is exceedingly improbable that the Shroud is a medieval forgery. First, there are no paints, dyes or other pigments on the Shroud. Second, the anatomical precision of the blood stains, which are real human blood that congealed on the Shroud before the formation of the image, are in precise anatomical correlation to the image itself. How could a medieval forger have accomplished this? Third, it is very difficult to explain how pollen grains indigenous to Palestine appeared in abundance on the Shroud of probable Semitic origin and how coins minted in A.D. 29 in Palestine appeared on the eyes of the man on the Shroud. How could a medieval forger have duplicated these first-century Palestinian characteristics of the Shroud? Fourth, the five enigmas of the image on the Shroud almost certainly preclude a forgery. How could a medieval forger have used vacuum ultraviolet radiation to discolor the cloth on the uppermost surface of the fibrils? How could he have created a perfect photographic negative image? How could he have created a double image on the frontal part of the Shroud? And how could he have known how to duplicate the interior and exterior of the hands in perfect proportion to each other? Therefore, it does not seem reasonable to believe that the Shroud is a medieval forgery.

Beyond this, there are three probative kinds of evidence pointing specifically to Jesus' place and time of origin and to His unique crucifixion and resurrection:

The material of the Shroud, the pollen grains on it and the coins on the man's eyes all have their origin in first-century Palestine, the place where Jesus was said to have died.

The blood stains come from crucifixion event identical to the one described in the four Gospels, which was very unusual, such as being crowned with thorns, being flogged, and being pierced with a Roman spear. The five enigmas of the Shroud's image point to a trans-physically caused burst of vacuum ultraviolet radiation from a mechanically transparent body. This is suggestive of the transformation of Jesus' body from a physical one to a spiritual-glorified one (as reported by St. Paul and the four Gospels).

The spiritual-glorified transformation of Jesus' body was unique to the Christian view of resurrection. Therefore, the enigmas on the Shroud's image point to the uniquely Christian view of resurrection implied by Jesus' risen appearance. Given all this, we might reasonably infer that the Shroud is the burial cloth of Jesus, which contains not only relic of His crucifixion but also His resurrection in glory. If so, it shows both the truth of the most significant event in human history as well as the accuracy of the Gospel accounts of it. As we read in Romans that "*If we suffer with him, that we may be also glorified with him*" (Romans 8: 17).

Let us take the story of Private Glenn Hockton, a soldier who was saved when his Rosary beads fell from his neck into the ground, which alerted him that he was standing on a landmine. Glenn Hockton joined the Coldstream Guards at the age of 16. His mother said that as a parent, it was the hardest thing she had to do. Being only 17, at the time, she had to sign to give permission for him to join the army. It was too painful for her to see Glenn leave for Afghanistan. There was one advice she remembered giving her son, she told him that Mother Mary suffered all the pains with Jesus in Calvary, and now she shares the glory of Jesus' resurrection from the dead. She told Glenn to entrance himself to Mother Mary as the Apostle John was to Mother Mary, and she told him to promise her to pray the Rosary every day and that Mother Mary will deliver him from every evil. Both Glenn Hockton and his family promised that they would pray the Rosary every day for each other as support and protection back home. Glenn's brothers and sisters worried about him but would always entrust him to Mother Mary. During the praying of the Rosary, eventually, the final test of their faith happened. One day, while his Platoon was on duty and while running and jumping on the terrain in the same time reciting the "Hail Mary", Glenn's Rosary fell from his neck (he had asked for the Rosary to take with him before being deployed to Afghanistan on the seven-month tour of duty with a Coldstream Guards in Helmand Province). When Glenn bent down to pick up the Holy beads, he realized he was stepping on a landmine. He thought to himself this is it, my life has ended. Yet he was grasping his Rosary, asking Mother Mary for protection. Glenn had to remain standing where he was for 45 minutes while constantly praying the Rosary. Thanks be to God, eventually, his colleagues came and successfully rescued him and detonated the landmine.

Saint Paul, by the power of Christ's resurrection, healed the cripple, to the point that the Hellenistic priests wanted to worship him as Hermes. Saint Peter also healed the cripple in the golden gate in the temple area in the name of the risen Christ. Glenn Hockton's miraculous deliverance from imminent death is the clear manifestation of Christ's resurrection even now. He has risen, He is alive. Mother Mary interceded for Her client to the Risen Lord Jesus. Why this power of intercession? Because Mary shared all the sufferings of Jesus and His Passion and Death, and so now She also shares the power of Christ's resurrection to heal, cast out demons, to convert sinners, and to save souls.

MEDITATION

Mother Mary revealed to St. Dominic many beautiful promises to those who prayed the Rosary. She said that whosoever shall faithfully serve Her by the recitation of the Rosary will receive signal graces. She promises before special protection and the greatest graces to all those who recite the Rosary daily and whoever shall recite the Rosary devoutly, applying himself to the consideration of the Sacred Mysteries shall never be conquered by misfortune. God will not chastise him and his justice, he shall not perish by an unprovided dead, and if he be just, he shall remain in the grace of God and become worthy of eternal life.

PRAYER

In all our trials and difficulties, let us pray the Rosary and invoke Mary's help always with this prayer from St. Bernard:

O most gracious Virgin Mary, that never was it known that anyone who fled to thy protection, implored thy help, or sought thy intercession was left unaided. Inspired with this confidence, I fly to thee, O Virgin of virgins, my Mother; to thee do I come; before thee I stand, sinful and sorrowful. O Mother of the Word Incarnate, despise not my petitions, but in thy mercy, hear and answer me. Amen.

DAY 24

MARY, HELP OF CHRISTIANS

"Now there stood by the cross of Jesus, his mother, and his mother's sister, Mary of Cleophas, and Mary Magdalen. When Jesus therefore had seen his mother and the disciple standing whom he loved, he saith to his mother: Woman, behold thy son. After that, he saith to the disciple: Behold thy mother. And from that hour, the disciple took her to his own." (John 19: 25-27)

Mary, the Help of Christians (Latin: Sancta Maria Auxilium Christianorum; Spanish: Nuestra Señora María Auxiliadora de los Cristianos), is a Roman Catholic Marian devotion with a feast day celebrated on May 24. Mary, Help of Christians, is very much rooted in a role as the Mother of God and Mother of the Church. As a Mother, She would do everything to protect Her spiritual children from the enemies of Christendom in their dire need since Her powerful intercession is unleashed through the Holy Rosary as manifested during the great battle of Lepanto in 1571. She is also referred to as Our Lady of the Rosary. The Catholic Commentary on John 19: 25 - 27 gives us a glimpse at the power of Mary so much so that Don Bosco said: "Just to utter the ejaculatory prayer, 'Mary, Help of Christians', is enough to make Satan bankrupt." Throughout the Gospel tradition, Mary has always been identified as the Mother of Jesus who is the Second Person of the Trinity, and therefore, the Mother of God. However, in John 19: 25-27, Mary's multifaceted role, which in the mind of God is already well defined even before She was born, is further revealed for the sake of the new disciples of Jesus. Jesus gives Mary a special motherly role at the initial moment of his glorification, which finds completion in the Resurrection. According to the Gospels, this is the great saving action of God. It signals a new era of faith and a new relationship, or Covenant, with God. God's glory made manifest in such a way may be understood as pointing to a New Jerusalem (Revelations 21: 9-11). Therefore, Mary is the foundational to this Covenant of Faith, a budding nation or community, and vital to its growth. As history has convincingly demonstrated, as the Christian community of followers grew into a Christian nation. By virtue of Jesus' words, Mary's role and popularity as Auxiliatrix of Christians has grown accordingly.

However, because of the bond with the Beloved Disciple, Jesus allowed Mary to move beyond the traditions of the great maternal figures of the Old Testament, who mothered ancient Israel. Because of His personal ties to the Beloved Disciple, Mary's motherhood becomes real and intimate. With Jesus' words, Mary's motherhood is being defined not as symbolic or distant, but as real and authentic, personal and loving. The fact that Jesus thought to care for His Mother at the moment of His death and in tremendous agony reflects the great love He had for Her.

Now, let us look at the Scriptural authority, the words of Jesus from the Cross to Mary and the Beloved Disciple culminate many Old Testament traditions, specifically regarding John 19: 25-27, we can see a parallel to Genesis 3: 15, as the victory over sin through the Cross can be paralleled to the victory over the serpent in Eden. In the Septuagint, which is the Greek version of the Hebrew Bible, the Genesis account is understood as saying that not the woman's offspring as a whole, but an individual offspring will be victorious over the serpent. According to Genesis 3: 15, the woman is also at war with the serpent and will share in the victory of her offspring over the serpent, this means that Mary's physical presence at the foot of the Cross connects Her perpetually with the victory of Jesus over Satan. This makes Mary the new Eve. However, unlike Eve of Genesis, Mary is a model of faith and obedience to the word of God as exemplified in Luke 1: 38. Also, unlike Eve, who was expelled from paradise where the victory was foretold, Mary is prominent at the place of victory, which is the Cross of Jesus. Because Mary's motherhood was defined from the Cross, the place of victory and glory in the Kingdom of Heaven, Her motherhood is entwined with Jesus' victory and glory, as King of the Universe.

While the image of Eve, the "mother of all life", provides a strong backdrop for St. John's definition of Mary's motherhood, he also uses the Old Testament imagery of the mother of Zion. In the midst of the intense and suffering, St. John draws our attention to Mary and the Beloved Disciple. The key to understanding this Zionist image of Mary is the presence of the Beloved Disciple. The Gospel depicts the Beloved Disciple as the Corporate Representation of the community of believers, the New Israel, or Zion.

If the Gospel casts the Beloved Disciple, the embodiment of Zion, as the new son of Mary, it follows that the Gospel casts Mary as the Mother of Zion.

Let us now look at the linguistic authority in Hebrew, the term for "Word" is "Dabar", in addition to "Word", this term connotes "Thing or Event". According to J.L. Mckenzie, in Dictionary of the Bible, there is a dynamic quality of the "Dabar". He argues that "the reality and power of the word are rooted in the personality" of the one who utters it. God spoke and Creation came into being and it was good. This means that creation is good, therefore, the word which generated it is good, and therefore, the one who uttered the word, God, is good.

It was also consistent with the Biblical view of family. According to Mckenzie and Dictionary of the Bible, the family was a religious unit, and the sense of solidarity was extremely close because the individual depended entirely on the family for support and protection, and life was not conceived as possible outside the family institution. The new Christian community of the baptized becomes, now, the new family of Jesus and Mary, of which She is the Helper of Christians. In this instance, Jesus is uttering words which would change the course of the lies of the Beloved Disciple and Mary, and therein, find fulfillment. It is in this moment when Jesus establishes this maternal bond between Mary and the Beloved Disciple, which we see the beginning of the redefining of Mary's motherhood to become a family of believers or Christians, where She operates as Auxiliatrix and Mother (John 19: 25-27). In the scene of two opposite emotional images: grief and joy, Mary undoubtedly was filled with grief and sorrow watching Her Son dying on the Cross. However, in this horrific moment, She is given another son, the son who represents all the followers of Jesus. Her grief will now be turned into joy. This echoes the mother Zion traditions of the Old Testament. Zion, in Her deep heartache and sorrow, must make room for a sudden increase and return of children. The sorrowful pain once felt is gone and replaced with exuberance and rejoicing. Mary is now deemed the Mother of all the followers of Jesus and Auxiliatrix, and Her motherhood is redefined in terms of discipleship. Overall, the Beloved Disciple is depicted as the ideal and representational Disciple of the Fourth Gospel. His actions and response to Jesus in faith secures his position in the new family of Jesus. Mary is not only a Disciple but Jesus' Mother with all the attendant images of love, auxiliatrix, and nurturing. From the Cross, She's made the Mother of all Christians, also the Help of Christians, always ready to accept and enlarge Her tent and Her heart to accommodate Her children given to Her through faith in Her Son Jesus Christ.

St. John Chrysostom was the first one to use the title "Mary, Help of Christians" in the year 345 as a devotion to the Blessed Virgin Mary. St. John Bosco also propagated Marian devotion under the title "Mary, Help of Christians "associated with the defense of Christian Europe, the North of Africa, and the Middle East from non-Christian people during the Middle Age. In 1572, during the expansion of the Islamic Ottoman Empire intended to invade Christian Europe, Pope Pius V invoked Christian armies, and his victory was attributed to the intercession of Mary under the title, "Help of Christians".

The tradition of this advocation goes back to 1571, the whole of Christendom was saved by "Mary, Help of Christians" when the faithful prayers of Catholics throughout Europe prayed the

Rosary. The great Battle of Lepanto occurred on October 7th, 1571. For this reason, this date has been chosen as the Feast of the Holy Rosary.

Near the end of the 17th century, when 200,000 Ottoman Turks had besieged the capital city of Vienna, emperor Leopold I of Austria took refuge in the Shrine of Mary Help of Christians at Passau. On September 8th, Feast of Our Lady's Birthday, plans were drawn for the battle. On September 12th, Feast of the Holy Name of Mary, the Turks was defeated and Vienna was finally freed through the intercession of Mary, Help of Christians. All of Europe had joined with the Emperor crying out "Mary, Help!" and praying the Holy Rosary. Therefore, Mary, Help of Christians should be a very special devotion in Europe for they owed their freedom from the Muslims to Mary under Her title the "Help of Christians".

In 1809, Napoleon's men entered to the Vatican, arrested Pius VII and brought him in chains to Grenoble, and eventually Fontainebleau. His imprisonment lasted five years. On May 24th, 1814, Pius VII returned in triumph to Rome. Twelve months later, the Pope decreed the Feast of Mary Help of Christians, be kept on the 24th of May.

St. John Bosco was a dynamic priest who founded of the Salesian Order in the XIX century in Italy. His many prophetic dreams and insights on how his ministry could defeat Satan in the future were inspired and guided by Mary Help of Christians. On May 14th, 1862, John Bosco dreamed about the final battles between the Church and Satan, in which the Pope of those days anchors the 'ship' of the Church between two pillars, one to the statue of Mary and the other to the large Eucharistic Host. St. John Bosco wrote about his congregation, the Daughters of Mary Help of Christians or Salesian of Don Bosco: "The principal objective is to promote veneration of the Blessed Sacrament and devotion to Mary Help of Christians. This title seems to please the august Queen of Heaven very much."

Vatican II, in the Constitution on the Church (sections 61, 62), cites this title of Mary, placing it in the context of Mary's maternal role: "In an utterly singular way she co-operated by her obedience, faith, hope and burning charity in the Savior's work of restoring supernatural life to souls. For this reason she is a mother to us in the order of grace...By her maternal charity, Mary cares for the brethren of her Son who still wander through this world in the midst of dangers and difficulties until they are led to the happiness of their heavenly home".

The number one challenge of the Church today is the youth. They could be like Absalom, rebellious son of King David, who destroys authority, proclaims himself as king, and threatens to kill his father and his brothers. All they could be as the Beloved Disciple John, the obedient and humble Disciple of Christ. Yet, full of power and wisdom in the Kingdom of God, but there is a need of a mother to guide the youth or else, if they are orphaned and without a mother, they will become wayward and delinquent. In Don Bosco's time, Mother Mary guided him in directing and sanctifying the young people who had fallen into mortal sins. Don Bosco and Mary Help of Christians were intertwined. In Don Bosco's dream, the Blessed Virgin Mary told him that the last anchors of salvation of believers of the Church against her enemies in the end times will be the Eucharist and the Immaculate Heart of Mary Help of Christians.

At the age of nine, Don Bosco had a vision of his future mission, he found himself amidst the crowd of children cursing, beating, and wounding each other. Don Bosco was shocked with their language that he jumped into their midst, swing wildly and shouting at them to stop. At that moment, Don Bosco heard a voice coming from a Man (Jesus) saying, "You will have to win these friends of your not with blows, but with gentleness and kindness. So begin right now to show them that sin is ugly and virtue beautiful." Jesus gave Don Bosco a shepherdess, the Mother, Help of Christians, to assist him and his future mission in molding these wild youngsters into meek and humble lambs. The Blessed Mother of God signaled to Don Bosco a vision of his mission. He saw many wild animals barking, growling, and biting each other, leaving a lot of them wounded or killed. Afterwards, these wild animals, suddenly, were transformed into meek and humble lambs. After seeing this vision, Don Bosco was perplexed, what can a nine-year-old boy do to remedy the problem? But Our Lady Helpful Christians told Don Bosco not to be afraid, saying: "In due time everything will be clear to you."

Years later, as the newly ordained priest, Don Bosco was vesting in the sacristy, he witnessed the sacristan chasing a young lad who happened to sneak inside the church looking for something, Don Bosco stopped the sacristan and told him that the lad was his friend. When asked for his name, the young boy said: "Bartholomew Garelli." This lad brought more of his friends to Don Bosco, and the first Oratory was organized, followed some years later, the initial foundations of the Salesian Order. Many of the young people of those times came from broken families being forced to the streets with nowhere to go, the oratorio which was inspired by the Blessed Virgin Mary became the very important solution in helping the young people to become good citizens. Through the guidance of the Blessed Mother, Don Bosco developed the Preventive System. Through this system which works by kindness, religion, and reason, he was able to draw the hearts of young people and prevent them from falling into sin. Don Bosco also was inspired to implement the Communion of Reparation Lifestyle to this youth by encouraging them to go to frequent confession, to adore the Lord frequently in the Blessed Sacrament, to pray the Holy Rosary every day, and to attend the Holy Sacrifice of the Mass every single day. By encouraging this simple lifestyle given by Mother Mary Help of Christians, Don Bosco was able to foster these youngsters into becoming good and holy citizens of the country and future citizens of heaven.

How is this communion of reparation lifestyle applied? The Blessed Mother works to inculcate in the youth the beauty of grace and virtue and ugliness of sin in vice.

In Don Bosco's time, sin had taken root in the structure of the society and in the life of the young people. Sin is the source of evil and all other evils.

According to Pope Paul VI in "Deliver Us from Evil", "Sin is the entry point of Satan." Joseph Cardinal Ratzinger stated that, "Sin is the cause of all afflictions in mankind." Sin causes all kinds of physical, psychological, moral, and spiritual sickness.

Don Bosco was the first Saint who was guided to implement the Communion of Reparation Lifestyle which is a Christo-Eucharistic Centered Lifestyle that incorporates the spirit of vigilance and reparation. The youth who would come to Don Bosco or who were brought to him by government authorities to live in his Oratory were often suffering from all kinds of sickness: physical sickness such as malnourishment, and all kinds of skin diseases; psychological sickness such as depression, many were suffering from trauma, sexual disorders and often spiritual sickness caused by infestation. For these abandoned children to be healed, the Vigilant Lifestyle produced an environment which made it virtually impossible for them to commit mortal sin and to live habitually in the state of sanctifying grace. A group of assistants armed with patience and kindness acted as shepherds assisting the youth at all hours of the day. The aim was to occupy every moment with prayers, acts of penance, works of mercy, and all with the motivation of loving and serving God. This Communion of Reparation Lifestyle healed all types of brokenness and sickness because it was virtually impossible for sin to thrive in the Oratory.

Let us take a closer look at the four elements of the Communion of Reparation Lifestyle, which are Confession, Adoration, Rosary, and Eucharist. In the spirit of vigilance and reparation, the person must make a good confession; a good confession should always include contrition of heart, verbal confession of sin, penance, and absolution. Contrition is the sincere sorrow for having offended God and the most important act of the penitent. There can be no forgiveness of sin if we do not have sorrow and firm result not to sin again. Confession is confronting our sins and the devil who is the tempter of sin. We accuse ourselves before God through the priests. Penance is an important part of our healing. It is imposed by the confessor in order for us to make reparation for our sins. Absolution is when the priest imparts the words which reconcile a sinner to God through the merits of Jesus on the Cross. In the Eucharist, Christ is really present: Body, Blood, Soul, and Divinity. When we go to Mass, we receive the Body of Christ with proper disposition, meaning: in the state of grace and without mortal sin. Then Christ, personally, will dwell in our hearts. *"It is no longer I that live; but Christ lives in me"* (Galatians 2: 20).

When Christ reigns in our hearts, we are moved to adore Him who is truly present in all the tabernacles throughout the world. When adoration develops into devotion, Christ becomes permanent in dwelling in our hearts, and Satan no longer has the power over the soul, then healing can take place.

During the battle of 1646 and 1647, Our Lady of the Rosary, Help of Christians, miraculously preserved the Philippines from that's protestant invasion through the prayer of the Rosary. General Lorenzo Ugalde de Orellana was the Commander-in-Chief of the Spanish fleet "Encarnación", and Sebastian Lopez was the admiral of the ship Rosario. In each ship, there were priors assigned to pray the Rosary.

First battle: On March 15th, 1646, at around 9:00 am, the Spanish fleet discovered one enemy vessel on oars, but it quickly took flight. At about 1:00 pm, four Dutch ships appeared, together with the smaller oared-vessel they had seen earlier. The two fleets came within firing range of each other between two and three o'clock in the afternoon. The first salvo came from the Dutch flagship but missed its mark. The Encarnación answered with two shots, hitting the Dutch flagship, and tearing open the forward edge of the ship's prow. The Dutch then focused on firing on the smaller ship Rosario, but it retaliated by firing a simultaneous volley cannons. On the other hand, the Encarnación fired freely at the four enemy vessels, inflicting severe damages and thus forcing the Dutch to disengage in battle. The second battle took place on July 25, beginning at dawn, the Dutch squadron was bound for Manila, and the Spanish fleet Encarnación and Rosario wasted no time and chased the enemy. On one occasion, as reported by one of the soldiers aboard, the Encarnación was the Dominican, prior father Juan de Cuenca who delivered "a very spiritual sermon" to the men, he said: "If you pray with me the Rosary devoutly, an assurance on the part of God and His Most Holy Mother, not only victory but also that no one will be killed in battle."

Three more battles were engaged but in all of these five encounters, the Dutch fleet was no match to the strong defense put up by the combined Spanish-Filipino fleet, whose secret weapon was in the continuous praying of the Rosary of the priors. Finally, the Dutch fire ship sunk, and the men on the Spanish flagship shouted: "*Ave Maria!*" (*Hail Mary!*) and "*Viva la fe Cristo y la Virgen Santisima del Rosario!*" means (*Long live the Faith in Christ and the Most Holy Virgin of the Rosary!*)

The Spanish-Filipino armada publicly declared that the victory belonged to Our Lady of the Rosary.

On January 20th, 1647, the victory was celebrated in the solemn feast by means of a procession, divine worship and a parade of the Spanish squadron with other demonstrations in fulfillment of the vow made to the Virgin of the Rosary, Help of Christians.

On April 9th, 1652, the battles of 1646 were declared miraculous by the Venerable Dean and Chapter and Ecclesiastical Governor in the vacant See of the Metropolitan Church of Manila.

Don Bosco made the following remark about the Communion of Reparation Lifestyle in the spirit of vigilance, he said: "I guarantee that no youth sent to the Oratory will become worse, instead they will become good and better. All the broken youth experience healing from their physical mental and psychological sickness, and were freed from satanic captivity becoming good and faithful Catholics."

MEDITAION

"The family that prays together stays together." (Fr. Patrick Peyton)

PRAYER

O Loving Mother, Mary Help of Christians, we have so many broken youth these days because of the terrible influence of atheism and Satanism. The youth are the future of the society. If we continue to have broken youth, we will have a broken society. If we have broken youth, we will have broken priests, bishops, and cardinals. As the shepherdess of the Oratory, you save everyone under your care. We have now the youth of our present generation gravely misled by the evil influence of our times. We entrust all the youth of our country today to Your Immaculate Heart of Mary Help Christians. Being such a powerful Mother, you will crush the head of the serpent as you promised in Genesis 3 15. We ask this through the most powerful intercession of Saint Joseph and through Jesus Christ, Our Lord. Amen.

DAY 25

ASCENSION OF JESUS

"Amen, amen I say to you, that you shall lament and weep, but the world shall rejoice; and you shall be made sorrowful, but your sorrow shall be turned into joy." (John 16: 20)

There are many lessons we can learn from the Ascension of Jesus into heaven:

First lesson, the Lord's Ascension tells us that Jesus' earthly life was always pointed to heaven. St. Paul said, *"Our citizenship is in heaven"* (Philippians 3:20). Our life on earth is a pilgrimage to heaven.

Second, the Ascension reveals the ultimate destiny of our human body to the Trinity. We read in the Catechism the Catholic Church that "The Father's power 'raise up' Christ his Son and by doing so perfectly introduced His Son's humanity, including His body, into the Trinity. Jesus is conclusively revealed as 'Son of God in power according to the Spirit of holiness by his Resurrection from the dead'" (CCC #648). "Christ's Ascension marks the definitive entrance of Jesus' humanity into God's heavenly domain, whence he will come again..." (CCC #665). Consequently, any claim that Christianity devalues the body or human nature is misguided. Pope Benedict XVI, in a homily in 2005, clarified: "Christ's Ascension means that He belongs entirely to God. He, the Eternal Son, led our human existence into God's presence, taking with Him flesh and blood in a transfigured form. The human being finds room in God; through Christ, the human being was introduced into the very life of God." The famed writer C.S Lewis adds: *"Next to the Blessed Sacrament itself, your neighbor is the holiest object presented to your senses."* Why?

Because Jesus in the Ascension introduced human existence into God's presence.

Third lesson, Christ's Ascension also signifies the beginning of the final hour of human history. By Christ's Ascension into Heaven the final age – indeed the final *"hour"* – of the world had begun. The Catechism states: "Since the Ascension God's plan has entered into its fulfillment. We are already at 'the last hour'. 'Already the final age of the world is with us, and the renewal of the world is irrevocably under way; it is even now anticipated in a certain real way, for the Church on earth is endowed already with a sanctity that is real but imperfect'" (CCC #670). All Christians are living in "end times," which means that we should be diligently preparing for the return of the Lord who is already present to us through the Holy Eucharist.

Finally, our Lord's Ascension shows that Jesus is the permanent King and High Priest of all creation There are powerful words in the Epistle to the Hebrews about Jesus' ongoing priestly ministry in Heaven (words that should really give us great encouragement!). In the seventh chapter of Hebrews we read: "... because Jesus lives forever [in Heaven], he has a permanent priesthood. Therefore he is able to save completely those who come to God through him, because he always lives to intercede for them" (Hebrews 7:24-25; CCC 519). Is it not incredibly encouraging to know that Jesus is always living to make intercession for you! Does not that revelation of his incessant intercession for you fill your heart with confidence!

Moreover, the author of Hebrews identifies Jesus' never-ending priesthood in Heaven as the true fulfillment of the Order of Melchizedek, the very first priesthood mentioned in the Old Testament (see Genesis 14). In fact, the Order of Melchizedek is mentioned multiple times in Hebrews! This is a very significant point for Catholics because the "thanksgiving offering" made by the priest Melchizedek in the Old Testament was that of bread and wine (Genesis 14:18), which constituted a "communion sacrifice" per Dr. Scott Hahn. Jesus is identified in Hebrews as "the mediator of a new covenant" (Hebrews 12:24). The true sacramental sign of this New Covenant is identified by Jesus as the Holy Eucharist (*"This cup is the new covenant in my blood, which is poured out for you"* – Luke 22:20). As such we are advised in Hebrews not to neglect 'to meet together" for the New Testament liturgy (Hebrews 10:25), the Mass, of our High Priest, Jesus Christ (see CCC 692). Jesus ascended into Heaven is the true High Priest at every Mass.

Pope Benedict XVI said at the Regina Coeli prayer on May 20, 2012 that "The Ascension of Jesus reminds Christians of the promise of Heaven and the power of earthly prayer." We read in Matthew 28: 20 that before Jesus ascended into heaven, He told his Apostles and Disciples to go make disciples of all nations, and remember I will be with you always until the end of times. Jesus always keeps His promise because He is really, truly, substantially present – Body, Blood, Soul, and Divinity in every Tabernacle in every church throughout the world, waiting for us with open arms to help us resolve any problem and challenge that we may encounter. We read in John 19: 25-27 that how Jesus before he died on the Cross, left us His Mother who would be with the Church. Although She assumed into Heaven, after some time in her resurrected body, She is present everywhere to those who pray to Her as a Mother for guidance and help until the end of times. Pope Benedict XVI told the pilgrims in St. Peter's Square on May 20, 2012 that "When he ascended into heaven, Jesus 'did not separate himself from our condition, in fact, in his humanity, he took mankind with him in the intimacy of the Father, and so has revealed the final destination of our earthly pilgrimage,'" the pope added that: "Jesse came down from heaven for us, and for us suffered and died on the cross, so for us he rose again and ascended to God, who therefore is no longer distant, but is 'Our God,' 'Our Father.'"

The Pope explained how "The Ascension of Our Lord marks the fulfillment of salvation which began with the incarnation. It is the ultimate act of our deliverance from the yoke of sin." Quoting Pope St. Leo the Great, Pope Benedict said that "The Ascension not only is the immortality of the soul proclaimed, but also that of flesh." Further, he added that "Today, in fact, not only are we confirmed possessors of paradise, but in Christ we also penetrated the heights of heaven."

There is no room for despair because Jesus did not abandon us. When he ascended into heaven, he said: *"A little while, and you shall not see me; and again a little while, and you shall see me? Amen, amen I say to you, that you shall lament and weep, but the world shall rejoice; and you shall be made sorrowful, but your sorrow shall be turned into joy. So also you now indeed have sorrow; but I will see you again, and your heart shall rejoice; and your joy no man shall take from you. And in that day you shall not ask me anything. Amen, amen I say to you: if you ask the Father anything in my name, he will give it you"* (John 16: 19-23). After His Resurrection and during His Ascension, Jesus introduced our humanity to the Trinity, and He now sits at the right hand of the Father to intercede for us always. And as He sits at the right hand of the Father, He also sits in all the tabernacles throughout the world until the end of time. Whatever trial, problem, challenge, or anything that we bring to Jesus in the tabernacle, where He is really, truly present – Body, Blood, Soul, and Divinity, therefore, is immediately presented to the Father in Heaven as we wait for His immediate response.

The Ascension also tells us that when we pray, "our humanity is brought to the heights of God, so every time we pray, the earth joins with Heaven." The Pope said of prayer, adding that "And like burning incense, its fragrant smoke reaches on high, when we raise our fervent and trusting prayer in Christ to the Lord, it crosses the heavens and reaches the Throne of God, it is heard by Him and answered." The Pope also said: "Let us beseech the Virgin Mary to help us contemplate the heavenly things, which the Lord promises us, and become more credible witnesses of divine life."

Let us learn about the approved Apparition of "Our Lady of Good Help" which happened in 1859 in Champion, Wisconsin:

On July 23, 1855, the Brice family moved from Belgium to the United States. On August 7 of that same year, Lambert and Marie

Brice purchased 240 acres of land in the Red River, Wisconsin region to establish their family farm. Every Sunday, their daughter Adele would walk 11 miles by herself to the nearest church.

In early October of 1859, Adele Brice, age 28, was taking some wheat to a grist mill along a four-mile Indian pathway. Just as Adele came to a clearing between a maple tree and a hemlock tree, she saw someone standing between the two trees. As she approached, her heart filled with fright, and she froze as she looked at the woman. The woman was all white with a yellow sash at her waist. Around her head was a crown of twelve stars. She was standing on a small cloud. She had yellow hair, blue eyes, and was surrounded by a bright light. Adele watched until the woman disappeared, and then she saw the cloud disappear as well. Adele went to the mill did her business and headed for home. When she arrived home, she told her parents what had happened. Her father suggested that it might be a poor soul that needed prayers, "so pray for her if you see her again." On October 9, 1859, Adele with her sister Isabelle (age 24), and their good friend, Mrs. Theresa Vander Niessen, were on their way to Sunday Mass at the nearest church in Bay Settlement. As they approached the spot where the two trees stood, Adele again saw the lady in white. She got excited and told her sister what she was seeing. Adele froze, staring at the woman, but the other two companions could not see anything. But they saw that Adele was indeed staring at something, and they could see fear in her eyes. Then the lady disappeared, and they all agreed to pray for the "poor soul." Adele confessed to the priest what she had seen, and the priest spoke to her about the matter, suggesting that she ask the lady who she is and what she wants. Adele felt comforted that Father Verhoeff believed her encounter. On the way home from the church, the three women were joined by a man who was clearing the land for the Holy Cross Fathers. When they came to the place with the two trees, Adele stopped because she again saw the lady who was dressed in a white gown which fell to her feet in graceful folds. There was a yellow sash around her waist. Long wavy golden hair fell loosely over her shoulders. On her head was a crown of twelve stars. The bright light surrounding her made it difficult for Adele to look at her for very long. Adele saw that the lady had a very sweet, gentle face. Surprisingly, she felt no fear this time. Instead, she was completely filled with joy and peace. She walked closer and fell to her knees before her. Kneeling before the lady, Adele asked: "*In God's name, who are you, and what do you desire of me?*" Speaking in a soft, sweet heavenly voice, the lady responded: "*I am the Queen of Heaven, who prays for the conversion of sinners, and I wish you to do the same. You were at Holy Communion this morning. You have done well, but I wish you to do more. Pray for nine days. Go and make a general confession and offer your Holy Communion for the conversion of sinners. If they do not convert themselves and do penance, my Son will be obliged to punish them.*" As Adele and the lady were speaking, the others could tell that Adele was seeing someone and talking with her. They kept asking her, "Who is she?" What is she saying? Is she the poor soul from Belgium? Who is it? Adele heard her friends and told them to kneel because "she was the Queen of Heaven." When Theresa complained about not being able to see her, Adele saw the Virgin Mary look kindly at Theresa and say, "*Blessed are they that believe and do not see.*" Then the Virgin Mary said to Adele, "*What are you doing here in idleness, while your companions are working in the vineyard of My Son?*" Adele cried, "*What more can I do, dear Lady?*" The Virgin Mary responded, "*Teach the children. Teach them their catechism, how to sign themselves with the sign of the cross, and how to approach the sacraments, that they may know and love My Son; otherwise, the people here will lose their faith.*" Promising to teach children about religion, Adele kept her vow to the Virgin.

Then the four walked home, and Adele told everyone about her encounter. Because of her character, most people believed her words. Her father had always believed her because she had always been a truthful girl. To show his support for his daughter and his love for the Virgin Mary, Adele's father decided to honor the location of the apparitions with a building of a very small chapel (10 feet x 12 feet) on the very spot. Adele offered to work hard for the busy pioneer families if they would let her teach their children the catechism and the rosary in their spare moments. She did so for seven years, bringing each child that was ready to Father Daems in Bay Settlement to test their knowledge before each one's First Communion. In 1861, the community built a larger chapel, more than twice as big as the first one that could hold a hundred people – and often did.

When doubters began to give Adele a hard time, miracle healings began occurring in the chapel when Adele asked for divine assistance. Blind visitors regained their sight, deaf people regained their hearing, the desperately sick were healed, and cripples would walk again, leaving their canes and crutches behind as evidence. Word spread across the Midwest of these divine healings near Robinsonville (later called Champion).

In 1864, Adele and the other religious women helping her became the Sisters of Good Help – and were accepted by the Bishop of Green Bay. In 1867, Adele opened a school next to the chapel and a boarding school, the St. Mary's Academy, in 1869. On Sunday, October 8, 1871, a deadly fire was created by a gale force wind that turned the prairies and forests of Wisconsin into a raging inferno. Fire tornadoes ripped throughout the area causing death and destruction everywhere. Flames jumped rivers, embers rained down, and small fires were whipped up into a giant fireball that destroyed homes, buildings, farms, factories, and entire towns. It was described as "a wall of flame a mile high, five miles wide, traveling 90 to 100 miles per hour, hotter than a crematorium, turning sand into glass." The heat was so strong that it killed people before the fire ever got to them. Approximately 2,500 people died, 12 towns were destroyed, and 1.2 million acres devastated – the deadliest fire in American history. The ground was burned to a depth of two feet deep in some places. Hiding in brick homes or underground basements did not help. Only those hiding in rivers had the best chance of survival.

Father Pernin of a local church made every effort to save the tabernacle from his church, but at the river his cart dumped, and it floated away as he watched helplessly. Many people lined the river banks, but the only ones who survived were those who jump into the water with Father Pernin. Three days later, among the blackened terrain and black ashes of everything destroyed, a pristine white tabernacle was discovered sitting upright on a log in the river. Its contents were unharmed from water or heat, and the people saw it as a miracle and a sign of hope.

Sister Adele decided it was impossible to flee the fire, so the sisters, the school children, the frantic neighbors gathered in the chapel in the five-acre grounds and prayed to Mary for help. Then Adele led a procession around the perimeter of the chapel grounds, carrying a statue of the Blessed Virgin Mary. The procession continued all night, praying the Rosary, all around the grounds. Everyone believed a miracle had occurred: the wind cooled, a heavy downpour drenched the fires, but this was long after the fires had stopped right the fence line surrounding the five acres. The outer side of the fence posts was charred while the inside was untouched. Everything surrounding their five acres, including the lush green forest, farm buildings, and homes were blackened, obliterated, and gone. Only the people and animals that had come to these grounds survived. The five-acre grounds that had been dedicated to Mary were green and untouched – "a glorious sight." Exhausted from their fears and night-long processions of prayers, the people praised God and retired to sleep. Twelve years ago, on this exact day, Mary had warned of a potential punishment.

Another miracle on the chapel grounds had to do with the chapel well. The weather had been extremely dry all summer with the deepest of wells in the region barely containing any water left. The shallow chapel well was only a few feet deep, and it was providing plenty of water to all the neighbors, their surviving livestock, and everyone else living on Mary's five acres. No one could explain how this small shallow well was able to serve so many people and animals for such a long time under dry conditions. People started taking some of the well water home as it was believed to have led to some healing miracles.

Many other miracles were documented. A 17-year-old boy developed pleurisy from double-pneumonia. Despite his lungs becoming extremely weak, he said a novena at the chapel, and he was completely healed. Another boy, Michael Fonde, age nine, fell from the barn and was crippled. Four years later, a group of women prayed a novena with him at the chapel, and he walked out healed, leaving scratches behind. Another miracle was when a little girl with bleeding sores, who had been treated by doctors for years, was completely healed after she and her mother made the pilgrimage to the chapel. Another small girl had become blind from a severe case of measles. When her mother brought her to this chapel to pray, she was instantaneously healed. And a deaf boy brought by his mother to the chapel completely regained his hearing.

On December 8, 2010, a historic event took place in this Shrine of Our Lady of Good Help near Champion, Wisconsin. Bishop David Ricken of Green Bay formally announced the approval of these apparitions: *"I declare with moral certainty and in accord with the norms of the Catholic Church that the events, apparitions, and locutions given to Adele Brice in October of 1859 do exhibit the substance of supernatural character, and I hereby approve these apparitions as worthy of belief by the Christian faithful."* This became the first approved Marian apparition in the United States of America.

Let us make our general Confession every time we have the opportunity, confessing all our sins since the age of reason. St. Francis of Sales recommended this practice on every Feast day of the Blessed Virgin Mary and Jesus Christ. This helps cleanse completely even the temporal punishment due to our sins or even remedy the bad confessions we made in the past because of shame and malice. Also, when we pray the Rosary, we remember that Mary sees to it that we are always in the state of grace so that we are ready anytime She comes to take us with her for eternity into Heaven. The Rosary connects us with Jesus so intimately that our union with our Mother Mary is a guarantee of our union with Jesus Christ who is inseparable with His Mother for eternity. When Christ ascended into Heaven, He did not leave His human nature behind; He brought that nature, our human nature, into Heaven with Him. By bringing His human nature into Heaven, Jesus Christ opened paradise for the human family. With a glorified human body and a human soul, the Second Person of the Holy Trinity sits at the right hand of God the Father for all eternity. This incorporation of the human and the Divine makes Him our presence in eternity, and the mediator between God and humanity. This is the pressing and inspiring lesson of the Ascension. It touches the core of the Christian faith, our own dignity as human beings and the life available to us after death. It is a strong reminder to us of how greatly we are loved, and how intensely God desires fellowship with us.

MEDITATION

"O sinner, be not discouraged, but have recourse to Mary in all you necessities. Call her to your assistance, for such is the divine Will that she should help in every kind of necessity." (St. Basil the Great)

"I am not only the Queen of Heaven, but also the Mother of Mercy." (Our Lady told St. Faustina)

"Prayer is powerful beyond limits when we turn to the Immaculata who is Queen of God's Heart." (St. Maximilian Kolbe)

PRAYER

O Blessed Virgin Mary, every time we pray our Rosary, you bless us with your loving presence. As we include in our prayer the petitions to our problems in this world, you console us and you clearly point out the solution to all our problems as a good mother does to the hapless child leaning and totally depending on his mother. You always bring me back to Jesus every time I fall away from Him, even from His state of grace. O Blessed Virgin Mary, I promise to pray always the Rosary because I know you are there so closely united with me every time I pray this beautiful prayer. I will try what St. Teresa of Avila tells me that I should always pray the Rosary during every idle moment of my life to increase the level of sanctity in the Kingdom of Heaven. I ask this through the intercession of St. Joseph, your chaste spouse, and in Jesus Christ, Our Lord. Amen.

DAY 26

DESCENT OF THE HOLY SPIRIT

"He said therefore to them again: Peace be to you. As the Father hath sent me, I also send you. When he had said this, he breathed on them; and he said to them: Receive ye the Holy Ghost." (John 20: 21-22)

What does it mean when St. John referred to "Breathing the Holy Spirit" to the Apostles? We remember that in the Old Testament there were two events when God breathed on creatures: 1) Creation; 2) Exile in Babylon.

Creation event, in the Old Testament, this breathing meant: God giving life to man whom he had fashioned from the dust of the ground. It was the first time divinity breathed on humanity. At Creation, *"the Lord God formed man of dust from the ground, and breathed into his nostrils the breath of life; and man became a living being"* (Genesis 2:7). We see this act as the clearest gesture of God's desire to impart His own life into man, who is made in His image and likeness.

The second event was in exile in Babylon. God breathed into humanity to signify a spiritual restoration and renewal of His life in us after man had fallen into sin. The fallen state of Adam and Eve and those in the exile in Babylon are all the result of their rebellion against God. The fall of Adam and Eve into sin robbed them (and us) of their inheritance as children of God. It also made us lose paradise, the original justice and holiness which is immortality freedom from concupiscence and natural sins. However, the entire story of salvation history reveals God's plan to restore and renew His life in us. So vivid is this image of God's breath in man that it appears again at the time of the prophet, Ezekiel. God's people, Israel, were in exile in Babylon; they had been ravaged by their enemies as punishment for the infidelity to the covenant. These Israelites represent all of us who are spiritually dead and entirely helpless. However, in His unrelenting determination to restore His people, God says to Ezekiel (whom He called "son of man"): *"'Son of man, can these bones live?' And I answered, 'O Lord God, Thou knowest.' Again He said, 'Prophesy to these bones, and say to them, O dry bones, hear the word of the Lord… Behold, I will cause breath to enter you, and you shall live…and you shall know that I am the Lord'"* (Ez 26:3-6).

When we read Acts 1: 8, we are reminded of the importance of the Holy Spirit because, at His Ascension, Jesus told the apostles not to start on their mission of making disciples of all nations until they received "power when the Holy Spirit has come upon you." When we read the New Testament, we can see how Christ's Resurrection changes the meaning of "breathing of the Holy Spirit:"

First, the breathing of the Spirit initiates the apostles and the disciples into the life of the Holy Spirit. It serves as a prelude to the Jewish feast of Pentecost, wherein the people received the full gift of the Holy Spirit; that was meant to assist them prior to their evangelization of the Jews and gentiles. The Jewish Pentecost celebration originally had been a harvest festival in the Jewish liturgical calendar. It was when the Jews from all nations assemble in Jerusalem to give thanks to the Lord for blessing them with rich harvest in their fields and preserving them from the slavery of sin. Gradually, this event became associated with a memorial celebration of God's giving of the Law to His people at Mount Sinai, when they had been delivered from slavery in Egypt. The Law, or Torah, gave the people a way of life that would distinguish them from all other peoples on earth. To seal this covenant between God and man, God came down on top of Mount Sinai, manifested in fire, smoke, thunder, an earthquake, and the loud sound of a trumpet (see Ex 19:16-19).

Second, in the New Testament, the breathing of God signifies receiving God's new Law of Love. This time nothing grave on stone but engraved in the hearts of men by the Holy Spirit.

On May 11, 2008, Pope Benedict XVI explained this meaning by drawing a parallel with God's visit to Mount Sinai: "Just as God's descent on Mount Sinai meant the formation of Israel as a nation, the descent of the Holy Spirit on Pentecost meant the formation of the Jews and Gentiles into the Church, the new Israel.

The events of Pentecost also evoke the deep symbolism of wind and fire which is present not just at Mount Sinai covenant but all throughout the Old Testament. At Creation, "the wind" of God (literally God's "breath") hovered over the waters of the earth, ready to do God's bidding as He brought forth life (Gen 1:2). The "wind" of God also blew apart the waters of the Red Sea so that God's people could escape from their enemies, the Egyptians. As for fire, recall that God first appeared to Moses, the deliverer of His people, in a fiery bush. Pope Benedict XVI continues in his parallel by mentioning how God's people had to follow a pillar of fire to make their way home to the Promised Land.

Third, the "breathing of the Holy Spirit" and the resting of the tongues of fire over each of the apostles signify how the apostles, now the Bishops, had become the burning fire. They will now be God's presence in His Church, leading His people on their journey home to heaven. That is why to this day, the bishops of the Church, who are the successors of the apostles, wear hats (we call mitres) in the shape of a flame of fire. With their miters, the bishops are marked out as our pillars of fire, leading us on our pilgrim journey home to heaven. Therefore, we can see how the more we know of the imagery representing God in the Old Testament, the more we can understand how the descent of the Holy Spirit on Pentecost as an explosion of fulfilled promises!

Fourth, the "breathing of the Holy Spirit" on Pentecost day is sent in the gifting of tongues to the 12 apostles and 120 disciples to provide unity in mind and heart of the new Israel (in Greek, "glossolalia"). Glossolalia is a supernatural gift of tongues from the Holy Spirit to the apostles that enabled them to speak their language to others and to still be understood by others in their own foreign language. The apostles were miraculously able to communicate the Gospel in the foreign tongues of the Jews assembled there. All male Jews were required to make a yearly pilgrimage to Jerusalem for this feast; that explains why "there were devout Jews from every nation" there. This immediately evokes the history of Babel (see Gen 11:1-9). There human pride made a grab at heaven by building a tower up to God. The solidarity of men (made possible by one language) was perverted to accomplish an evil end. God broke it by confusing the one language into many. Now, in the fullness of time, God grants the human solidarity for which man longs (because he is made for that) but which he cannot naturally achieve. The Holy Spirit creates supernatural solidarity, represented here by all men being able to hear, in their own language, the mighty works of God. This time, God reaches down to man rather than man trying to climb up to God.

Fifth, St. Luke, in his writing, conveys the fundamental idea that the act itself of the "breathing of the Holy Spirit" and the "gift of tongues" initiates the birth of the Church, which was already Catholic or universal. During the coming of the Holy Spirit with "*glossolalia*", the existing multiple languages and different cultures that divide peoples suddenly united the Jews and foreigners into one mind and heart, thus making them the Church. Peoples of different nationalities then can now understand and make each other fruitful. This group of 12 apostles and 120 disciples constitutes an authentic "QAHAL", an assembly on the model of the first covenant. The community convoked to hear the voice of the Lord and to walk His way.

St Augustine spoke of the early Church in one of his sermons, the *Societas Spiritus (Society of the Spirit)*. However, prior St. Augustine's sermon, St. Irenaeus had already taught that "Where the Church is, there also is the Spirit of God; where the Spirit of God is, there is the Church and every grace; and the Spirit is truth; to distance oneself from the Church is to reject the Holy Spirit", and thus "exclude oneself from life" (*Adversus Haereses* III, 24, 1).

Let's take this story which manifests strongly the power of the Holy Spirit through the Blessed Mother's Rosary, the power of victimhood and the power of love:

In 1842, in Rome, Italy, a young man Alphonse Ratisbonne was touring Europe before settling down for marriage and assuming a partnership at his uncle's bank. Alphonse was the youngest Jew of an important banking family in Strasbourg, a close relation of the Rothschild. Ratisbonne was a strongly anti-Catholic and libertine in his customs. Ending his tour in Rome, he was well received by the local French diplomatic circle residing there He reluctantly made a call on Baron Theodore de Bussières, a very fervent Catholic. Even though the Jew seemed quite far from any conversion, the Baron, undaunted by his sarcasm and blasphemy, saw in him a future Catholic and encouraged his visits. One afternoon, Baron Theodore challenged Ratisbonne to wear the Miraculous Medal and recite the *Memorare* once a day, wanting to prove the ineffectiveness of such religious medals and prayers. Ratisbonne agreed and allowed the Baron's young daughter to put the medal around his neck. He also promised to recite the Memorare each day. Meanwhile, the Baron and his friends increased their prayers, especially their Rosary for the conversion of Ratisbonne. Notable among them was a devout Catholic who was seriously ill, Count Laferronays, who offered his life for the conversion of the "young Jew." On the same day he entered a church and prayed more than 20 Memorares for this intention, he suffered a heart attack, received the last Sacraments, and died.

On January 20, 1842, as the Baron was meeting to make arrangement for the Count's funeral the next day in the Basilica of St. Andrea delle Fratte when he met Ratisbonne. He asked Ratisbonne to accompany him and wait in the church until he had arranged some matters with the priest in the sacristy. While waiting, Ratisbonne wandered through the church, admiring the beautiful marbles and the various works of art. As he stood before a side altar dedicated to St. Michael the Archangel, Our Blessed Virgin Mary suddenly appeared to him. Standing over the altar, Our Lady wore a crown and a simple long white tunic with a jeweled belt around her waist and blue green mantle draped over her left shoulder. She gazed at him affably; her hands open spreading rays of graces. Her height and elegance gave the impression of a great lady, fully conscious of her own dignity. She transmitted both grandeur and mercy in an atmosphere of great peace. She had some of the characteristics of Our Lady of Graces. Ratisbonne saw this figure and understood that he was before an apparition of the Mother of God. When the Baron came back to the church, he found Ratisbonne on his knees in prayer. This sight moved him to tears. In Ratisbonne's own word: "I was scarcely in the church when a total confusion came over me. When I looked up, it seemed to me that the entire church had been swallowed up in shadow, except one chapel. It was as though all the light was concentrated in that single place. I looked over towards the chapel whence so much light shone, and above the altar was a living figure, tall, majestic, beautiful, and full of mercy. It was the Most Holy Virgin Mary, resembling her figure on the Miraculous Medal. At this sight, I fell on my knees right where I stood. Unable to look up because of the blinding light, I fixed my glance on her hands, and in them, I could read the expression of mercy and pardon. In the presence of the Most Blessed Virgin, even though she did not speak a word to me, I understood the frightful situation I was in, my sins and the beauty of the Catholic Faith." At that moment, he knelt down before her and he was converted.

Returning from the sacristy, the Baron was surprised to see the Jew fervently praying on his knees before the altar of St. Michael the Archangel. He helped his friend to his feet, and Ratisbonne immediately asked to go to a confessor so he could receive Baptism. Eleven days later, on January 31, he received Baptism, Confirmation and his First Communion from the hands of Cardinal Patrizi, the Vicar of the Pope. Eventually, Ratisbonne became a Jesuit priest. Ten years later, he and his brother Theodore, who also had converted from Judaism to Catholicism, founded a religious congregation – the Congregation of the Daughter of Sion, whose mission was to convert Jews. Ratisbonne's conversion had an enormous impact throughout Europe and the Catholic world. He was an influential figure who not only renounced his engagement and worldly possession but also embraced religious life. Obviously, that apparition represented a great benefit for the soul of Ratisbonne. It also represented a benefit for the Catholic Church with the foundation of the Congregation of Sion, with its special mission to work for the conversion of the Jews. This congregation expresses well the Church's position toward the Jews. Her position is not to hate the Jews, but rather to defend herself against their attacks. To the measure that they attack the Church, she defends herself. But above all, she desires their conversion, the eradication of Judaism as a religion, and the entrance of the Jews into the Catholic Church, which is the true continuation of the chosen nation.

All those who enter the Alliance with the two hearts of Jesus and Mary and now promote the communion of reparation and consecration are instruments of the Holy Spirit to unite all the people in the world in Christ Jesus. Through Our Lady of Fatima's message of core care, Jesus and Mary have given us the instrument to save atheistic countries before Christ comes again.

MEDITATION

"The Rosary is a powerful weapon to put the demons to flight and to keep oneself from sin...If you desire peace in your hearts, in your homes, and in your country, assemble each evening to recite the Rosary. Let not even one day pass without saying it, no matter how burdened you may be with many cares and labors." (Pope Pius XI)

PRAYER

Offer your own prayers and intentions to Our Virgin Mary in silence...

We ask this through the most powerful intercession of the Blessed Virgin Mary, in the name of Jesus Christ, Our Lord. Amen.

DAY 27

THE ASSUMPTION OF THE VIRGIN MARY

"And blessed art thou that hast believed, because those things shall be accomplished that were spoken to thee by the Lord.

And Mary said: My soul doth magnify the Lord.

And my spirit hath rejoiced in God my Saviour.

Because he hath regarded the humility of his handmaid; for behold from henceforth all generations shall call me blessed.

Because he that is mighty, hath done great things to me; and holy is his name.

And his mercy is from generation unto generations, to them that fear him. He hath shewed might in his arm: he hath scattered the proud in the conceit of their heart." (Luke 1: 45-51)

When Mary was in Nazareth and Jerusalem, she could only assist her holy family relatives and her friends in Israel, but she could not assist us the modern gentiles who were outside Israel. The Assumption of the Virgin Mary, body and soul, to Heaven is a joyful reminder for all of us baptized Christians that Our Lady can already assist her spiritual children anywhere in the world if only we put our trust in her mercy as the Heavenly Mother of God and Mother of the Church. Like Jesus after resurrection, Mary, with her Assumption into Heaven, body and soul, she is no longer constrained by time and space; she could already be in all places at the same time to assist her children in the Church.

Since the dogma of the Assumption is not directly found in the Scripture but simply in the tradition of the people of God and the Fathers of the Church. It is important to see the Theology of the Assumption used by Pius XII. In his Encyclical *Mediator Dei*, #38, the Pope wrote that "the evidence of the Scripture shows

Mary 'as most intimately joined to her divine Son and as always sharing His lot.' In Romans 6: 4-13, St. Paul assures that through Baptism they are joined to Christ and share His victory over sin. Mary's unique similarity to Christ began with her conception. Since sin it is and its consequent punishment in death and corruption that delay the final triumph of the ordinary Christian, it is implicit that anyone perfectly free from sin, like Christ, would be free from the deferment of the resurrection of the body, as Christ was. Mary is surely an exception to the rule (MD#5), portrayed perhaps (MD#27) in Revelations 12: 1 as the great sign in the heavens, a woman clothed with the sun, the moon under her feet, and her head crowned with 12 stars. That St. John was primarily here describing the Church in ultimate victory is generally agreed, but that he was also describing the personification of the Church in Mary, the eschatological image of the Church, a prototype already enjoying the glory that the Church will eventually share, has been seriously proposed and defended.

However, the most significant evidence, implied in Scripture and specific already in patristic writings, for accepting and understanding something of the mystery of the Assumption, is that of Mary as the New Eve. Three times in his Encyclical Mediator Dei #27, #30, #39, the Holy Father accepted this teaching as an obvious deduction from Scripture and a logical development of tradition. St. Paul reminds us in Romans 5:18-19 that 'as from the offense of the one man the result was unto condemnation to all men, so from the justice of the one the result is unto justification of life to all men. For just us by the disobedience of the one man the many were constituted sinners, so also by the obedience of the one the many will be constituted just." The first Eve proved not to be the 'mother of the living' but rather, in a sense, the mother of the dead, for she led Adam into sin and became his accomplice in bringing all men to the punishment of death and the dominion of Satan. In contrast, Mary, the New Eve, by her obedience to the Annunciation of the angel, brought life to men in having conceived the person of the New Adam and in having united herself to the principal acts of His redemptive mission.

Just as Eve cooperated not only in the original sin but also shared with Adam his subsequent life, parenthood, and the sufferings that were sin's punishment, so Mary cooperated with Christ not only in the role of giving Him birth but also cooperated with Him, evidently in a secondary and unessential – but actually necessary and important – roles, in the significant events of His life, the Presentation, one of His first miracles, the Crucifixion, the Ascension, and, later in the beginnings of His Church at Pentecost. More truly than Eve ever would have been, at Nazareth, at Bethlehem, and at Calvary, Mary became in an ever fuller sense, the mother of all the members of the Mystical Body. Hence as things said of Adam apply also, but proportionately, to Eve, so things said of Christ apply also, but proportionately, to Mary. The author of the Epistle to the Hebrew 2: 14 had said 'that through death Christ might destroy him who had the empire of death, that is, the devil.' Christian intuition, guided by the Holy Spirit, gradually came to see that Mary's share in Christ's victory over sin began with her conception in the state free from all sin (the state in which Eve was created), and ended with her miraculous Assumption (an immunity from death and corruption which Eve enjoyed until the Fall)."

Pope Pius XII repeatedly refers to Mary's being the Mother of God as the theological reason (for Christ's unique love for and union with Mary and) for the Assumption (MD #6, 14, 21, 22, 25), it is like a superlative application of what we read in Sir 3: 11, "His father's honor is a man's glory; disgrace for her children, a mother's shame." The Pope continued, "For Mary was united to all three Persons of the Blessed Trinity in a unique relationship – as privileged daughter, mother, and spouse, privileges that involved her body and soul, that implicated her in extraordinary sufferings and joys" (MD#14). That is why from the earliest times the Church Fathers defended Mary's perpetual virginity as a proof of divinity of her offspring, as evidence of her exemption from painful parturition, which is the punishment for sin (see Gen 3:16), as the effect of a sinlessness that, negatively, preempts her from the curse of death and that, positively, merits for her the immediate contemplation (after this life), in body and soul, of God. Ezekiel 18: 4 teaches us that God's justice would not inflict punishment (pain, death, corruption) on one innocent of the crime (sin) is being punished: "For all lives are mine; the life of the father is like the life of the son, both are mine; only the one who sins shall die." Briefly and simple explanation of the propriety of the Assumption is the fact that Christ loved Mary and united her in His mysteries makes it proper that the woman He had created sinless, that the virgin whom He had chosen for His mother, be, like Him, completely triumphant over death in her Assumption as He had triumphed over sin and death in His Resurrection.

Mary, in her Assumption, but even if Mary was assumed body and soul into heaven, what difference does it make? On November 1st, 1950, Pope Pius XI gave us the answer as he proclaimed in the dogma that "Mary, having completed the course of her earthly life, was assumed body and soul into heavenly glory" (MD#44). From this dogma, came for the following papal teachings that show the importance of the Assumption. Pope Pius XII taught that Mother Mary, who was installed by Jesus before He died on the Cross at Mount Calvary, is the Mother of the Church, and because of her Assumption into heaven, she is more available to all her children, most especially, those who are diabolically harassed, gravely ill, abandoned, and in need of her motherly assistance.

Ted Bundy was one of the worst serial killers in history. On the night of January 15, 1978, at 3:00 am, Bundy murdered two girls in the Chi Omega sorority house at Florida State University – he entered the third room, but fled when he saw a girl clutching a rosary in her hands. Later the girl explained that she had promised her grandmother to pray the rosary every night when she went to bed, even if she fell asleep while praying. Years later, when Bundy was awaiting his execution, he asked for a priest. The priest, Fr. Esper, asked him what happened that night. Bundy said he intended to murder the girl, but "some mysterious power prevented him."

On August 15, 2012, Pope Benedict XVI explained in his homily that "This truth of faith was known by the Tradition of the Church, was affirmed by the Fathers of the Church and was above all a relevant aspect of the devotion to the Mother of Christ. This liturgical element was the driving force that leads to the formulation of this dogma: it is an act of praise and exaltation of the Holy Virgin". This Dogma on Mary's Assumption teaches the importance of fidelity to one's call to holiness, which we are reminded of in Matthew 5: 48 that "Be holy as the heavenly father is holy." Let us remember that every sacrifice that we exert to remain faithful to the call to holiness will be compensated by God. Pope Benedict XVI further explained how the Assumption "appears as an act of praise and exaltation of the Holy Virgin," for her fidelity to Jesus while on earth is now being rewarded with eternal bliss of heaven. The Apostolic Constitution affirms that the Dogma of the Assumption of Mary – body and soul into Heaven is proclaimed for "the honor of her Son... for the increase of the glory of that same august Mother, and for the joy and exultation of the entire Church. Since Mary is God's masterpiece of creation, if she perseveres until the end in doing God's Holy Will, her fidelity reveals also the greatness of God who supplied Mary with all the heavenly graces that shone forth during her life on earth. Pope Benedict XVI also explained how Mary, herself prophetically pronounces a few words that orientate us in this perspective. She says: "For behold, henceforth all generations will call me blessed" (Luke 1:48). These words of the *Magnificat,* recorded by St. Luke, indicate that praising the Blessed Virgin, Mother of God, ultimately united to Christ her Son, regard the Church of all ages and of all places.

But why is Mary glorified by her Assumption into Heaven? St Luke, as we have heard, sees the roots of the exaltation and praise of Mary in Elizabeth's words: "Blessed is she who believed" (Luke 1:45). And the *Magnificat*, this canticle to God, alive and active in history is a hymn of faith and love, which springs from the heart of the Virgin. She lived with exemplary fidelity and kept in the inmost depths of her heart the words of God to his people, the promises he made to Abraham, Isaac and Jacob, making them the content of her prayer: the Word of God in the *Magnificat* became the word of Mary, the lamp for her journey, thus preparing her to receive even in her womb the Word of God made flesh.

But now let us ask ourselves: how does the Assumption of Mary help our journey? The first answer Pope Benedict XVI is: in the Assumption we see that in God there is room for man, God himself is the house with many rooms of which Jesus speaks (see John 14:2); God is man's home, in God there is God's space. And Mary, by uniting herself, united to God, does not distance herself from us. She does not go to an unknown galaxy, but whoever approaches God comes closer, for God is close to us all; and Mary, united to God, shares in the presence of God, is so close to us, to each one of us. St. Gregory the Great says that the heart of St. Benedict expanded so much that all creation could enter it. This is even truer of Mary: Mary, totally united to God, has a heart so big that all creation can enter this heart, and the ex-votos in every part of the earth show it.

Let us remember that Mary is close, she can hear us, she can help us, and she is close to every one of us. In God, there is room for man and God is close, and Mary, united to God, is very close; she has a heart as great as the heart of God.

But there is also another aspect: in God not only is there room for man; in man there is room for God. This too we see in Mary, the Holy Ark who bears the presence of God. In us there is space for God and this presence of God in us, so important for bringing light to the world with all its sadness, with its problems.

Let's take the story of Our Lady speaks to Russia on October 13, 1960. Most of us remember the time when Nikita Khrushchev visited the United Nations in October, 1960 and boasted that "they would bury us" – would annihilate us! And to emphasize his boasting, Khrushchev took off his shoe and pounded the desk before the horrified world assembly. This was no idle boast. Khrushchev knew that his scientists had completed their work on a nuclear missile and had planned to present it to him on

November, 1960, during the 43rd anniversary of the Bolshevik Revolution. But here's what happened. Pope John the XXIII had opened and read the third secret of Fatima given the Sister Lucia. He authorized the bishop of Leiria (Fatima) to write to all the bishops of the world, inviting them to join with the pilgrims of Fatima on the night of October 12-13, 1960, in prayer and penance for Russia's conversion and consequent world peace. On the night of October 12-13, about a million pilgrims spent the night outdoors in the Cova de Iria at Fatima in praying the Rosary and doing penance before the Blessed Sacrament. Countless people went to Confession. They prayed and watched despite a penetrating rain which chilled them to the bone. At the same time, at least 300 dioceses throughout the world joined with them. Pope John XXIII sent a special blessing to all taking part in this unprecedented night of reparation. And as the reparation vigils went on, Khrushchev suddenly pulled up stakes and enplaned in all haste for Moscow, cancelling all subsequent engagement, Why? Marshall Nedelin, the best minds in Russia on nuclear energy and several government officials were present for the final testing of the missile that was going to be presented to Khrushchev. When countdown was completed, the missile, for some reason or other, did not leave the launch pad. After 15 or 20 minutes, Nedelin and all the others came out of the shelter. When they did, the missile exploded killing over 300 people. This set back Russia's nuclear program for 20 years, prevented all-out atomic warfare, the burying of the U.S.—and this happened on the night when the whole Catholic world was on its knees before the Blessed Sacrament, gathered at the feet of our Rosary Queen in Fatima. Our Lady does not want nuclear war.

Today, there is much discussion about the better world that awaits us, a better world that we all hope for. If and when this better world comes, we do not know. All we know is that a world which distances itself from God does not become better, but instead it becomes worse. Only God's presence can guarantee a better world. Let us leave it at that. Pope Benedict XVI said: "One thing, one hope is certain: God expects us, waits for us, we do not go out into a void, and we are expected. God is expecting us and ongoing to that other world we find the goodness of Mother Mary, we find our loved ones, and we find eternal love. God is waiting for us: this is our great joy and the great hope that is born from this Feast. Mary visits us, and she is the joy of our life and joy is hope."

MEDITATION

"Mary is the dawn and the splendor of the Church triumphant; she is the consolation and the hope of the people still on the journey" (Pope Benedict XVI).

PRAYER

O Blessed Mother Mary assumed into Heaven, now that both your body and soul are in heaven. You can make yourself available to all your children who call on you for help. It's true that many will try to give a helping hand in times of great necessities, your help as the Mother of God weighs more than all our charitable works. With your most powerful intercession of Blessed Virgin Mary, we are confident that you will grant us your peace and joy in serving God and neighbor. We ask this through Christ, Our lord. Amen.

DAY 28

MARY, QUEEN OF MERCY

"And a great sign appeared in heaven: A woman clothed with the sun, and the moon under her feet, and on her head a crown of twelve stars." (Revelation 12:1)

We reflect on how Mary, Virgin without stain, has made up for the fall of Eve. She is the daughter of God, Mother of God, and spouse of God who has crushed the head of the hell's serpent with her immaculate heal. The Father and the Son and the Holy Spirit have crowned her with the rightful empress of the universe. St. Josemaria Escriva wrote about Mary: "And the Angels render homage unto her as her subjects... and the patriarchs and the prophets and the Apostles... and the martyrs and the confessors and the virgins and all the saints... and all sinners and you and I." What is the relevance of the queenship of Mary? St. Alphonsus de Liguori wrote in the "Glories of Mary" as Queen of all creatures: "Mary is a mild and merciful queen, desiring the good of us poor sinners."

Why does the Church call Mary the "queen of mercy?" Saint Bernard answers that it is because we believe that Mary opens up the vaults of God's mercy to anyone she likes, when she likes, and as she likes. There is not a sinner, he adds, no matter how wicked, who is lost as long as Mary protects him.

One of the stories in the book the "Glories of Mary" show how merciful is the heart of the Blessed Mother. There was a prostitute named Anna who was censored publicly by her parish priest for refusing to amend her life, even the convent where Anna sought refuge refused to accept her. She found herself outside the parish alone, dejected, and condemned in isolation. She had one recourse that had always given her consolation in the midst of her afflictions and misery. She would always call on Mary, the Queen of Mercy and compassion. Anna did one act of piety faithfully. She would pray the Rosary daily with all her heart, begging God for mercy. It was her only recourse as the parish priest would no longer absolve her of her sins, and she remained ostracized by parishioners, and even the sisters. She became very sick and died all alone in her little small shop outside of the parish. Three days after her death, she appeared to St. Elizabeth of St. Augustine, the superior of the convent, and told her that because she faithfully prayed the Rosary every day, she had been saved from damnation by Mary. However, she was in purgatory and asked for fifty Masses to be saved. St. Elizabeth sent petitions to celebrate fifty Masses to priests in town. After a month, Anna appeared to her again from heaven in bright white clothes to thank her for the Masses she offered on her behalf.

St. Bernardin of Siena said: "Mary, from her 'Fiat' to God the Father at the Annunciation, was already the Queen of Heaven, earth, and under the earth.

In his February 11, 2018 Decree on "Mary, the Mother of the Church," Pope Francis said: "the Angel Gabriel at the Annunciation already called her 'Hail Mary, full of grace, the Lord is with thee, blessed art thou among women.' Because being the Mother of God, she would also be the Mother of the Church." Therefore, all creatures are subject to her. But this title never took effect in Mary until Jesus spoke at the foot of the Cross on Mount Calvary as His last will and testament. Before He died, Jesus said to His disciple John who represented all disciples and believers of Jesus in the future: "*Woman, behold thy son. And to the disciple He loved: Behold, thy mother. And from that hour, the disciple took her to his own*" (John 19: 25-27).

As Mother, the Queen of Mercy, she can remove all miseries from the creatures under her reign. All we need to do is to invoke Mary, the Queen for help and she will be there to assist us. There is an example of this power during the visit of the International Centennial Pilgrim Image of Our Lady of Fatima to South Florida in July, 2017. A Vietnamese woman related the story of her brother's conversion from Marxist Atheism to Catholic faith after the visit of the Centennial Image. During the visit, the woman prayed to the Blessed Mother for the conversion of her brother to Catholicism. Coming from a communist country and although baptized as a Catholic, her brother never renounced his belief in Marxist Atheism. The woman, a devout Catholic, invited her brother to spend a vacation with her in Florida where she then lived. It was during this time too, the Centennial Pilgrim Image of Our Lady of Fatima was visiting their parish, and families were being imposed with the brown scapular. She asked the parish priest for an extra scapular for her fallen away brother. As soon as her brother received the scapular as a gift from the Queen of Peace, she said she felt Mother Mary touch his heart deeply. Right there and then, he went to church and attended the community preparation vigil which lasted until one o'clock in the morning. Her brother went to confession, renounced Marxist Atheism and renewed his baptismal promises. Since then, he frequently goes to church, attends the Holy Sacrifice of the Mass, adores the Blessed Sacrament, and praise the holy Rosary daily with his sister.

St. Thomas Aquinas said: "There are four mysteries that beseech mankind because of sin: First, suffering due to human miseries; Second, suffering due to catastrophe tribulation or disaster; Third, suffering caused by persecution from religion, culture, language, nationality, or other reasons; Fourth, suffering due to mortal sin." While only God can remove the suffering from mortal sin, still, through Mary's intercession. Jesus makes sure that the repentant client of Mary will have the Sacrament of Baptism or Confession, necessary for salvation. Mary's queenship has certain essential elements. St. Albert relates how she is compassionate making provisions for the poor. In this way, Mary differs greatly from the tyrannical severity and rigor of an empress. St. Alphonsus Liguori writes that Mary, as Queen, comforts us wretched creatures.

The anointing of a King with oil symbolizes mercy, which

denotes that the King should above all things cherish thoughts of kindness and goodness towards his subjects as he reigns. A King occupies himself with works of mercy, but not to neglect of justice towards the guilty, when it is required. Not so Mary, who, although queen, is not queen of justice, intent upon the punishment of the guilty, but queen of mercy, solely intent upon compassion and pardon for sinners. Accordingly, the Church clearly requires us all to make recourse to her as Queen of Mercy. Mary, the Queen, is the manifestation of God's Kingdom of mercy.

The High Chancellor of Paris, John Gerson, meditating on the words of David, as accounted in the book the Glories of Mary, said: "These two things have I heard, that power belongs to God, and mercy to thee, O Lord." The Kingdom of God consisting of justice and mercy, the Lord God has divided it: He has reserved the Kingdom of justice for Himself in our particular and general judgment, but He has shared the Kingdom of Mercy to Mary, ordaining that all mercies which are dispensed to men should pass through the hands of Mary, and should be bestowed according to her good pleasure. In the book the Glories of Mary, St. Thomas Aquinas confirms John Gerson's reflection by teaching in his preface to the Canonical Epistles that the Holy Virgin, Queen of Mercy, when she conceived the divine Word in her womb, she obtained half of the Kingdom of God by becoming Queen of Mercy, and Jesus remaining the King of Justice. St. Bonaventure happily repeats the same traditional teaching by saying: "Give to the king thy judgment, Oh God, and to the mother thy mercy." Ernest, Archbishop of Prague, says, "that the eternal Father in heaven has given to the Son the office of judging and punishing, and to the mother the office of compassionating and relieving the wretched." Again, in the Glories of Mary, St. Alphonsus Ligouri said: "The Prophet David predicted that God himself, if I may thus express it, would consecrate Mary queen of mercy, anointing her with the oil of gladness, in order that all of us miserable children of Adam might rejoice in the thought of having in heaven that great queen of mercy, so full of the unction of mercy and pity for us; as St. Bonaventure says: 'Oh Mary, so full of the unction of mercy and the oil of pity, that God has anointed thee with the oil of gladness.'"

St. Alberlus Magnus said while reflecting on the Book of Esther, chapter 4: "that in the reign of King Assuerus, there went forth, throughout his kingdom, a decree commanding the death of all the Jews." Then Mordochai, who was one of the condemned, committed their cause to Esther, the Queen, that she might intercede with the king to obtain the revocation of the sentence. At first, Esther refused to take upon herself this office, fearing that it would excite the anger of the king more. But Mordochai rebuked her, and bade her remember that she must not think of saving herself alone, as the Lord had placed her up on the throne to obtain salvation for all the Jews: "Think not that you may save your life only, because you are in the king's house, more than all the Jews." Thus we poor sinners might also say to our Queen Mary, if she were ever reluctant to intercede with God for our deliverance from the just punishment of our sins. Assuerus, when he saw Esther before him, affectionately inquired of her what she had come to ask of him: "What is your petition?" Then the Queen answered, "If I have found favor in your sight, oh King, give me my people for which I request." Assuerus heard her, and immediately ordered the sentence to be revoked. Now, if king Assuerus granted to Esther the salvation of the Jews, because he loved her, will not God graciously listen to Mary, in his boundless love for her, when she prays to him for those poor sinners who recommend themselves to her, she would say to him: "If I have found favor in your sight, oh King, my King and my God, if I have ever found favor with Thee (the divine mother knows well that she is the Blessed, the fortunate, the only one of the children of men who found the grace lost by man; she knows that she is the beloved of her Lord, more beloved than all the saints and angels united), give me my people for which I request." Because of this, she is our greatest and our powerful intercession to her Beloved Son. "If you love me," she prays to him, "give me, oh my Lord, these sinners, in whom behalf, I entreat you." Is it possible that God will not graciously hear her? St. Alphonsus relates in the Glories of Mary that "Every prayer of Mary is as a law established by our Lord, that mercy shall be exercised towards those for whom Mary intercedes."

Some may wonder what the queenship of Mary is. It is our tradition that after Mary assumed into Heaven, body and soul, no sooner was she also decreed by God the Father as Queen of Heaven and earth. Mary is also the Queen of all creatures in the universe. As we know that in any monarchy, the queen has so much influence in the kingdom. For example, Queen Mary or Queen Elizabeth in England, so too, Mary, being the Queen of all creatures in the universe, has also a great influence towards them. Others may ask: How? When? And why is it so? St. Athanasius explains that: "If the Son is the King of kings, so Mother Mary must necessarily be considered and entitled Queen." St. Bernardin said, "From the moment that Mary consented to become the mother of God at the Annunciation, she merited the title of queen of the world and of all creatures." The saint also relates that, if Jesus is the king of the whole world, Mary is also queen of the whole world: therefore, all creatures who serve God ought to serve Mary; for all angels and men, and all things that are in heaven and on earth being subject to the dominion of God, are also subject to the dominion of the glorious Virgin. St. Arnold, abbot, says: "If the flesh of Mary was the flesh of Jesus, how can the mother be separated from the Son in his kingdom? Hence it follows that the regal glory must not only be considered as common to the mother and the Son, but even the same." Hence Guerric, abbot, tells us Mary securely the queen of heaven, on earth and under the earth, since everything is created by God and belonging to Jesus, the only begotten Son of God, being the mother of the King of the world, the kingdom and power over all creatures is due to Mary as queen.

There is a remarkable miracle through the intercession of Mary in the Heroic History of the Small Mediterranean Town. At first glance, the town of Mosta in Malta appears to be nothing but an average sized market town in the middle of the island with shops and roads and people going to work and school. But upon a closer look, there are two stunning features that draw visitors to Mosta time after time – the magnificent 19th century domed church at its center and the story of the 1942 miracle of Mary the queen of heaven, which saved not only the magnificent church but most importantly the lives of the people in Mosta. In 1942, as World War II spread over Europe, the Allied forces led by Great Britain, and the Axis forces led by Germany and Italy, fought hard over the island of Malta, for the island nation holds a strategic geographical location between Europe, North Africa, and the Middle East. Hitler and the Axis forces with their allies surrounded the island of Malta, threatening to wipe out all its people, battleships, submarines, fighter planes, and bomber planes dangerously encircled the tiny island. People heard explosions from machine guns and grenades everywhere throughout the night. The dead lay in the streets and in open marketplaces. On April 9, 1942, a congregation of over 300 people was inside the church, praying continuously the Rosary before exposed Blessed Sacrament. They begged the Queen of Heaven and Mother of Mercy for protection from harm. Four bomber planes attacked the church, each carrying a bomb that weighed one thousand pounds. Enemy planes launched an aerial attack and aimed directly at the church in the center of Mosta. Several bombs were dropped; one of the enemy bombs came through the roof of the Mosta church's dome and bounced off two of the interior walls before landing inside the church. In the panic, several people died to protect themselves from danger, fearing the bomb would ignite and explode inside the church. However, they refused to stop praying the Rosary; some courageous people even remain kneeling to pray the Rosary louder. The Queen of Heaven with her army of angels was already present to protect her children. Miraculously, the bomb did not explode. This miracle was attributed to Mary, the Queen of Mercy, and all because of the unfading faith of the people of Malta to Mary, which is expressed in their continuous daily Rosary. This miracle is truly a lesson that Mary will always keep her word which she gave St. Dominic. Some of these promises were fulfilled in the miracle of

Mosta, Malta. First, whoever shall faithfully serve the Blessed Mother by the recitation of the Rosary shall receive signal graces or miracles. Second, the Blessed Mother promises to give her special protection and the greatest graces to all those who shall recite the Rosary. Third, whosoever shall recite the Rosary devoutly and applying himself to the consideration of his sacred mysteries shall never be conquered by misfortune. God will not chastise him in His justice. He will not perish by an unprovided death, if he be just he shall remain in the grace of God and become worthy of eternal life.

People have been praying the Rosary daily in the church of Mosta, even before the bombs fell. During March and April of 1942, as the Axis forces continually build up their aggressive forces in the Mediterranean Sea around Malta, the Blessed Mother faithfully protected her children when the bombs were dropped on and near the church. No one was hurt. The two other bombs failed to detonate in the crowded marketplace. The fourth bomb landed in the nearby field. There were no casualties from any of the four bombs. These miracles strengthened the resolve and faith of the Maltese people to fully trust in God and their Heavenly Mother. Ultimately, with the grace of God and the strong Marian spirit of the Maltese people, the tide turned in favor of the Allied forces that eventually defeated the Axis forces. More Masses and Rosaries were offered in thanksgiving to the Blessed Virgin Mary for protecting her subjects under the Kingdom of God. She is truly a Mother, always interceding for her subjects.

The lesson we learned from this story is we should never despair. If we have devotion to Our Lady, the Queen of Heaven, there is nothing she cannot obtain. Praying the Rosary daily is what Mary wants from her children, and in return, she will be our protective heavenly Queen in moments of wars or calamities. Even when the verdict is already given by Jesus for the condemnation of the sinner, like in the case of the prostitute and the dangerous threat against the island of Malta, with Mary's intercession, Jesus could still reverse the decision. Her children, the ordinary people, must give faith and believe that their mother will never fail them. If they persevere to remain faithful in praying to her, praying her Rosary.

MEDITATION

"The faithful children of the Rosary shall merit a high degree of glory in heaven." St. Dominic

"The fervent prayer of the 'Hail Mary' increases the degree of glory in Heaven. Had I known this truth earlier, I would have prayed more Rosaries when I was on earth." St. Teresa of Avila

PRAYER

Hail Holy Queen, Mother of Mercy, I know that thou, being queen of the universe, art also my queen; and I, in a more especial manner, would dedicate myself to thy service; that thou mayest dispose of me as seemeth best to thee. Therefore I say to thee with St. Bonaventure, Oh, Lady, I submit myself to thy control, that thou mayest rule and govern me entirely. Do not leave me to myself. Rule me, oh my queen, and do not leave me to myself. Command me, employ me as thou wilt, and punish me if I do not obey thee, for very salutary will be the punishments that come from thy hand. I would esteem it a greater thing to be thy servant than Lord of the whole earth. Thine I am, save me! Accept me, oh Mary, for thy own and attend to my salvation, as I am thine own. I no longer will be my own, I give myself to thee. And if hitherto I have so poorly served thee, having lost so many good occasions of honoring thee, for the time to come I will unite myself to thy most loving and most faithful servants. No one from this time henceforth shall surpass me in honoring and loving thee, my most lovely queen. This I promise, and I hope to perform with thy assistance. Amen.

DAY 29

THE HUMILITY OF MARY

"And Mary said: My soul doth magnify the Lord. And my spirit hath rejoiced in God my Saviour." (Luke 1: 46-47)

We have reason to give prayerful reflection to the Magnificat. The Magnificat is Mary's perfect act of humility, and a profound humble adoration of a great God: "My soul proclaims the greatness of the Lord, for he has looked with favor on his lowly servant." The Magnificat reveals to us the humble heart of Mary expressed in a beautiful prayer. It is a prayer inspired by the Holy Spirit to Mary who was then carrying the Divine Child in her womb. This is the longest discourse recorded of Mary in the Scripture. This prayer has been part of the Church's liturgy since the first centuries. It has been recited or sung daily by ancient monks and hermits and other Religious who have consecrated themselves to God. Father John Harden, S.J. once said that "The Magnificat is indeed the prayer of consecrated souls and all clients of Mary." Humility is defined as a supernatural virtue, by which a person has a lowly opinion of himself, and willingly submits himself to God and to others for God's sake considering his own defects. St. Bernard defines it as "A virtue, by which a man knowing himself as he truly, is abases himself." St. Thomas also said: "The virtue of humility consists in keeping oneself within one's own bounds, not reaching out the things above one, but submitting to one's superior." St. Bernard tells us that "Humility is the foundation of all virtues, without it, any other virtues will collapse." After Mary, our Queen and Advocate, rescues a soul from Lucifer and unites a soul to God, she wishes the soul to imitate her virtues, the foremost being her humility. St.

Thomas Aquinas notes: "Whereas saints excelled in one or two particular virtues, the Blessed Virgin Mary, because of her humility excelled in all virtues."

Humility, which is necessary for salvation, is unknown in the world. Then Jesus came to earth to teach us how we can imitate Him in His virtue: "Learn from Me because I am meek and humble of heart." Mary is the perfect reflection of the virtues of Jesus. St. Teresa of Avila said: "Mary knew she never offended God. She received greater graces from God than all creatures, but rather than being proud of them, the Virgin Mary instead the infinite greatness and goodness of her God, and at once, her own nothingness. Therefore, she humiliates herself as revealed in the Canticles: "Do not consider me that I am brown, because the sun hath altered my colour" (Song of Solomon 1:6). And therefore, says St. Bernardine, "no creature in the world has been more exalted, because no creature has ever humbled herself more than Mary."

Mary, in the Gospel, manifested her act of humility by concealing the extraordinary gifts of heaven, such as being Mother of God. St. Joseph did not even know she was made the Mother of God, although it seemed necessary for Mary to reveal it to him in order to remove his suspicion when he saw her pregnant. St. Joseph, ignorant of the mystery, in order to free himself from perplexity, and without putting Mary to shame, planned to put her away privately. Without an order from God, Mary did not reveal anything to St. Joseph, instead, God sent his angel to tell him that his spouse's pregnancy was caused by the power of the Holy Spirit. And if the angel had not revealed to him that his spouse was pregnant by the operation of the Holy Spirit, he would really have left her. Moreover, a humble soul also refuses praise, and gives it all to God. Behold, Mary is disturbed at hearing herself praised by St. Gabriel.

St. Alphonsus wrote that when St. Elizabeth called the Virgin Mary, "Blessed art thou among women... Mary returned all these praises to God, answering with humble Magnificat: My soul doth magnify the Lord, as if Mary had said: You praise me, oh Elizabeth, but I praise the Lord, to whom alone honor is due; you wonder that I come to you, and I wonder at the divine goodness in which alone my spirit exults. And my spirit hath rejoiced in God my Saviour. You praise me because I have believed; I praise my God because He has wished to exalt my nothingness; because He hath regarded the humility of His handmaid."

St. Thomas Aquinas said that "The greatest sin is pride. Pride is an inordinate esteem of oneself. It is inordinate because it is contrary to truth. It is essentially an act or disposition of the will desiring to be considered better than a person really is. Pride may be expressed in different ways: by taking personal credit for gifts or possessions, as if they had not been received from God; by glorifying in achievements, as if they were not primarily the result of divine goodness and grace; by minimizing one's defects or claiming qualities that are not actually possessed; by holding oneself superior to others or disdaining them because they lack what the proud person has; by magnifying the defects of others or dwelling on them."

A prime example of pride can be found in Peter Shaffer's Play, Amadeus. It is a portrait of the composer of moderate ability Antonio Salieri who yearned after the kind of admiration deserving only of a truly great composer. Salieri recognized the greatness of a young Wolfgang Amadeus Mozart, but realized that he could never imitate or equal him, he plotted to murder Mozart. But not before he extracted from him the glorious Requiem, he would then perform this composition at Mozart's funeral as his own creation, and when, at last, the glory that is prized so ardently craved. However, Salieri's plans went all wrong; he suffered a mental and emotional breakdown and was sent to an asylum, where he would go around in his wheelchair forgiving his fellow inmates of the sin of mediocrity. Even in his madness, he retained his pride though it was given a different form of expression. This time, he presumed to have the power to forgive sins reserved only to God for a condition that only he imagines to be a sin.

According to St. Thomas Aquinas, "Humility is truth and

justice." It is in the proper connection between these two things of truth and justice against deceit and injustice, which makes a human act humble or proud. An act against truth is when one excels in a gift he stole from others. For example, in the story, Salieri stole the Requiem from Mozart and claim it was his own in order to earn fame. This is pride. When St. Elizabeth proclaimed Mary to be "blessed among women...," immediately, Mary sung the Magnificat to praise God in her nothingness: "My soul proclaims the greatness of the Lord, for He has looked on his servant in her nothingness." This is humility. But humility is also justice. A parent can be proud of his child when his child's life conforms to the standard of moral excellence. For example, a person can be justly proud over the fact that he is a Catholic, proud over his family, his country, or his neighborhood. The key term here is justified.

According to St. Alphonsus Ligouri, we can deduce the following lessons from Mary's life:

First, be careful never to boast of anything. Any virtue we possess is a gift of God. Therefore, we should not boast of something that belongs to God lest we steal the glory that belongs to God alone. Whenever St. Teresa of Avila performed a good work or saw an act of virtue performed by others, she immediately praised God and referred the whole work to God as the author. The graces God bestows on us should lead to twofold actions: 1) Humility in which we draw the line between what belongs to God and what belongs to us; 2) Gratitude to thank God for the gifts He bestows on us and worthy do we are.

Second, never trust your own strength. Trusting in one's own strength leads to temptation. Remember how St. Peter protested that not even that would induce him to deny his Master, but because he trusted in himself. St. Peter having no sooner entered the house of the high priest, denied Jesus Christ three times. Therefore, never trust in your own resolutions or in your own dispositions, rather place all your trust in God alone. St. Paul said: *"I can do all things in him who strengthens me"* (Philippians 4:13). If we cast away all self-confidence and place all our hopes in the Lord, we will do great things for God. Prophet Isaiah said that "He that hopes in the Lord shall renew their strength (see Isaiah 40:31). St. Joseph Calasanz also said: "He who seeks to be an instrument of God, should seek to be the lowest of all." We remember the example of St. Catherine of Siena, who when was tempted to vainglory, made an act of humility by saying: "I am nothing, good for nothing, worth nothing; all good things belong to God, and therefore, all glory praise, honor, worship, and adoration are due to God alone." When she was tempted to despair, the saint would make an act of confidence in God by saying: "God is my strength, my fortress, my stronghold." When the devil would intimidate her, saying that she does not know how to attack him, the saint make an act of abandonment to God by saying: "In you, oh Lord, I place all my hopes." Therefore, when Satan tells you that you are not in danger of falling into sin, you must tremble. Remember that if God were to ever abandon us, even for just a moment, we would be lost.

Third, Should you be unfortunate as to commit a fault, take care not to give way to diffidence or lack of confidence, by either: 1) not caring anymore because your conscience is dead; 2) by getting discouraged because you tried so hard and did not succeed in overcoming the sin. To overcome the first type of diffidence, you would need to avail of deliverance or exorcism prayer and a good confession. To overcome the second type of diffidence, humble yourself, repent, and with a stronger sense of your own weakness, throw yourself into the arms of the Lord. Some people would bend their heads on the wall out of anger for having committed the same fault, but this is pride. When we get angry after a fall, it draws us to despair, because we cannot seem to rise above our weaknesses. This is merely the devil's ploy to pull us down in despair after we have advanced in virtue. When the soul is sustained, and one washes it with a good Confession, the soul becomes cleaner than before it was sustained. How? It is because the soul that commits the fault, after being purified by repentance, made more pleasing in the eyes of God than it was before its transgression. To teach them to distrust themselves and to confide only in God, God permits His servants, particularly those who are not well granted in humility to fall into some defects. When you commit a fault, you endeavor to repair it immediately by an act of love or an act of sorrow; and resolve to amend and redouble your confidence in God. St. Catherine of Genoa prayed the following prayer every time she fell after trying so hard in virtue: "Lord, this is the fruit of my garden. If you do not protect me, I shall be guilty or be still more grievous offenses. But I shall try to avoid this fault in the future, and with the aid of Your grace, I hope to keep this resolution."

Fourth, Should you ever see another commit some grievous sins, take care not to indulge in pride or to be surprised at her fall. Be scandal proof. When someone falls, pity his misfortune and trembling for yourself, say the words of David: *"Unless the Lord had been my helper, my soul had almost dwelt in hell"* (Psalm 93:17). Never think that you are exempted from falling into the same sins or weaknesses that others do. For, otherwise, the Lord will allow that you do, just that, to teach you a good lesson on humility. For example, St. John Cassian narrated that a certain young monk, being molested by a violent temptation to impurity, sought the advice of an aged father who was scandalized. In punishment for his pride, the Almighty permitted the aged monk to be assailed by the spirit of impurity to such a degree that he ran like a madman throughout the monastery. In correcting sinners, we should not treat them with contempt. Otherwise, who knows God allows us to fall into the very same sin, and our situation turns out to be worse than those we correct. *"Before we correct others, we should consider ourselves as miserable and as liable to sin as our fallen brothers"* (Galatians 6:1).

Fifth, consider yourself the greatest sinner of all on this earth. They, who are truly humble because they are most perfectly enlightened by God, possess the most perfect knowledge, not only of divine perfections, but also of their own miseries and sins. Hence, notwithstanding their extraordinary sanctity, the saints, not in the language of exaggeration, but in the sincerity of their souls, called themselves the greatest sinners in the world. St. Francis of Assisi called himself the worst of all sinners. St. Thomas of Villanova was kept in a state of continual fear and trembling by the thought of the account he was one day to render to God of his life; which, through full of virtue, appeared to him very wicked. St. Gertrude considered it a miracle that the earth did not open under her feet and swallowed her up alive, in punishment of her sins. St. Paul, the first hermit, continually exclaimed: "Woe to me, a sinner, who am unworthy to bear the name of a monk." St. Mary of Avila mentioned of a great saint who besought the Lord to make known to her the state of her soul. Her prayer was heard, when she saw her soul after committing venial sins, she cried with horror: "For mercy's sake, oh God, take away from before my eyes the representation of this monster!"

Sixth: Beware, never to prefer yourself to anyone. To steam yourself better than others, is abundantly sufficient to make you the worst of all others. "You have despised; you have become worse than others." To entertain a high opinion of your own gifts, is enough to deprive yourself of all merit. Humility consists principally in a sincere conviction that we deserve only reproach and chastisement. If, by preferring yourself to others, you have abused the gifts and graces which God has conferred upon you, they will only serve for your greater condemnation at the hour of judgment. But it is not enough to abstain from preferring yourself to anyone; it is, moreover, necessary to consider yourself the last and the worst of all your sisters in religion. Why? First, because in yourself you see with certainty so many sins; but the sins of others you know not, and their secret virtues, which are hidden from your eyes, may render them very dear in the sight of God. Second, with all the helps and graces that God has given you, you should be a saint by now! Had they been given to an unbeliever, he would have become an angel by now, and still you are so miserable and full of defects. Third, your ingratitude should be sufficient to make you always regard yourself as a fit object of scorn to the whole Community: for, as St. Thomas Aquinas teaches, the malice of sin increases in proportion to the ingratitude of the sinner. One of your sins, therefore, may be more grievous in the sight of God than a hundred sins of another less favored than you have been.

Seventh: lesson on humility. We ought to be inspired by the humility of Mary who has so many titles yet she never spoke about them. Her sense of unworthiness should inspire all of us, her spiritual children, to follow her. We may think that we had received all imaginable insults, and were confined in the bottom of hell, under the feet of all the damned, in humility, we should reflect that all of these would be but little in comparison with what we truly deserve as ungrateful servants of the Lord. From the bottomless abyss of our own miseries, we should continually cry out, with holy David: "Incline unto my aid, O God; O Lord, make haste to help me" (Psalm 66:1). St. Bernard says: "In the soul no humiliation, however great, is to be feared; but the least elation is to be regarded with horror." Yes, for the smallest degree of arrogance may lead us into every evil.

The following story will shows us the greatness of humility:

In 1746, France Duke of d'Anville sailed for New England, commanding the most powerful fleet of the time, consisting of 70 ships with 13,000 troops. His mission was to recapture Louisburg, Nova Scotia, Canada, and to destroy everything from Boston to New York, all the way to Georgia. The Massachusetts Governor William Shirley, a very humble and Marian man, who upon learning of this invasion plan, knelt in church before the altar and in front of the statue of the Virgin Mary, acknowledged his helplessness and unpreparedness to defend the state of Massachusetts. He repeated Mary's response to the angel Gabriel: "I am the slave of the Lord, let this be done unto me according to Thy word." Then he told the Virgin Mary: "Mother, your humility obtained everything from God, because it is written in James 4:6, 'God loves the humble but hates the proud.' I am nobody. Who am I to defend this State? Please intercede for me, because before your humility, I am the proudest and dirtiest man in this country. I am nothing, and who could listen to me in heaven in my desperate need? No one, because I'm so proud, so I beg of you, O

Lady, to intercede for me." Then William Shirley prayed the Rosary together with his staff and the parish priest of the area. Afterwards, he called on all the citizens of Massachusetts to pray the Rosary and fasting. He declared a Day of Prayer and Fasting on October 16, 1746. So that all might pray the Rosary for deliverance from France's most powerful navy which was about to invade them. Everyone responded generously to the Governor's request. In Boston's Old South Meeting House, Father Thomas Prince prayed the Rosary together with his parishioners, with the following intentions: "Send Thy tempest, Lord, upon the water...scatter the ships of our tormentors!" Historian Catherine Drinker Bowen related that with the prayers of Governor William Shirley and Father Thomas Prince and his parishioners finished praying, the sky darkened, winds shrieked, and church bells rang "a wild, uneven sound...though no man was in the steeple." Suddenly, a hurricane sank and scattered the entire French fleet. With 4,000 sick and 2,000 dead, including the Duke of d'Anville, Vice-Admiral d'Estournelle threw himself on his sword. Some years later, Henry Wadsworth Longfellow wrote in his Ballad of how the French fleet suffered the most humiliating defeat brought on by the power of the Rosary: "Admiral d'Anville had sworn by cross and crown, to ravage with fire and steal our helpless Boston Town... From mouth to mouth spread tidings of dismay, I stood in the Old South saying humbly: 'Let us pray!' Like a potter's vessel broke, the great ships of the line were carried away as smoke or sank in the brine."

We can see that God truly exalts the humble. Mary's subject humility is the reason why she always obtains what she requests from Jesus, her Son. It was truly God who wrought the unalterable damage to the proud French navy. However, it was Mary who obtained this favor from God by the humble praying of the Rosary by Governor Shirley and Father Prince. This is why after the Battle of Lepanto, St. Pius V concluded that "the Rosary is more powerful than any powerful armada in the world."

MEDITATION

"You shall obtain all you ask of me by the recitation of the

Rosary." Blessed Alan de la Roche

PRAYER

Mother of Jesus and Mother of God, teach us something of your quiet peacefulness and childlike confidence in your Son. Help us to trust Him, especially when things seem to go wrong. Help us to believe in Him as you did, that the promises He makes to us He will fulfill. Help us never to worry or be sad but always rejoice like you, in God, your Savior and ours, your beloved Son and our dearest Lord. Amen.

DAY 30

THE VISITATION OF MARY

"And Mary rising up in those days, went into the hill country with haste into a city of Juda. And she entered into the house of Zachary, and saluted Elizabeth. And it came to pass, that when Elizabeth heard the salutation of Mary, the infant leaped in her womb. And Elizabeth was filled with the Holy Ghost: And she cried out with a loud voice, and said: Blessed art thou among women, and blessed is the fruit of thy womb. And whence is this to me, that the mother of my Lord should come to me? For behold as soon as the voice of thy salutation sounded in my ears, the infant in my womb leaped for joy." (Luke 1: 39-44)

What importance do we attach to the Feast of Mary's Visitation to St. Elizabeth? This Feast renews our missionary zeal of charity with joy, a disposition very much needed today to evangelize the secularized world, says the Holy Father.

As we meditate today on the Visitation of Mary to her cousin Elizabeth, we can ask ourselves that what prompted the celebration of the Feast of Mary's Visitation to Elizabeth.

On May 31, 2004, at Lourdes Grotto in the Vatican Gardens, Pope John Paul II taught us that "this Feast of the Visitation reminds us of the breath of the Holy Spirit that impels Mary and with her, the Church, to take on the highways of the world to bring Christ, the hope of humanity, to everyone." We find Mary's immediate and joyful response to the inspiration of the Holy Spirit to set out for the country of Judea on the mission of charity to her elderly relative, who became mysteriously pregnant despite being barren and advanced in age. Mary knew how difficult it would be for Elizabeth all that she was to be pregnant and to go through labor, and yet still, having to care for her equally elderly weak and mute husband, Zechariah. We read how Mary's missionary service to Elizabeth brought so much joy because of the Gospel she was to announce to her.

It is written in Luke 1:41 that Mary's visit to Elizabeth made John leap for joy in his mother's womb. In Luke 1:47 of her song of praise, Mary proclaimed: "My spirit hath rejoiced in God my Saviour." Jesus's born from Mary was the perfect prototype of joyful evangelization. When Jesus began His missionary ministry, John cried out: "This my joy therefore is fulfilled" (John 3:29). Jesus himself was said to have rejoiced in the Holy Spirit (see Luke 10:21). Then, again, Jesus said: "These things I have spoken to you, that my joy may be in you, and your joy may be filled" (John 15:11). In order for all baptized to carry the good news of salvation with joy when they evangelize to all peoples, the Church gives Mary as the model of joyful evangelization, and this we find in the Visitation of Mary to her cousin Elizabeth. This occasion reminds and inspires us to carry our missionary labor of evangelization with joy to reach out to all peoples who are in dire need of God.

The Feast of Visitation is a medieval origin the Order of Friars Minor observed this Feast before 1263, when St. Bonaventure recommended it, and the Franciscan Chapter adopted it. The Franciscan Breviary spread it to many churches to inspire them on how Mary brought the good news of salvation with joy. In 1389, Pope Urban VI extended the feast to the entire Church, with the hope that Christ and Our Lady would put an end to the Great Schism that was threatening the Church at the time. The feast was originally assigned to July 2, the day after the octave of St. John, which is estimated to be around the time that Mary returned to Nazareth. However, during the Schism, many opposing bishops refused to adopt the feast, until it was confirmed at the Council of Basle in 1441. Pius IX raised the feast to the rank of a double of the second class on May 13, 1850. In 1969, the revision of the calendar, Pope Paul VI moved the Feast of the Visitation to May 31, between the Solemnity of the Annunciation of the Lord on March 25 and the Nativity of St. John the Baptist on June 24 to harmonize better with the Gospel story. The Catholic Church in Germany together with the Lutheran Church has, and with the consent of the Holy See kept the July 2 date as the national variation of the general Roman calendar. July 2 is also observed by traditionalist Catholics who use a pre-1970 calendar, and by Anglicans who use the 1662 Book of Common Prayer. In some Anglican traditions, it is merely a commemoration rather than a feast day.

During the general audience of May 31, 2013, Pope Francis reflected on the significance of the Feast of the Visitation, he said that the theme of the Feast of the Visitation centers on Mary's responding promptly to the inspiration of the Holy Spirit to set out on a mission of charity.

In general, this mystery of the Visitation shows how Mary faced her mission of charity to Elizabeth as well as her life's missionary journey with Jesus with great realism, humanity, and practicality. For the Pope, three words sum up Mary's attitude: Listening, Decision, and Action, which offers us a way or disposition how we can face what the Lord God gave us in our mission life after Baptism.

Listening: What gave rise to Mary's missionary act of going out to visit her cousin Elizabeth? It was the word from God's angel. Mary knew how to listen to God, but she must remember that listening and hearing are totally different actions. Hearing is superficial; on the other hand, Listening consists of attention, acceptance, and availability to God. Mary did not listen in the distracted way with which we sometimes listen to the word of the Lord or others: that is when we only hear their words, but do not really listen. Mary, on the other hand, was attentive to God. She listened to God. However, Mary listened not only to God but also to the facts by reading the events of her life. She was attentive to concrete reality and did not stop at the surface but went to the depths of these realities so that she can grasp its meaning. Her kinswoman Elizabeth, who was already elderly, was expecting a child: this is the event. But Mary was attentive to the meaning of Elizabeth's pregnancy. She was able to understand it, because she remembers what the angel said: "No word shall be impossible with God" (Luke 1:37). This is also true in our life: listening to God who speaks to us, and also listening to daily reality. It means paying attention to people, to events, because the Lord is knocking at the door of our hearts in countless ways. He puts signs on our path; He gives us the capacity to see them. Mary is the Mother of attentive listening to God and of equally attentive listening to the events of life. She is our great example.

Decision: Mary did not live "with haste," with breathlessness, but, as St. Luke emphasizes, she "kept all these things, pondering them in her heart" (Luke 2:19, 51). Moreover, at the crucial moment of the angel's annunciation, Mary also asks, "How shall this happen?" (Luke 1:34). But she does not just stop at the moment of reflection, she goes a step further: she decides. She does not live in haste but "goes with haste" only when necessary. Mary does not let herself get dragged along by events; she does not avoid the effort of taking a decision. And the Virgin Mary made both in the fundamental decision that changed her life: "I am the handmaid of the Lord" (Luke 1:38), and in her daily decision, routine but also full of meaning. The account of the wedding feast at Cana (John 2:1-11) showed the realism, humanity, and practicality of Mary, who was attentive to events, and to problems. She saw and understood the predicament of the young married couple when the wine ran out at a wedding feast. Thinking about it and knowing that Jesus could do something, she decided to ask her Son to intervene by saying, "they have no more wine."

Looking at our own situation, we find ourselves at times in difficulty making decisions. We often tend to put them off, or to let others decide instead. We frequently prefer to let ourselves be dragged along by events, or just go with the flow to make life easier. At times we know what ought to do, but we have no courage to do it, or it seems difficult to make a decision because it means swimming against the tide. In the Annunciation, in the Visitation, and at the wedding at Cana, Mary went against the tide; she listened to God, she reflected and sought to understand the reality of the angel's message and decided to entrust herself totally to God. Although she was with child, the Virgin Mary decided to visit her elderly relative, and she decided to entrust herself to her Son with insistence so as to preserve the joy of the wedding feast.

Action: According to Luke 1: 39, Mary set out on the journey and went "with haste." Despite the difficulties and the criticism, she would have faced because of her decision to go and visit her cousin. Mary did not let anything stop her rather she left "with haste." Mary was never in a hurry. She thought and meditated on the facts of her life, because she did not let herself be swept away by the moment, and she did not let herself be dragged along by events. However, when she has understood clearly what God was asking of her, she did not delay but instead she went "with haste." Mary's action was a consequence of her obedience to the angel's words but was combined with charity: she went to Elizabeth to make herself useful; and in going out of her home, of herself, for love, she took with her the most precious possession: Jesus, her Son. At times, our challenge is that, sometimes, we stop listening and thinking about what we must do. We may even be certain about decisions we have to make, yet we do not move on to take action. We do not take towards others "with haste" to bring them our help, our understanding, and our love; to bring them like Mary the most precious thing we have received: Jesus and His Gospel. This we preach with words, and most of all, with the tangible witness of what we do. Here we see why God gave us Mary as our Model for listening, for making decisions, and making definitive actions.

Mary, the woman of listening opens our ears; she teaches us how to listen to the words of her Son Jesus among the thousands of words competing for her attention. Our prayer ought to be how we learn to listen to the reality of the present moment; to listen to every person we encounter, especially, to those who are poor, in need, and in difficulty.

Mary, the woman of decision illuminates our minds and our hearts so that we may know how to obey the word of her Son Jesus without hesitation. She gives us the courage to decide and to not let ourselves be dragged along because of others who dictate upon our lives.

Mary, the woman of action grants that our hands and feet move with haste towards others to bring them the charity and love of her Son Jesus; to bring like you the light of the Gospel into the world.

This story recalls how the Rosary saved a man's life on the ill-fated day known as September 11:

A fallen away Catholic from New York, who had not been to confession for years, met the America Needs Fatima Custodian, Jose Ferraz. After the visit, the New Yorker took home a Rosary and Rosary Guide and started praying the Rosary. He began to return to the sacraments. Months later, on September 11, 2001, he was at the World Trade Center at the very moment when the terrorist attack took place. Seeing the fireball and smoke from the crash, the man fled from his office started running down the stairs to safety. However, he was stuck before a big obstacle and with the fire doors locked. He found himself trapped in the stairwell, listening to the screams of burning people who were still inside the building, unable to escape death. The scene was horrific because any attempt to pry open the fire doors with bare hands would be futile. With Our Lady's help, instead of panicking, he felt calm. He took his Rosary and started praying to the Blessed Mother for help. At that moment, he was ready for anything: life or death, whatever was the will of God, as long as he was with Mother Mary. He continued to hear more explosions in the background: the wailing, groaning, screaming, shouting, and cries for help increased amid the suffocating smoke and fire. But he remained there, kneeling, and praying for all the others in the building who were trapped in the fire with no way out. And within minutes, firemen reached his floor, broke down the fire doors and set him free. Since most of the firemen were Catholics, they were amazed to see a man so calm praying the Rosary on his knees. As they lifted him up, one fireman said: "Yes, sir. Mother Mary took us to this floor first and we did not know why. But when we saw you praying the Rosary, we knew she had brought us here because you were calling out for help from her with your Rosary which she could not refuse." Amidst falling debris and smoke, the man ran downstairs to safety before the whole building collapsed. The man's prayers were answered thanks to the power of the Most Holy Rosary, with which Mother Mary has promised, "You shall obtain all you ask of me by the recitation of the Rosary." In thanksgiving, this man immediately went to the nearby Catholic church to make his confession and attended Mass.

MEDITATION

"Whoever shall faithfully serve the Virgin Mary by the recitation of the Rosary, shall receive signal graces or miracles. The Blessed Mother will give a special protection and the greatest graces to all those who shall recite the Rosary." (Blessed Virgin Mary's promises)

PRAYER

O Blessed Virgin Mary, God sends you to help us since you are the spouse of the Holy Spirit, the New Eve. We know that you will never abandon us since you are the most generous Mother and Queen of the world. Visit us with your missionary zeal for charity and kindle again our hearts with the fire of courage, patience, and perseverance. So that we, the missionaries and evangelizers of old, may enjoy once again that great faith and joy of saving souls. We ask this through the Most Powerful Intercession of the Blessed Virgin Mary, with St. Joseph, in the name of Jesus Christ, Our Lord. Amen.

In the name of the Father, and of the Son, and of the Holy Spirit. Amen

Ad Jesum Per Mariam!

Printed in Great Britain
by Amazon

78948850R00139